To the Texas Health Student,

What does *health* mean to you? You might think it means how well your body works. However, as you read *Health & Wellness* you will learn that *health* has to do with your body, your mind, your relationships, your safety, and the world around you.

What foods can help you be as healthy as you can be? How can you become physically fit? What can you do to be safe if there is a fire or an earthquake? *Health & Wellness* answers these questions and more. *Health & Wellness* also teaches life skills, such as how to communicate and set health goals. You can practice these skills to benefit your health throughout your life.

Read *Health & Wellness* with your teachers and parents or guardian. These responsible adults can guide you in making responsible decisions and setting health goals. They are your partners in health.

Are you ready? Read for health—your most precious possession!

Macmillan / McGraw-Hill

Health & Wellness

TEXAS

Linda Meeks
The Ohio State University

Philip Heit
The Ohio State University

Macmillan McGraw-Hill

About the Authors

Professor Linda Meeks and Dr. Philip Heit

Linda Meeks and Philip Heit are emeritus professors of Health Education in the College of Education at The Ohio State University. As faculty members, Linda and Philip held joint appointments in Health Education in the College of Education and in Allied Medicine in the College of Medicine. Linda and Philip are America's most widely published health education co-authors. They have collaborated for more than 25 years, co-authoring more than 300 health books that are used by millions of students preschool through college. They are co-authors of an organized, sequential K–12 health education program, *Health and Wellness,* available from Macmillan/McGraw-Hill.

Together, they have helped state departments of education as well as thousands of school districts develop comprehensive school health education curricula. Their books and curricula are used throughout the United States, as well as in Canada, Japan, Mexico, England, Puerto Rico, Spain, Egypt, Jordan, Saudi Arabia, Bermuda, and the Virgin Islands. Linda and Philip train professors as well as educators in state departments of education and school districts. Their book, *Comprehensive School Health Education: Totally Awesome® Strategies for Teaching Health,* is the most widely used book for teacher training in colleges, universities, state departments of education, and school districts. Thousands of teachers around the world have participated in their *Totally Awesome® Teacher Training Workshops.* Linda and Philip have been the keynote speakers for many teacher institutes and wellness conferences. They are personally and professionally committed to the health and well-being of youth.

Chapter 6 outlines emergency care procedures that reflect the standard of knowledge and accepted practices in the United States at the time this book was published. It is the teacher's responsibility to stay informed of changes in emergency care procedures in order to teach current accepted practices. The teacher also can recommend that students gain complete, comprehensive training from courses offered by the American Red Cross.

The McGraw·Hill Companies

 **Macmillan McGraw-Hill**

Published by Macmillan/McGraw-Hill, of McGraw-Hill Education, a division of The McGraw-Hill Companies, Inc., Two Penn Plaza, New York, New York 10121.

Printed in the United States of America   ISBN 0-02-280375-0/4

6 7 8 9 079 09 08 07 06 05

learning through listening

Students with print disabilities may be eligible to obtain an accessible, audio version of the pupil edition of this textbook. Please call Recording for the Blind & Dyslexic at 1-800-221-4792 for complete information.

Contributors

Celan Alo, M.D., MPH
Medical Epidemiologist
Bureau of Chronic Disease and Tobacco
  Prevention
Texas Department of Health
Austin, Texas

Danny Ballard, Ed.D.
Associate Professor, Health
Texas A&M University
College of Education
College Station, Texas

Lucille Villegas Barrera, M.Ed.
Elementary Science Specialist
Houston Independent School District
Houston, Texas

Gus T. Dalis, Ed.D.
Consultant of Health Education
Torrance, California

Alisa Evans-Debnam, MPH
Dean of Health Programs
Fayetteville Technical Community College
Fayetteville, North Carolina

Susan C. Giarratano-Russell, MSPH, Ed.D., CHES
Health Education, Evaluation & Media
  Consultant
National Center for Chronic Disease
  Prevention & Health Promotion
Centers for Disease Control & Prevention
Glendale, California

Donna Lloyd-Kolkin, Ph.D.
Principal Associate
Public Health Applications & Research
Abt Associates, Inc.
Bethesda, Maryland

Mulugheta Teferi, M.A.
Principal
Gateway Middle School
Center for Math, Science & Technology
St. Louis, Missouri

Roberto P. Treviño, M.D.
Director, Social & Health Research Center
Bienestar School-Based Diabetes
  Prevention Program
San Antonio, Texas

Dinah Zike, M.Ed.
Dinah Might Adventures LP
San Antonio, Texas

Content Reviewers

Mark Anderson
Supervisor, Health Physical
  Education
Cobb County Public
  Schools
Marietta, Georgia

Ken Ascoli
Assistant Principal
Our Lady of Fatima High
  School
Warren, Rhode Island

Jane Beougher, Ph.D.
Professor Emeritus of
  Health Education,
  Physical Education,
  and Education
Capital University
Westerville, Ohio

Lillie Burns
HIV/AIDS Prevention
  Education
Education Program
  Coordinator
Louisiana Department
  of Education
Baton Rouge, Louisiana

Jill English, Ph.D., CHES
Professor, Soka University
Aliso Viejo, California

Elizabeth Gallun, M.A.
Specialist, Comprehensive
  Health Education
Maryland State Department
  of Education
Baltimore, Maryland

Brenda Garza
Health Communications
  Specialist
Centers for Disease Control
  and Prevention
Atlanta, Georgia

Sheryl Gotts, M.S.
Consultant, Retired from
  Milwaukee Schools
Milwaukee, Wisconsin

Russell Henke, M.Ed.
Coordinator of Health
Montgomery County Public
  Schools
Rockville, Maryland

Kathy Kent
Health and Physical
  Education Teacher
Simpsonville Elementary
  School at Morton Place
Simpsonville, South
  Carolina

Bill Moser, M.S.
Program Specialist for
  Health and Character
  Education
Winston-Salem Forsyth City
  Schools
Winston-Salem, North
  Carolina

Debra Ogden
Curriculum Coordinator
District School Board of
  Collier County
Naples, Florida

Thurman Robins
Chair/Professor
Health and Kinesiology
  Department
Texas Southern University
Houston, Texas

Sherman Sowby, Ph.D., CHES
Professor, Department of
  Health Science
California State University,
  Fresno
Fresno, California

Greg Stockton
Health and Safety Expert
American Red Cross
Washington, D.C.

Deitra Wengert, Ph.D., CHES
Professor, Department of
  Health Science
Towson University
Towson, Maryland

Susan Wooley-Goekler, Ph.D., CHES
Adjunct Faculty
Kent State University
Kent, Ohio

Medical Reviewers

Celan Alo, M.D., MPH
Medical Epidemiologist
Bureau of Chronic Disease
  and Tobacco Prevention
Texas Department of
  Health
Austin, Texas

Donna Bacchi, M.D., MPH
Associate Professor of
  Pediatrics
Director, Division of
  Community Pediatrics
Texas Tech University
Health Science Center
Lubbock, Texas

Olga Dominguez Satterwhite, R.D., L.D.
Registered Dietitian and
  Diabetes Educator
Baylor College of Medicine
Houston, Texas

Roberto P. Treviño, M.D.
Director, Social & Health
  Research Center
Bienestar School-Based
  Diabetes Prevention
  Program
San Antonio, Texas

Contents

CHAPTER 2 Family and Social Health

LOG ON www.mmhhealth.com
For more on Unit A Mental, Emotional, Family, and Social Health.

CHAPTER 3 Growth and Development

CHAPTER 4 Nutrition

LOG
ON www.mmhhealth.com
For more on Unit B Growth and
Nutrition.

UNIT C Personal Health and Safety

CHAPTER 5 Personal Health and Physical Activity

CHAPTER 6 Violence and Injury Prevention

 LOG ON www.mmhhealth.com
For more on Unit C Personal Health and Safety.

UNIT D Drugs and Disease Prevention

CHAPTER 7 Alcohol, Tobacco, and Other Drugs

CHAPTER 8 Communicable and Chronic Diseases

LOG ON www.mmhhealth.com
For more on Unit D Drugs and Disease Prevention.

CHAPTER 10 Environmental Health

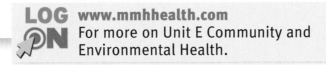

LOG
ON   www.mmhhealth.com
      For more on Unit E Community and
      Environmental Health.

Features and Activities

Features and Activities

Learning Life Skills

Make Responsible Decisions, **E14**
Use Communication Skills, **E32**

Life Skills Activities

Make Responsible Decisions, **E7**
Set Health Goals, **E13, E45**
Access Health Facts, Products, and Services, **E21**
Resolve Conflict, **E31**
Access Health Facts, **E39**

Build Character

Citizenship, **E17, E30**

Cross Curricular Links

Art, **E5, E36**
Math, **E10, E41**
Physical Education, **E29**
Science, **E36**
Write About It!, **E18, E38**

On Your Own for School or Home

Time for Family, **E11**
Battery Disposal, **E44**

Consumer Wise

Ask Five Questions, **E6**
Look Before You Buy, **E42**

Health Online

Locate Your Community Hospital, **E20**
Providing Clean Air, **E37**

Life Skills

Life Skills are actions you can take to improve and maintain your health. The life skills that are taught in this text are listed below.

- Make Responsible Decisions, **E14**
- Use Resistance Skills, **D22**
- Practice Healthful Behaviors, **B32**
- Analyze What Influences Your Health, **B60**
- Access Health Facts, Products, and Services, **C40**

- Resolve Conflicts, **A56**
- Be a Health Advocate, **C78**
- Manage Stress, **A38**
- Use Communication Skills, **E32**
- Set Health Goals, **D54**

Using **Foldables™** To help you learn these life skills, each of the Learning Life Skills features in this book includes Foldables™. Foldables™ are three-dimensional graphic organizers you will make. They will help you understand the main points of each life skill.

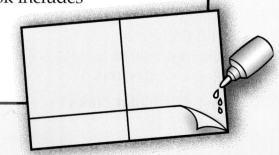

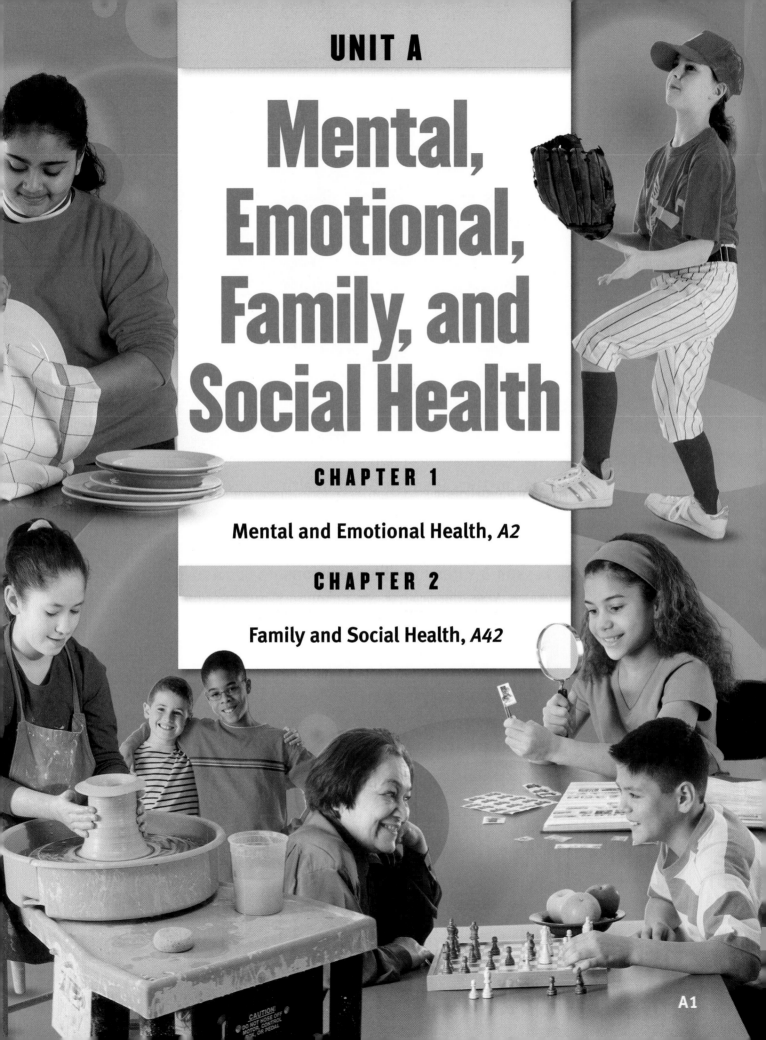

UNIT A

Mental, Emotional, Family, and Social Health

CHAPTER 1

Mental and Emotional Health, *A2*

CHAPTER 2

Family and Social Health, *A42*

CHAPTER 1

Mental and Emotional Health

What Do You Know?

Read each statement. Answer each question **yes** or **no.**

A friend wants to copy your work. What do you say? __?__

You are having trouble remembering your lines for the school play. Do you ask for help? __?__

Your baseball team loses a game. Do you try harder next time? __?__

Being able to say "no," ask for help, and try harder are skills every healthy person should have. Read **Mental and Emotional Health** to learn more.

LOG ON
www.mmhhealth.com
Find out more about mental and emotional health.

A3

A Plan for Good Health

You will learn . . .

- to identify three parts of total health.
- how to improve health.
- what steps to follow to practice healthful behaviors.

Think about the things that are important to you. Do you take good care of them? Your health is important, too. How well do you take care of your health?

Vocabulary

- **health**, A5
- **health goal**, A5
- **wellness**, A6
- **healthful behavior**, A6
- **risk behavior**, A6
- **life skill**, A7

Three Parts of Total Health

Many people think being healthy means having a strong body. But **health** is the condition of your body, mind, and relationships. *Total health* is made up of three parts: physical health, mental and emotional health, and family and social health. To be healthy, you must care for each part of health.

Physical health is how well your body works. When you have good physical health, you have energy. Your body is strong. You are free from illness.

Mental and emotional health is how well your mind works. It's also how you show your feelings. When you have good mental and emotional health, you can think clearly. You perform better at school. You express your emotions in healthful ways.

Family and social health is how well you get along with others. When you have good family and social health, you have strong relationships.

▲ Total health includes your ① physical health, ② family and social health, and ③ mental and emotional health.

Setting Health Goals

You improve your total health by setting health goals. A **health goal** is something you work toward to promote health. Suppose that your health goal is "I will get enough rest and sleep." If you get plenty of rest and sleep, you will not be tired. You will have energy for work and play.

What is health?

Improving Health and Wellness

ACTIVITY

Science
LINK

A Glass of Health

Fill a glass with water. The water represents the three parts of health. Drop green food coloring in the water. The green food coloring represents a healthful behavior. What happened? It affected all parts of health. Drop blue food coloring in the water to represent a risk behavior. What happens?

Wellness is the highest level of health you can reach. When you have a high level of wellness, all three parts of total health are present. You can rate your total health using the Wellness Scale. *The Wellness Scale* measures your health on a scale of 0 to 100. The goal is to choose behaviors that keep your health near the wellness end. To do this you need to practice healthful behaviors and avoid risk behaviors.

A **healthful behavior** is an action that increases the level of health for you and for others. Being physically active every day is a healthful behavior. It leads to a higher rating on the Wellness Scale.

A **risk behavior** is an action that can be harmful to you and others. Smoking is a risk behavior. Choosing friends who don't obey family guidelines is a risk behavior. It causes a person's rating on the Wellness Scale to decrease.

▶ Where would you rate yourself on the Wellness Scale?

Poor Health

High Level Wellness

0 10 20 30 40 50 60 70 80 90 100

The Wellness Scale

Life Skills

Using life skills also improves your health and wellness. A **life skill** is a healthful action to learn and practice to improve and maintain your health. Here are the ten life skills.

- Access Health Facts, Products, and Services
- Practice Healthful Behaviors
- Manage Stress
- Analyze What Influences Your Health
- Use Communication Skills
- Use Resistance Skills
- Resolve Conflicts
- Set Health Goals
- Make Responsible Decisions
- Be a Health Advocate

▲ Practicing life skills promotes and protects health and wellness.

You will use one or more life skills on most days. For example, suppose a friend asks you to ride double on a scooter. Which life skill might you use? First, you might use the life skill "Make Responsible Decisions" to decide what to do. Suppose your friend pressures you to ride double after you decided it is not a responsible decision. You might use the life skill "Use Resistance Skills." This life skill helps you say "no." Then you might use the life skill "Use Communication Skills" to clearly state your reasons for saying "no." This book includes steps to follow in order to use each life skill.

 **What is wellness?**

Practicing Healthful Behaviors

Practice Healthful Behaviors

1. Learn about a healthful behavior.

2. Practice the behavior.

3. Ask for help if you need it.

4. Make the behavior a habit.

Do you remember how hard it was to learn to write in cursive? You had to practice many times. It was the same with learning to solve math problems. Some skills were easy to learn. Some took more time.

The key to learning any new skill is practice. You get better at a skill by repeating its steps. This is how you learn life skills, too. When you master life skills, you practice healthful behaviors instead of risk behaviors.

ACTIVITY

On Your Own

FOR SCHOOL OR HOME

Drink Water for Health

Drinking six to eight glasses of water is a healthful behavior. Do you practice this behavior? Count the number of glasses of water you drink each day for three days. Did you drink six to eight glasses of water each day? If not, how will you make this healthful behavior a habit?

◄ Drinking water is a healthful behavior.

Ways to Practice Healthful Behaviors

Suppose that you spend several hours a day watching television. This causes your rating on the Wellness Scale to drop. You decide to make the following health goal: "I will get plenty of physical activity."

You decide to practice healthful behaviors to reach this health goal. You learn about different ways to be physically active. You make a list of ways to spend your free time being active. Each day, you choose one of the activities. As you practice this healthful behavior, it becomes a habit. You reach your health goal.

 What is the first step in practicing a healthful behavior?

Practice Healthful Behaviors

Many of your classmates have colds. You want to stay healthy. Use this activity to help you practice a healthful behavior.

1. **Learn about a healthful behavior.** On a sheet of paper, trace and cut out the shape of your hand. On each finger write the day of the week starting with Monday and ending with Friday.

2. **Practice the behavior.** For each day, make a tally mark each time you wash your hands before and after a meal.

3. **Ask for help if you need it.** Add up the tally marks at the end of each day. How are you doing? Who might you go to for help in making the healthful behavior a habit?

4. **Make the behavior a habit.** Explain how and why you made hand washing a habit.

LESSON REVIEW

Review Concepts

1. **List** the three parts of your total health.

2. **Explain** how to improve health and wellness.

3. **List** the steps to follow in order to practice healthful behaviors.

Critical Thinking

4. **Analyze** Suppose that your health goal is "I will eat healthful meals and snacks." Which life skills will you use to reach your health goal?

5. **LIFE SKILLS** **Practice Healthful Behaviors** Your parents work long hours. What healthful behavior can you practice that would show your family that you care about them?

Good Character and Your Health

You will learn . . .

- to identify personality traits.
- to identify the six traits of good character.
- how to use self-statements.

Vocabulary

- **personality,** *A11*
- **self-respect,** *A11*
- **values,** *A11*
- **character,** *A12*
- **responsible,** *A13*
- **self-statement,** *A14*

Look in the mirror. What do you see? A person who looks like no one else? Who is that person? What makes you special?

Your Personality

No other person is exactly like you. No other person shares your personality. Your **personality** is made up of how you look, think, act, and feel. It also includes your likes and dislikes. Your personality can affect your total health. Your personality is influenced by the following:

- **heredity**, such as height, eye color, and talents, such as being able to play the piano.

- **emotions,** such as how you express yourself.

- **strengths and weaknesses,** what you do well and not so well. There are parts of your personality that make you proud. These are your strengths. There are other parts that you would like to improve. These are your weaknesses.

- **values** such as showing respect for yourself and others. **Values** are the beliefs that guide a person's behavior.

Self-Respect

Working to improve your strengths and weaknesses helps you develop self-respect. **Self-respect** is thinking highly of yourself. Do you always act in responsible ways? Does your family always approve of your actions? Do your actions match your values? If you have self-respect, you promote and protect your total health. You practice healthful behaviors. You avoid risk behaviors. You make responsible decisions.

 **What makes up your personality?**

Art
L I N K

Design a Coat of Arms

Make a coat-of-arms that describes you. A coat-of-arms is a shield with symbols on it. The symbols represent a person or a family. Draw six pictures on your shield. Have each picture show a part of your personality that makes you feel proud. Explain to a friend what each picture tells about you.

When You Have Good Character

Your words and actions show your character. **Character** is the qualities that make a person different from others. You have good character when you show the following traits.

Trustworthiness You are honest. You keep promises. You are brave enough to do the right thing even when it is hard.

Respect You show that you think highly of others by being polite and using good manners. You consider other people's feelings.

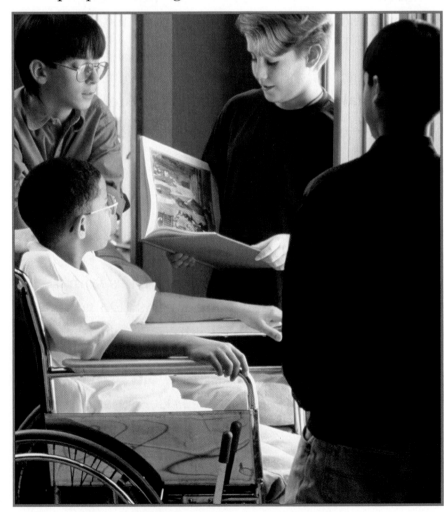

▶ Being polite and using good manners when someone else is talking shows good character.

Responsibility When you are **responsible**, you are able to be trusted with a job, duty, or concern. You can be counted on to do what you say you will. You take ownership of your actions.

Fairness You play by the rules. You share and take turns.

Caring You are kind to others and help those in need.

Citizenship You follow the rules of your family, your school, and your community. You are a good neighbor. You do your share to make the world a better place.

What does it mean to be responsible?

BUILD ACTIVITY

Character

List Ways to Show Respect

Respect Showing respect means that you think highly of others. You are polite and you use good manners. You consider other people's feelings. Work with a group of four students. Try talking all at the same time. What happened? Now try taking turns. Raise your hand and wait to be called on if you want to speak. Pay attention to what your classmates are saying. How is showing respect in class helpful?

Helping others in your community shows good citizenship.

A13

Staying on Track

ACTIVITY

On Your Own
FOR SCHOOL OR HOME

Hang on to Good Character

Make a "Good Character" tag. Using cardboard, scissors, markers or crayons, design a tag to hang on your doorknob. Write *Good Character Traits* at the top followed by a list of the six traits that make up good character. Place it on the doorknob in your room to remind you to show good character every day.

Your character is always being tested. Good character takes effort. To help keep good character, use a **self-statement**, or a reminder to yourself as to what you should do. Self-statements help you build and keep good character.

Suppose that your friend forgot to do her homework. She asks to copy yours. This request is a test of your character. You want to help, but you also want to keep your self-respect. You remember that a person of good character is honest. What could you do?

You could use a self-statement. You might say, "I want to show good character. I will be trustworthy and caring." You suggest to your friend that she complete the assignment after eating lunch. You offer to wait for her. Your actions show that you are a person of good character.

▶ **Waiting for a friend to complete her homework before you go out to play shows that you care.**

A14

Self-statements help you keep your self-respect. Sticking to your values helps you to have good feelings about yourself.

There are other actions that you can do to build good character. You can set health goals. Build on your strengths. Work on improving your weaknesses. If you have trouble reaching a health goal, ask for help. Learn from your mistakes. These actions can benefit the three parts of total health.

 How might you build good character?

Set Health Goals

Suppose you want to show good character. Use this activity to help you reach this health goal.

1 **Write the health goal you want to set.** I will show good character.

2 **Explain how your goal might affect your health.** Draw a large star on the paper. In the middle of the star explain how this health goal might affect your health.

3 **Describe a plan you will follow to reach your goal. Keep track of your progress.** Label each point with a good character trait. Write a paragraph to tell what you can do to show each trait. Make a star next to the trait each time you demonstrate it.

4 **Evaluate how your plan worked.** At the end of the week, add up your stars. Are you a "star" for good character?

LESSON REVIEW

Review Concepts

1. **Discuss** what influences personality.

2. **List** the six traits of good character.

3. **Define** a self-statement.

Critical Thinking

4. **Contrast** Select two of the six character traits. Give examples that demonstrate each trait. Show the differences between the traits.

5. **LIFE SKILLS** **Set Health Goals** You have trouble paying attention to math at school. Describe a plan to reach this health goal. "I will pay attention in math class."

Responsible Decisions

You will learn . . .

- how to tell the difference between a responsible decision and a wrong decision.

- what factors influence decisions.

- to identify the steps to making responsible decisions.

Vocabulary

- **responsible decision**, *A17*

- **wrong decision**, *A17*

- **resistance skills**, *A19*

You make decisions every day. You may decide what to wear to school. You may choose what to eat. Some decisions are easy. Others are not so easy. Making responsible decisions means knowing what to do in difficult situations.

Kinds of Decisions

A **responsible decision** is one that is healthful and safe. It follows school rules. It follows community laws. A responsible decision shows that you respect yourself and others. It follows family guidelines. It shows that you have good character.

A **wrong decision** is one that is harmful and unsafe. It breaks school rules or community laws. A wrong decision does not show respect for yourself or others. It does not follow family guidelines. A wrong decision does not show good character.

Use Health Facts to Make Responsible Decisions

You can tell whether a decision is responsible by using the *Guidelines for Making Responsible Decisions*™ on page A21. Before answering the questions, you may need health facts. You can do this by accessing health facts. To access (AK•sess) means to be able to obtain something that you need. First, identify when you need health facts. Then determine where you can find the health facts you need. You might read about the topic in books or pamphlets. You might ask a health care professional, such as a school nurse. You might find health facts in your library or clinic. Next, evaluate the health facts. Then you can use these health facts to help you make responsible decisions.

What is a responsible decision?

Social Studies LINK
ACTIVITY

List Voter Questions

What health issues are important to you and your classmates? Select an issue and find out all you can about it. Then present your findings to your classmates and have them vote "for" or "against" the health issue.

Access Health Facts, Products, and Services

1. **Identify when you might need health facts, products, and services.**

2. **Identify where you might find health facts, products, and services.**

3. **Find the health facts, products, and services you need.**

4. **Evaluate the health facts, products, and services.**

Factors that Influence Decisions

Many factors affect, or influence the decisions you make. Health knowledge is one factor. Your family also influences your decisions. Your family has certain values, such as obeying the laws of your community. Another family value might be respecting others. Your family expects you to act in ways that show these values. They expect your decisions to be based on these values. Knowing and using your family's values helps you make responsible decisions.

Your friends and classmates also might influence the choices you make. You might make a responsible decision together. You might decide to spend time studying for a test. You may help each other avoid making a wrong decision. You can keep each other from breaking family guidelines. In this way you influence each other in positive ways.

ACTIVITY
Con$umer Wi$e

Analyze Media Messages

Find an advertisement in an old newspaper or magazine that shows a well-known sports star. Cut out the advertisement. Paste it on a sheet of construction paper. Refer to the steps to "Analyze What Influences Your Health" below. Respond to each step while looking at the ad.

Analyze What Influences Your Health

1. **Identify people and things that can influence your health.**

2. **Evaluate how these people and things can affect your health.**

3. **Choose healthful influences.**

4. **Protect yourself against harmful influences.**

▼ **Your family has a positive influence on your health choices.**

Whenever anyone tries to get you to make a wrong decision, use resistance skills. **Resistance skills** are ways to say "no" to risk behaviors. Use resistance skills when someone tries to get you to do something:

- harmful,
- unsafe,
- unlawful,
- disrespectful,
- that does not follow your family's guidelines, or
- that does not show good character

Use Resistance Skills

Use these four steps to say "no."

1. Look at the person. Say "no" in a firm voice.

2. Give reasons for saying "no."

3. Match your behavior to your words. Keep away from situations in which someone might try to talk you into a wrong decision.

4. Ask an adult for help if you need it.

 **What are resistance skills?**

Analyze What Influences Your Health

Have a panel discussion with your class to determine what influences your food choices.

1 **Identify people and things that can influence your health.** Work in groups of three. Have each group member list either a specific person, a TV commercial, or a magazine or billboard that influences his or her food choices.

2 **Evaluate how these people or things can affect your health.** Look at the influences you identified. Did the person, TV commercial, or ad try to influence you to choose healthful foods? Write a sentence telling how much influence each one had on your decision.

3 **Choose healthful influences.** The healthful choice influenced you to eat healthful foods. Discuss which influences you will pay attention to.

4 **Protect yourself against harmful influences.** Choose actions to protect against harmful influences. Suppose an ad tempts you to eat high-fat food. What might you do? Discuss with the class how to protect against harmful influences.

Making Responsible Decisions

You are working on a report for school. It's due the next day. You really want to get a good grade. Your friends come to your house. They want you to play basketball. You want to play with them. You remember that basketball is a way of being physically active. You remember that exercise is good for your health.

But then you remember your report. You still have to finish it. If you join your friends, you won't have enough time to do a good job on the report. What should you do?

▼ The first step to making responsible decisions is to identify your choices.

A20

Steps to Make Responsible Decisions

The first step in making a decision is to identify your choices. Your choices are—1) You can play basketball. 2) You can work on your report. When you know what your choices are, you are ready for step two. Use the *Guidelines for Making Responsible Decisions*™ to evaluate your choices. Ask yourself the questions shown here on the clipboard, filling in the blanks for each choice. Some of the questions may not apply to your situation.

If you answer "no" to one or more questions, rethink your choice. Return to step two. If you answer "yes" to all six questions, then you can take step three. Identify the responsible decision. Then in step four, tell how the decision worked out.

 What is the first step in making a responsible decision?

> ### Guidelines for Making Responsible Decisions™
>
> - Is it healthful to ___?
> - Is it safe to ___?
> - Do I follow rules and laws if I ___?
> - Do I show respect for myself and others if I ___?
> - Do I follow my family's guidelines if I ___?
> - Do I show good character if I ___?

LESSON REVIEW

Review Concepts

1. **Discuss** the difference between a responsible decision and a wrong decision.

2. **List** three factors that influence the decisions you make.

3. **Name** the four steps to follow in making responsible decisions.

Critical Thinking

4. **Discuss** Why is it important to choose friends who have values that your parents or guardian want you to demonstrate?

5. **LIFE SKILLS** **Analyze What Influences Your Health** Suppose you want to try a new brand of toothpaste. List two people or things that might influence your decision.

Your Self-Concept

You will learn . . .

- how to have a healthful self-concept.
- what steps to follow in setting health goals.
- how to make a health behavior contract.

Vocabulary

- **self-concept**, *A23*
- **long-term goal**, *A24*
- **short-term goal**, *A24*

You make plans every week. You may plan a project. You may plan a report. You may even plan a party. A plan can help you reach a goal. A plan can help you develop a healthful self-concept.

Healthful Self-Concept

Your **self-concept** is what you think about yourself. A healthful self-concept protects your mental and emotional health.

Actions for a Healthful Self-Concept

People who have a healthful self-concept behave in certain ways. Here is what they do.

- **Show good character.** Words and actions that show good character build a healthful self-concept. Showing good character allows others to respect you.

- **Make responsible decisions.** Follow the *Guidelines for Making Responsible Decisions*™ when making decisions.

- **Choose actions for a healthy mind.** Replace negative thoughts and feelings with positive ones. Work on your strengths and weaknesses. Develop an "I-can" attitude by trying to do your best. Use your mind to solve problems.

- **Practice life skills.** Practicing life skills promotes and protects your total health.

- **Set health goals.** Achieving health goals gives you a sense of accomplishment.

- **Practice healthful behaviors.** When you practice healthful behaviors, you take care of yourself.

BUILD ACTIVITY

Character

Make a Blue Ribbon

Responsibility Think of a time when you have shown that you are responsible. A responsible person is dependable. Cut a blue ribbon from construction paper. On the ribbon, write "I am a Responsible Person for ____". Fill in the blank with a description of what you did. Put the ribbon in a place where you will see it every day.

What is self-concept?

Set Health Goals

Setting health goals helps you practice healthful behaviors and choose responsible actions.

Health goals may be long-term or short-term. A **long-term goal** takes a long time to reach. A long-term goal may be to become physically fit or to get better grades in school. A **short-term goal** is reached in a short time. It may help you work toward a long-term goal. A short-term goal may be to ride your bike for one week. It may be to write your spelling words five times every day. Accomplishing many short-term goals can help you reach a long-term goal.

A health behavior contract can help you reach either type of goal. Steps for making a contract are shown on the next page. After you write a health behavior contract, ask a responsible adult to review and approve it. Then follow your plan to reach your goal.

 What is a short-term goal?

Set Health Goals

1. Identify the health goal you want to practice.

2. Explain how your goal might affect your health.

3. Describe a plan you will follow to reach your goal. Keep track of your progress.

4. Evaluate how your plan worked.

ACTIVITY

LIFE SKILLS

CRITICAL THINKING

Set Health Goals

Your sister has set a long-term goal to eat more fruit. How can she reach this goal? Write a skit to help her.

1 **Write the health goal you want to set.** I will eat healthful meals and snacks.

2 **Explain how your goal might improve your health.** If your sister eats fruits for snacks, she will get vitamins and minerals. This will improve her physical health.

3 **Describe a plan to reach your goal. Keep track of your progress.** Use a Health Behavior Contract. Use the sample on the next page as a guide. Include how to make a contract in your skit.

4 **Evaluate how your plan worked.** You will need to explain how to decide if a goal is met. What can you suggest? Where could your sister get help if she needs it?

Health Behavior Contract

Name _____ Date _____

1 Health Goal   I will eat healthful meals and snacks.

2 Effect on My Health   Eating healthful snacks will help me stay at a healthful weight. I will be less likely to get cavities. My body will get the vitamins and minerals it needs.

3 My Plan   I will choose healthful snacks from the list below. I will use a calendar every day for one week. I will write the healthful snacks I chose on my calendar.

My Calendar

Sun.	Mon.	Tues.	Wed.	Thurs.	Fri.	Sat.

milk   cottage cheese   carrot sticks
apple   plain popcorn   low-fat frozen yogurt
celery   peanut butter   low-fat cheese
banana

4 How My Plan Worked   Did I choose healthful snacks every day? How can I make my plan work better?

1. Write the health goal you want to set.

2. Explain how your goal might affect your health.

3. Describe a plan to reach your goal. Keep track of your progress.

4. Evaluate how your plan worked.

LESSON REVIEW

Review Concepts

1. **List** two actions that you can do to keep a healthful self-concept.

2. **Explain** why you need to set health goals.

3. **Explain** how making a health behavior contract improves self-respect.

Critical Thinking

4. **Assess** Does setting health goals help build a healthful self-concept? Tell why or why not.

5. **LIFE SKILLS** **Set Health Goals** List the four steps to follow to reach the health goal: I will get plenty of physical activity.

Expressing Emotions

You will learn . . .

- about different kinds of emotions.
- some healthful ways to express emotions.
- some healthful ways to prevent boredom.

Vocabulary

- **emotion**, *A27*
- **fear**, *A27*
- **caring**, *A27*
- **joy**, *A27*
- **sadness**, *A27*
- **grief**, *A27*
- **bored**, *A30*

Think about your emotions. What makes you feel joy? What makes you sad? People express emotions differently. Expressing emotions in healthful ways keeps you healthy.

Kinds of Emotions

An **emotion** is a feeling inside you. Everyone has them. There are many different kinds of emotions. Examples of emotions are fear, caring, joy, sadness, and grief.

Fear is a feeling of danger. People can be afraid of other people. You might be fearful of strangers. People can be afraid of certain things. Your brother or sister might be afraid of thunderstorms. Your friend might be afraid to read to the class.

Caring is being kind to someone. You feel it when you like someone or something. You might feel this emotion when you see a relative. You can feel caring when a friend is kind to you. In addition to caring, you may feel joy. **Joy** is a feeling of great happiness. You might feel joy when you do well on a test. You might feel joy when your team wins a game.

Sadness is a feeling of sorrow or unhappiness. You might feel sad when your best friend moves away. Some people feel sad when things don't work out the way they had hoped. Grief is a stronger emotion than sadness. **Grief** (GREEF) is the discomfort a person feels after a loss. You may feel grief after a loved one or a pet dies.

All your emotions are felt inside you. You express your emotions through your words and actions. You will read how expressing your emotions in healthful ways promotes and protects health. It helps you communicate well with others.

 **What are five types of emotions?**

▲ **When you are confused, talking to a parent or guardian can help you to sort out your feelings.**

Health Online
Dealing With Grief

Grief is the discomfort a person feels after a loss, such as the death of a grandparent. Use the e-Journal writing tool to write a report about how people deal with grief. Visit **www.mmhhealth.com** and click on **e-Journal**.

Expressing Emotion

✏️ Write About It!

Write a Story Write a story about a character of your choice. Describe the feelings the person experiences. Explain how the person expresses his or her feelings in healthful ways.

Expressing emotion means that you show how you feel. Expressing your emotions in healthful ways has three benefits.

- **Expressing emotions helps you relate to others.** *Relate* means how you talk, listen, and act with others. Suppose you are angry and refuse to talk about what is making you angry. This may only make things worse. But when you talk about your anger, the other person can respond. You relate to each other and work things out.

- **Expressing emotions helps you solve problems.** Life events can affect your emotions. Suppose your best friend moves away and you feel sad. Talking about how you feel helps you deal with this life event.

- **Expressing emotions benefits your health.** Keeping your emotions inside can affect your physical health. You may get a headache or stomachache. You may have difficulty sleeping or doing homework. When you express your emotions in healthful ways, you protect your health. You also reduce stress.

◀ **It's okay to feel sad when a friend moves away.**

Healthful Ways to Express Emotions

Expressing emotions healthfully protects your mental and emotional health. It also can protect physical health. Here are some examples of emotions that people express.

Fear Talk to your parents or guardian or another responsible adult. Talking to someone you trust allows you to be honest. The adult you talk to may be able to help you overcome your fear.

Caring If you care for someone, tell him or her. Write the person a note, send a card or draw a picture.

Sadness or Grief Let your emotions out by crying. Talk to a responsible adult about the pain you feel. He or she may suggest you that keep a private journal. Then you can write about your feelings.

Joy When you feel joy, show it. You might smile or laugh. You might have more energy. Don't try to hide how you feel. Your joy and happiness could make others feel happy.

 Name a healthful way to express fear, caring, sadness, and joy.

CAREERS
Teacher

Your teacher helps you to learn life skills. Your teacher also helps protect your health and safety. He or she gets help if you become ill or get injured during school hours. Your teacher is a responsible adult whom you can talk to if you are having problems.

LOG ON www.mmhhealth.com
Find out more about careers in health.

Dealing with Boredom

Have you ever been bored on a Saturday afternoon? Being **bored** is feeling restless and not knowing what to do. Maybe all your friends were busy. Maybe family members were doing chores.

Everyone gets bored from time to time. Most people find healthful ways to beat boredom. You might read a book, write in a journal, or shoot hoops. However, some people might choose risk behaviors instead. They might try smoking. But risk behaviors are not the answer to boredom. Healthful behaviors keep your mind alert. Healthful actions beat boredom.

Healthful Ways to Prevent Boredom

To prevent boredom, choose behaviors and a variety of activities that promote health. Here's a few ideas.

- **Try a new physical activity.** Take a jog around your neighborhood. Visit a local gym or YMCA. Kick a soccer ball. Walk a neighbor's dog. Exercise. Physical activity releases substances into the bloodstream that improve mood.

- **Express yourself through a creative activity.** Paint a picture. Build a birdhouse. Make a card for someone. Write a song or poem. Learn a new hobby. You might discover a hidden talent.

- **Do something to help others.** Scrub the bathtub. Rake leaves. Organize a closet. These actions will show others that you care about them. It also provides you with health benefits. You feel good about yourself when you help others.

 What does being bored mean?

A30

Use Communication Skills

Brainstorm events that trigger emotions, such as finding a $10 bill, getting lost in the woods, or breaking a friend's toy. Use the events to play a game to practice communication skills.

1 **Choose the best way to communicate.** Work with three other classmates. Have each group member cut a sheet of paper into four squares. On each square, each member is to write one of the events listed.

2 **Send a clear message. Be polite.** Clearly identify an emotion that might be felt with each event. Write that emotion on the opposite side of the square.

3 **Listen to each other.** Put all the squares in a hat or box. Then, have one person in your group select a square and communicate the emotion triggered by the event described on the paper without using words. Ask group members to tell the emotion.

4 **Make sure you understand each other.** The first group member to correctly name the emotion selects a new square. Continue the activity until every team member has had a turn.

LESSON REVIEW

Review Concepts

1. **Discuss** how joy and sadness are alike. How do they differ?

2. **Identify** three benefits of expressing emotion in healthful ways.

3. **List** two ways to beat boredom.

Critical Thinking

4. **Apply** Your friend Justin is bored. He wants to come over to your house to skate. You're not allowed to go outside today. What might you and Justin do?

5. **LIFE SKILLS** **Use Communication Skills** How can you communicate to a younger brother or sister that you care?

Reducing Stress

You will learn . . .

- how your body responds to stress.
- what steps to follow to manage stress.
- why you need to have a positive attitude.

Vocabulary

- **stress**, *A33*
- **stressor**, *A33*
- **attitude**, *A36*

Most people your age have busy schedules. You have to get to school on time. You have to complete your homework on time. You might play sports. You may be involved in a club. Having too many demands on your time can cause stress.

What Happens When You Feel Stress?

Think about a time when you felt anxious or nervous. Did your heart beat faster? Did you start to breathe more quickly? Did your hands get moist? These are ways your body reacts when you feel stress. **Stress** is the response to any demand on your mind or body. Everyone feels stress. It is a natural part of life. That's because you deal with stressors every day. A **stressor** is something that causes stress. Being late for class may be a stressor for one person. Giving a speech may be a stressor for another. Playing in a baseball game may be a stressor. Certain things may be stressors for some people, but not for others.

Your body reacts when you feel stress. It produces chemicals that help you take quick action. The chart shows some of the body's reactions to stress.

 How might a person's body react under stress?

The Body's Reaction to Stress
Your heart beats faster.
More sugar goes into your bloodstream.
More blood flows to your muscles.
Your muscles get tense.
You breathe faster.
Your hands get moist.
Your mouth gets dry.

ACTIVITY

Art LINK

Picture Stress

On a sheet of paper, draw a picture of someone in a stressful situation. Then write a paragraph describing how the body reacts to stress. Does your drawing show these reactions?

▲ When you feel anxious, your body reacts.

Ways to Manage Stress

Stress that lasts a long time can harm your physical health. You can get headaches and stomachaches. You can have difficulty sleeping. Your body's ability to fight illness might decrease.

Your mental and emotional health also can be harmed by stress. You might have trouble concentrating. You might have trouble learning new things. You may feel worried and nervous. Your family and social health also might be harmed. You might snap at someone.

Steps to Manage Stress

These steps can help you manage stress.

1. **Identify the signs of stress.** Suppose that tomorrow you have a test in your least favorite subject. You start to get a headache. You have difficulty sleeping. These are signs that you are feeling stress.

2. **Identify the cause of stress.** When you feel stress, you need to determine what's causing it. Perhaps you feel pressure to do as well as your classmates. Or maybe you haven't studied enough. When you know the cause of the stress, you can take action to reduce the stressor.

Manage Stress

- Identify the signs of stress.
- Identify the cause of stress.
- Do something about the cause of stress.
- Take action to reduce the harmful effects of stress.

3. **Do something about the cause of stress.** If you are worried about a test, make a list of things you need to know. Call a classmate and help each other review all the items.

4. **Take action to reduce the harmful effects of stress.** The night before the test, go to bed a little early. Eat a healthful breakfast in the morning. Say to yourself, "I can do this. I know what to expect."

Other Healthful Ways to Manage Stress

There are a number of healthful ways to manage stress. Here are some options.

● **Get regular exercise.** Exercise lessens muscle tension. It uses up extra sugar in your bloodstream. It helps you sleep better.

● **Make a daily plan.** List the things you have to do. As you finish each task, cross it off your list. At the end of the day, review your list and note how much you've accomplished.

● **Get plenty of rest and sleep.** When you are rested, your body can respond to stressors better. This will help keep you healthy.

● **Do healthful activities with your friends.** Ride bikes, take a walk, play tag, or kick a soccer ball around. At the same time you enjoy the activity, you get support and encouragement.

 **What are the four steps to follow in order to manage stress?**

ACTIVITY

Physical Education **L** **I** **N** **K**

Stress Buster

One common reaction to stress is muscle tension. You can release muscle tension through relaxation exercises. You might begin by tensing your leg muscles. Hold for 10 seconds then let go and relax for 15 to 20 seconds. Move on to the next muscle group.

Your Attitude and Stress

ACTIVITY

On Your Own
FOR SCHOOL OR HOME

Attitude Adjustment

Draw a stick figure to represent YOU. Place three (+) signs and three (–) signs around the head of the figure. The + represent things about which you have a positive attitude. The – represent things about which you have a negative attitude. Write a label next to each sign. For example, you might write "my schoolwork" next to a + sign to show you have a positive attitude. Identify ways to change the – signs to + signs. Ask your family members to do the same.

Suppose that you're working on your homework. You have to get the work done before your scout meeting. Your mom is cooking. She's trying to prepare dinner for you. She calls you to come set the table. You are not done with your work. The pressure starts to build inside you. You get mad. You angrily place the dishes on the table. You shout, "Why am I always the one who gets stuck doing the work around here?"

This reaction shows a negative attitude toward dealing with stress. **Attitude** is your way of thinking, acting, and feeling. Everyone has a bad day once in a while. Being unpleasant and not helpful most of the time shows a negative attitude. A negative attitude can lessen your ability to manage stress. A negative attitude can prevent you from reaching your goals.

▶ **A positive attitude helps you manage your stress.**

Suppose that you are not doing well in reading. You tell yourself, "I can't read. I'm not good at this." You approach reading expecting to fail. You might even use risk behaviors, such as breaking class rules, to cope with your stress. This shows a negative attitude.

With a positive attitude, you take action to improve your weakness. You might tell yourself, "I can't be good at everything, but I can try!" You seek help from a teacher or classmate. You now approach reading, thinking you'll succeed. You use healthful behaviors to deal with your stress. Your positive attitude helps you manage stress and reach your goals.

 What three actions can you take to show a positive attitude?

ACTIVITY

LIFE SKILLS

CRITICAL THINKING

Manage Stress

Your friend's older brother is supposed to pick you up after soccer practice. He is late. You and your friend are anxious.

1. **Identify the signs of stress.** Role-play two friends telling ways they feel stress. Act out ways they show stress.

2. **Identify the cause of stress.** Have the friends state what has happened (the brother is late) and how they feel about it.

3. **Do something about the cause of stress.** In your role-play, the brother will arrive late. The two friends must share their stress.

4. **Take action to reduce the harmful effects of stress.** In your role-play, the two friends will go home with the brother. On the way they will discuss what they will do as soon as they get home to relieve the stress that has built up.

LESSON REVIEW

Review Concepts

1. **Name** four changes that occur in your body when you feel stress.

2. **List** three healthful ways to manage stress.

3. **Define** the word attitude.

Critical Thinking

4. **Explain** Is it possible to feel stress without a stressor? Tell why or why not.

5. **LIFE SKILLS** **Manage Stress** You and your friend Trina are studying for a test. She seems calm while you are getting a headache. How will a positive attitude help you manage stress?

Manage Stress

Problem Jenna has a leading role in the school play. Everyone expects her to do well. On the day of the play, she wakes up with a headache. She is anxious and can't remember her lines. Does she have signs of stress?

Solution Jenna talks to her parents or guardian about her feelings. Then she follows the four steps to manage stress that are described on the next page.

Learn This Life Skill

Follow these four steps to manage stress.

1 **Identify the signs of stress.**

Jenna has a headache. She is anxious and cannot remember her lines. These are signs of stress.

2 **Identify the cause of stress.**

Jenna is anxious about the school play. She is afraid of performing in front of a large audience.

3 **Do something about the cause of stress.**

Jenna can talk to her parents or guardian. She can ask them to go over her lines with her.

4 **Take action to reduce the harmful effects of stress.**

Jenna does something to take her mind off the school play. She decides to take a walk around the block.

Practice This Life Skill

With your classmates, make a list of stressful situations. You might include singing in front of other people or playing a sport. Then make a Foldable™ using the situation and applying the four steps to follow to manage stress.

Use Vocabulary

character, *A12*

emotion, *A27*

healthful behavior, *A6*

life skill, *A7*

resistance skills, *A19*

risk behavior, *A6*

stressor, *A33*

wellness, *A6*

Choose the correct term from the list to complete each sentence. Write the word on a separate sheet of paper.

1. A(n) __?__ is something that causes stress.

2. A healthful action to learn and practice that increases and maintains your health is a(n) __?__.

3. An action that increases the level of health for you or for others is a(n) __?__.

4. A(n) __?__ is a feeling inside you.

5. An action that can be harmful to you or others is called a(n) __?__.

6. Your __?__ are ways to say "no" to risk behaviors.

7. The qualities that make one person different from another is called __?__.

8. The highest level of health you can have is __?__.

Review Concepts

Answer each question in complete sentences.

9. What are ways to improve life skills?

10. Describe how your mental and emotional health can be harmed by stress.

11. What two parts of your total health does your personality impact?

12. How does having self-respect improve your health?

13. Give three reasons why you need to express emotions in healthful ways.

14. How do you show respect for others?

Reading Comprehension

Answer each question in complete sentences.

All your emotions are felt inside you. When you express your emotions, you let these feelings out. You do this through your words and actions. Expressing your emotions in healthful ways promotes and protects health. It helps you communicate well with others.

15. How do you express emotions?

16. What happens when you express emotions in healthful ways?

17. What do you think might happen if you kept your emotions bottled up inside of you?

Critical Thinking/Problem Solving

Answer each question in complete sentences.

Analyze Concepts

18. You haven't been getting enough sleep lately. You are tired in class. You get angry easily. What part(s) of your total health are affected?

19. You want to get plenty of physical activity. How might you practice this healthful behavior?

20. You and your sister have the same parents. However, you have very different personalities. Why is this?

21. You've been working hard to improve your grades. How does this action affect your self-concept? Why?

Practice Life Skills

22. **Access Health Facts, Products, and Services** Grief is the discomfort a person feels after a loss. During periods of grief, a person might become very tired and have little energy. Name three places where you can find other health facts about grief.

23. **Practice Healthful Behaviors** You want to express anger in a healthful way. List the four steps to follow to practice this healthful behavior. Discuss what you will do for each step.

24. **Make Responsible Decisions** A classmate suggests doing something daring to stop boredom. He dares you to smoke a cigarette. Ask and answer the six questions in the *Guidelines for Making Responsible*

Decisions™ to evaluate this action as a way to overcome boredom.

Read Graphics

In a survey of fourth graders each student chose his or her most common reaction to stress. Use the chart below to answer questions 25–27.

Common Reactions to Stress

25. Which reaction to stress is the most common? Which is the least common?

26. How many more students chose the most common reaction than the least?

27. Which reaction to stress was two times more common than dry mouth?

 www.mmhhealth.com
Find out how much you know about emotions, character, and health.

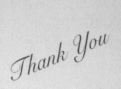

CHAPTER 2

Family and Social Health

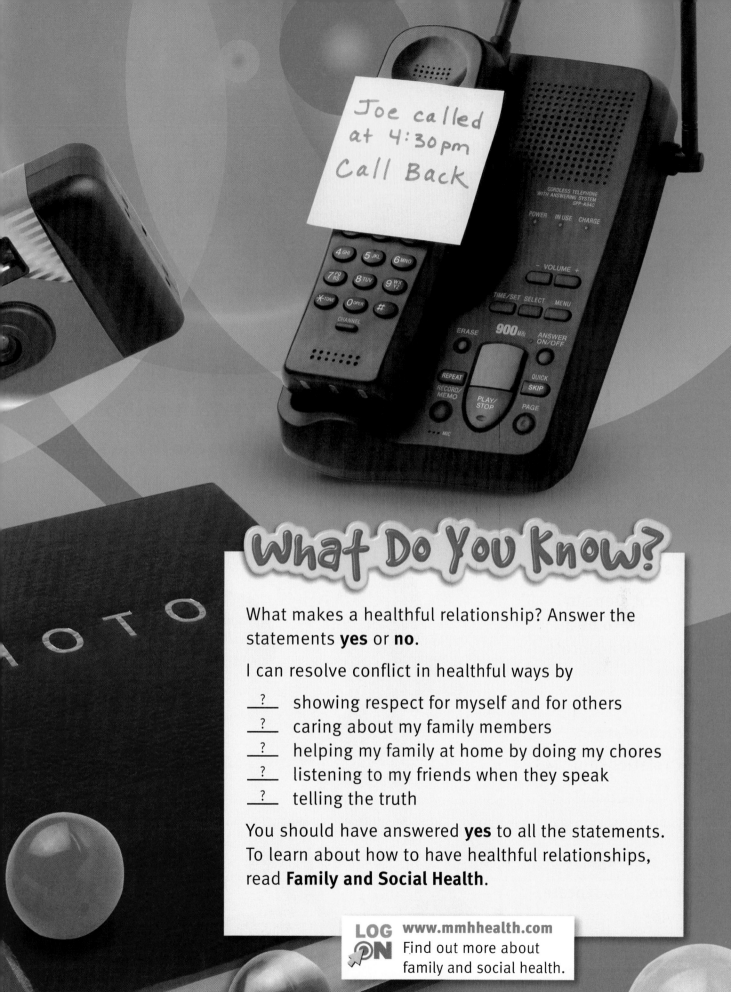

Joe called
at 4:30pm
Call Back

What Do You Know?

What makes a healthful relationship? Answer the statements **yes** or **no**.

I can resolve conflict in healthful ways by

__?__ showing respect for myself and for others
__?__ caring about my family members
__?__ helping my family at home by doing my chores
__?__ listening to my friends when they speak
__?__ telling the truth

You should have answered **yes** to all the statements. To learn about how to have healthful relationships, read **Family and Social Health**.

LOG ON www.mmhhealth.com
Find out more about family and social health.

Your Relationships

You will learn . . .

- ways to show respect in relationships.
- what steps to follow to improve your communication skills.
- what steps to follow to be a health advocate.

Parents or guardians, brothers, sisters—these were your very first relationships. Later, you learned how to make friends. Having healthful relationships improves your family and social health.

Vocabulary

- **relationship**, *A45*
- **respect**, *A45*
- **communication**, *A46*
- **I-message**, *A46*
- **health advocate**, *A48*
- **role model**, *A48*

Respect in Relationships

A **relationship** is a connection you have with another person. You have relationships with members of your family. You have relationships with students and teachers at school. You have relationships with people in your community. Each relationship you have is different. All relationships, however, are built on respect.

Respect is treating others as you want to be treated. Some people earn your respect. They show good character by being honest with you. They act in responsible ways.

Some people may not treat others with respect. They might interrupt when others speak. They might not be fair. They might be unkind. They may show disrespect for teachers.

When people are disrespectful, be careful how you respond. Although you don't like their actions, you must treat them with respect. Don't interrupt, be unfair, or be unkind. Instead, ask them to treat you with respect.

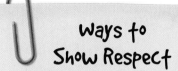

ways to Show Respect

- **Treat people the same way that you would like to be treated.** If you want others to treat you with kindness, be kind. If you want respect, show respect.

- **Be understanding of other people's ways of life.** Put yourself in another person's place. Try to understand why the person sees things a certain way.

 How do people earn your respect?

◄ **Friends respect each other.**

Use Good Communication Skills

Communication is important in healthful relationships. **Communication** is the sharing of feelings, thoughts, or information. Here are steps to follow to improve your communication skills.

1. **Choose the best way to communicate.** You communicate mostly by talking with a person face-to-face. This allows you to communicate easily and get a quick reply. However, you may choose to communicate in other ways, such as by writing notes and letters, talking on the phone, or sending e-mails. *Body language* is another way to communicate with other people using movements or gestures.

2. **Send a clear message. Be polite.** Be honest about what you are feeling. An **I-message** is a healthful way to communicate about a problem and how it affects you. For example, you might say, "I feel hurt when I'm treated with disrespect." I-messages let others know what you think and how you feel. Then others can respond to your thoughts and feelings.

3. **Listen to each other.** Look directly at the person. Pay attention. Try not to think of other things. Listen even when you don't agree. Allow the person to finish talking before you speak.

4. **Make sure you understand each other.** Tell the other person what you heard. Ask questions if you need to. Ask the other person what he or she heard from you. Give the other person a chance to share his or her thoughts and feelings.

Use Communication Skills

- **Choose the best way to communicate.**
- **Send a clear message. Be polite.**
- **Listen to each other.**
- **Make sure you understand each other.**

ConSumer WiSe

Communication at the Doctor's Office

You can make the most of your doctor visits by knowing what you want to say ahead of time. Talk to your parents or guardian about what you will need to tell the doctor. Write a conversation that might take place between you and the doctor. What questions might you ask? Write your questions on index cards.

Learning to communicate takes practice. You must be willing to share what you are thinking and feeling. This is easy at times when you feel happiness or joy, or when talking with friends and family. It may be harder when your emotions are strong, such as when you are angry. It also may be difficult when you feel anxious, such as when you are giving a report in front of classmates. With practice, however, your communication skills will improve.

 Why is it important to share your feelings when you communicate with others?

BUILD Character
Be a Friend

Respect You can show respect for someone who has difficulty communicating. To *stutter* is to repeat words or sounds several times when speaking. A person who stutters faces a challenge when communicating.

- Listen closely to the person as he or she is speaking.

- Be patient. Do not finish a sentence for the person or call attention to the person's stuttering.

- Do not make fun of him or her.

◀ **Communicating takes work by both the speaker and the listener.**

Be a Health Advocate

Be a Health Advocate

- Choose a healthful action to communicate.
- Collect information about the action.
- Decide how to communicate this information.
- Communicate your message to others.

ACTIVITY

Art LINK

A Classroom Advocate

Promote a positive attitude in your classroom. Make a poster or banner promoting the value of cooperation, communication, respect, and responsibility.

In a healthful relationship, two people encourage each other to choose healthful behaviors. A person who helps another person choose healthful behaviors is a **health advocate**. Here are a few steps to follow to be a health advocate.

1. **Choose a healthful action to communicate.** Think of a healthful behavior to help an inactive friend become more active. You might invite your friend to bike ride after school. You might ask your friend to join your soccer team. What other physical activities might you do together?

2. **Collect information about the action.** After you choose a healthful behavior, look for information on the topic. Visit the library. Find a book on bicycling or soccer. Think about other sources you could rely on for information.

3. **Decide how to communicate this information.** You might communicate by talking to your friend. You might write the information on a piece of paper and give it to your friend. You might communicate by being a role model. A **role model** is someone who shows behavior that other people copy. You are a role model when you play soccer and your friend decides to join the team.

▶ An older sister or brother can be a positive role model for a younger brother or sister.

4. Communicate your message to others. Now it is time to follow through. Set time aside to talk with your friend. Give your friend the information you collected. Invite your friend to watch you play soccer.

✓ **What is a health advocate?**

CRITICAL THINKING
LIFE SKILLS — ACTIVITY

Be a Health Advocate

Some of your friends just watch TV after school. How can you encourage them to be more physically active?

1 **Choose a healthful action to communicate.** Work with a partner. Choose a healthful action that promotes physical activity, such as skating. Suggest other healthful behaviors.

2 **Collect information about the action.** Find out about the importance of physical activity. You might go to the library or conduct research on the Internet. You might talk with your physical education teacher.

3 **Decide how to communicate this information.** Make flyers to give to your friends. How else might you get your message to others?

4 **Communicate your message to others.** Now take action. Make your flyers. Share your flyers with your friends.

LESSON REVIEW

Review Concepts

1. **Identify** two ways to show respect.

2. **List** four steps to follow to improve your communication skills.

Critical Thinking

3. **Synthesize** Why is it better to be a role model than to just tell someone how to improve their health?

4. **LIFE SKILLS** **Be a Health Advocate** You want to help your friend Brad choose healthful snacks. What could you tell Brad to convince him to eat more healthful foods?

5. **LIFE SKILLS** **Use Communication Skills** You trip while running and some students laugh at you. Write an I-message to express your feelings.

Managing Your Emotions

You will learn . . .

- reasons to maintain self-control.
- how to manage anger.
- steps to follow in resolving conflict and avoiding fights.

Joy, anger, surprise, sadness—you feel a range of emotions in healthful relationships. Some of these emotions, such as anger, may be strong and hard to manage. To keep healthful relationships, you need to learn ways to manage strong emotions.

Vocabulary

- **self-control**, *A51*
- **conflict**, *A53*
- **mediation**, *A54*

Aim for Self-Control

You are in charge of your actions, and you can decide what you will or will not do. Deciding not to say or do something that you know you shouldn't is called **self-control**.

Reasons to Maintain Self-Control

There are several reasons why it is important to maintain self-control.

- **It keeps you from doing things that you may regret.** Sometimes classmates may push or shove one another while playing at recess. You may want to push or shove back, but instead you show self-control. You stop before saying or doing something that you may regret. Instead you ask them to stop.

- **It keeps you from doing too much of something.** Without self-control, it could be very easy to eat an entire bag of pretzels or to hog the ball when playing basketball. When you use self-control, you eat only a serving of the pretzels and you play ball like a team player. You know how to keep from doing too much of something.

- **It helps you manage your emotions.** You experience many emotions throughout the day. Self-control allows you to show the right amount of any given emotion in a healthful way.

One way to help maintain self-control is to use *self-statements.* Before eating that entire bag of pretzels, say to yourself, "I will not eat all these pretzels. I want to stay at a healthful weight." Self-statements remind you to maintain self-control.

 Name three reasons why you should maintain self-control.

Music LINK

Share the Music

Volunteer to bring in a tape or CD of your favorite music. Get an okay from your teacher first. Play it for the class. Talk about how the music makes you feel. Ask your classmates how the music makes them feel.

▲ **Self-control keeps you from eating too much food.**

Manage Anger

Anger is a strong emotion that develops when you feel upset or hurt. Everyone feels angry at times, and that's okay. However, acting on your anger by yelling or hitting is not okay. If you yell or hit, you have lost self-control.

How to Manage Anger

You can manage angry feelings. You can stay in control.

- **Stop what you are saying or doing.** If you don't, it is likely you will say or do something that you may regret later.

- **Take time out to cool down.** Try taking several deep breaths or counting slowly to 10. This gives you time to calm down.

- **Think about the situation.** Decide how you could best respond in a healthful way before you act on your decisions.

  - **Act on your decision.** You may decide to talk about your feelings. If you do, use I-messages. In some cases, it may be better just to walk away. This gives you even more time to calm down. Then you can work out the problem later.

✓ **What are two ways to cool down when you are angry?**

◀ Taking time to cool down helps you to manage anger.

Avoid Fighting

A **conflict** is a strong disagreement or fight. Such disagreements can be verbal—yelling and shouting, or physical—pushing and kicking. You can avoid fights by learning how to resolve conflicts. Here's how.

1. **Stay calm.** Use self-control and self-statements to remind yourself not to fight.

2. **Talk about the conflict.** It takes at least two people to fight. Tell the other person involved that you will not fight. Suggest talking out the conflict instead. Listen to the other person's point of view. Then express your point of view without using put-downs.

Resolve Conflicts

- Stay calm.

- Talk about the conflict.

- List possible ways to settle the conflict.

- Agree on a way to settle the conflict. You may need to ask a responsible adult for help.

▶ **What types of actions can cause conflict on a playground?**

"Cut It Out"

Playground conflicts were making many Valdez Elementary School students feel unsafe. Students listened to counselors from a conflict center and the Denver Police. They learned ways to resolve conflicts and prevent violence. Then they began an advice column, called "Cut It Out," in their school newspaper. What actions did these students take that worked well to reduce conflict?

3. **List possible ways to settle the conflict.** Evaluate each solution on your list. Use the *Guidelines for Making Responsible Decisions*™ on page A55 to help you. Make sure the solution is healthful and safe. It must follow rules and laws and show respect for yourself and others. It should follow family guidelines and show good character, too.

4. **Agree on a way to settle the conflict. You may need to ask a responsible adult for help.** A parent, guardian, teacher, or other responsible adult might need to be a mediator. **Mediation** is a process in which a responsible person helps settle a conflict.

 What are four steps to follow to resolve conflict without fighting?

ACTIVITY
Conşumer Wişe

Returns

If you buy a product that doesn't work, return it to the store. Role-play with a parent or guardian what to say to a salesperson or customer service manager in order to get your money back or an offer to replace the product. A receipt is usually needed. How does having a receipt when you return a product help prevent conflict?

Make Responsible Decisions

Suppose you are standing in line for lunch when a classmate cuts in front of you. Your friends push the classmate out of line. What should you do? Write a skit to tell how you could handle the situation.

1 **Identify your choices.** One choice might be to ask the classmate to go to the end of the line. Another choice might be to join your friends and push the classmate out of line. What are some other choices?

2 **Evaluate each choice. Use the *Guidelines for Making Responsible Decisions™*.** Narrow down your choices.

3 **Identify the responsible decision.** Explain why it is responsible. You might consider whether your decision shows respect for others. Check this out with your parents or guardian or other responsible adult.

4 **Evaluate your decision.** Explain what might happen if you make this decision. Does your decision help you show self-control and resolve the conflict?

Guidelines for Making Responsible Decisions™

- Is it healthful?
- Is it safe?
- Do you follow rules and laws?
- Do you show respect for yourself and others?
- Do you follow family guidelines?
- Do you show good character?

LESSON REVIEW

Review Concepts

1. **Discuss** how a self-statement helps you maintain self-control.

2. **Tell** how to manage anger.

3. **Explain** what mediation is.

Critical Thinking

4. **Analyze** When might it be better to just walk away from a situation when you're angry?

5. **Infer** Why is it important not to use put downs during a conflict?

6. **LIFE SKILLS** **Make Responsible Decisions** You are playing basketball with friends. A classmate asks to join the game. The other players tease the new player. Refer to the *Guidelines for Making Responsible Decisions™* above. Explain what you will do.

Learning LIFE SKILLS

Resolve conflicts

Problem Sarah and Jake are playing a board game. Jake loses and accuses Sarah of cheating. They start to argue. How can they resolve this conflict?

Solution Family members can resolve conflict without fighting. Use the four steps on the next page to resolve conflicts when they occur.

Foldables™ To Learn Life Skills

Learn This Life Skill

Follow these four steps to help you resolve conflicts.

1 **Stay calm.**

Sarah is angry because Jake accused her of cheating. She yelled at him. What are ways Sarah could have used to stay calm?

2 **Talk about the conflict.**

Sarah decides to talk with her brother about what he said. Write an I-message Sarah might use to tell him how she feels. What might Jake say?

3 **List possible ways to settle the conflict.**

Sarah could suggest that they both say, "I'm sorry." They could play another game. Use the *Guidelines for Making Responsible Decisions*™ to evaluate each way you list.

4 **Agree on a way to settle the conflict. You may need to ask a responsible adult for help.**

Sarah and Jake choose a responsible way to settle the conflict. They decide to play again. When might they need to ask a parent or guardian for help?

Practice This Life Skill

Work with a group of four. Describe a conflict that might happen between classmates. How might you use the four steps to resolve the conflict? Role-play using these four steps to resolve conflict.

A57

How a Healthy Family Functions

You will learn . . .

- why it is important to be close to family members.

- how your family affects your health.

Vocabulary

- **family**, *A59*
- **family guidelines**, *A59*
- **heredity**, *A60*
- **environment**, *A60*

In a healthful family, members have close relationships. They support each other. They give love and attention to one another. They spend time together doing chores, sharing meals, or playing games.

Being Close to Family Members

A **family** is a group of people who are related in some way. Families may include different family members. There are four types of families that people might have. These include nuclear, single-parent, extended, and blended families.

- A *nuclear family* has a husband and wife who raise one or more children.

- A *single-parent family* has one parent who raises one or more children.

- An *extended family* includes a husband and wife and children as well as other relatives, such as grandparents, aunts, and uncles, who might act as guardians in some cases.

- A *blended family* is formed when one or both parents have been married before. It may include children from a previous marriage.

Being close to your family helps you feel safe and secure. Family members experience good times and bad times together, making them stronger.

Family members also follow **family guidelines**, or rules set by parents or guardians that tell children how to act. Family guidelines can help you resolve conflicts and get along with other family members. By following family guidelines, you show that you respect your parents or guardian. You stay healthy and safe, and form healthful habits.

On Your Own
ACTIVITY
FOR SCHOOL OR HOME

Write Your Family's Guidelines

Discuss family guidelines with your parents or guardian. Make a list and hang the guidelines in your home where everyone can see them. Having family guidelines posted serves as a good reminder. Review the family guidelines often. Make changes if they are needed.

 Why is it important to follow family guidelines?

How a Family Influences Your Health

ACTIVITY

Art

L I N K

Make a Mobile

Make a mobile to show traits you inherited and habits you developed from your family. Cut out strips of construction paper. On one side write a talent or healthful habit (for example "Has perfect teeth"). On the other side write the name of the person with whom you share the trait (for example "Mom"). Tape string to the paper strips and tie to a hanger.

You may share some of the same looks or talents as one or both of your birth parents. You look the way you do because of **heredity**, or the traits passed on to you from your birth parents. The **environment**, or everything around you, also influences your health and the talents that you develop.

Your heredity gives you your eye and hair color. It's the reason you may have a strong body that easily fights off disease. You can find out more about your heredity and health from your parents or guardian.

Your parents or guardians try to provide a healthful and safe environment for you. The health habits that the adults in your household have affect your health. Suppose that these adults do not smoke and get plenty of exercise. You may copy these healthful habits. On the other hand, if the adults smoke and do not exercise, their children may someday copy these harmful habits.

Where a family lives also affects health. Environments with very little crime reduce a family member's risk of being harmed by violence.

▶ **Children share many of the same traits as their birth parents.**

How family members interact affects health. In most families, members are warm and caring. They praise each other for good efforts and help each other when they make mistakes. They encourage self-respect and improve each family member's overall health. However, in some families, the adults may use put-downs. They may be unkind. Children who live in these families are more likely to get headaches and stomachaches. They may feel sad and lonely.

 What is heredity?

ACTIVITY LIFE SKILLS · CRITICAL THINKING

Analyze What Influences Your Health

The television programs you watch or books you read feature many types of families. Use this activity to find out how books and television influence your health.

1 **Identify people and things that can influence your health.** Choose a television program or a book that features a family.

2 **Evaluate how these people and things can affect your health.** Watch the program, or read the book. Take notes on how family members affect one another.

3 **Choose healthful influences.** Review your notes. Write down healthful ways family members influence one another.

4 **Protect yourself against harmful influences.** Review your notes again and write down any harmful influences. How might you protect yourself from these influences in the future?

LESSON REVIEW

Review Concepts

1. **Explain** reasons to be close to family members.

2. **Identify** two ways that your family influences your health.

3. **Tell** how you can get along with family members.

Critical Thinking

4. **Analyze** What might happen if you did not have family guidelines?

5. **LIFE SKILLS** **Analyze What Influences Your Health** Suppose that an adult family member enjoys playing sports. How might this adult's activities influence your choice of activities?

How Families Change

You will learn . . .

- ways family members work together.
- how a family adjusts to change.
- ways to adjust if parents separate or divorce.
- how families adjust to new members.

Vocabulary

- **separation**, *A65*
- **divorce**, *A65*
- **adoption**, *A66*
- **foster child**, *A66*

Part of being in a family means sharing responsibilities around the home. Think of some of the things you do to help your family. Working together helps family members adjust to change during difficult times.

Family Members Work Together

Family members have to work together. Maybe you help your family by washing the dishes. Maybe you take out the trash. You may be expected to keep your room clean. Both adult family members may work outside of the home. At home they cook, clean, care for their children, and run necessary errands. You can help your family by doing your chores. Here are ways family members work together.

- **Take turns and share.** Suppose that you and your sister both want to take a shower at the same time. Or maybe you both want the rest of the potatoes at dinner. How will you decide who goes first? Will you divide the potatoes? Think about being fair. Take turns and share.

- **Resolve conflict.** Suppose that your younger brother keeps interrupting you. Calmly explain to him how this makes you feel. Find solutions to conflicts.

- **Visit relatives and share work.** Perhaps you have helped your family by visiting an ill relative in a hospital or spending time with a grandparent. You may go shopping together for food or clothing. It takes a lot of work to meet the needs of a family, but the work is much easier when it is shared.

 Name two ways family members work together.

Math LINK

Share the Pie

Plan a pizza party. There are 28 students and 1 teacher in your class. Each pizza pie is divided into 8 slices. How many pizza pies will you need to make sure each person gets a slice? How many carrots will you need to make sure everyone gets 3 carrots?

▲ Family members can work together to get a job done.

Adjusting to Change

Families often face changes. Healthful families talk about change. They share their feelings and ask questions. They learn to *adjust*, or change and make things better.

Change can bring family members closer. Family members can look for the good in difficult times. They can offer each other support.

Moving Some families move, making it hard to see friends. To adjust, family members talk about ways to keep in touch. They make new friends at their new home.

Losing a Job When a parent or guardian loses a job, he or she experiences a great deal of pressure. To adjust, family members offer support and encouragement. They cut back on spending.

Illness When a family member becomes ill, other family members spend time with that person. They offer help. They take on more chores.

Death The death of a family member may cause sadness. To adjust, family members talk about the person and cry together. They share memories.

▼ **Spending time together brings family members closer. It makes their relationships stronger.**

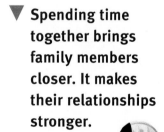

What are ways a family might change?

Separation and Divorce

All married couples have times when they disagree. Most of the time they are able to work out their disagreements. Sometimes they decide to take time away from each other. A **separation** is when a couple is still married but living apart. During this time they try to work things out. Some married couples who separate get back together again. Others are unable to resolve their conflicts. They get a **divorce**, or a legal end to a marriage.

Separation and divorce might be hard for family members. Children might feel sad, angry, and confused. They might feel guilty and think that they are responsible. Children whose parents separate or divorce might do the following to help adjust. They might share their feelings with their parents or guardian. They might ask questions so they know what to expect. They might pay attention to their health habits in order to stay strong and healthy.

 What might children do if their parents become separated or divorced?

CAREERS

Social Worker

A social worker is trained to help families who are unable to adjust to certain changes or problems on their own. A social worker knows where families can get help when they need it. Social workers may work in hospitals, community clinics, mental health centers, schools, or social service agencies.

LOG ON www.mmhhealth.com
Find out more about health careers.

A65

When a Family Grows Larger

Families face changes when there are new family members. This can happen several different ways.

- **The addition of a newborn baby.** A family changes with the birth of a baby. Older children may need to help care for the baby. Parents or guardians may have less time to spend with their older children.

- **The addition of an adopted child. Adoption** is legally taking a child of other parents into the family. This child becomes a permanent member of the family. Family members can make the change smoother by making the child feel welcome.

- **The addition of a foster child.** Parents or guardians might decide to have a foster child live with the family. A **foster child** is a child who lives with a family without being related by birth or adoption. A foster child stays with the family until a permanent home is found.

- **The addition of children as a result of marriage.** Sometimes parents remarry. The family becomes a blended family. Both parents may have children from another marriage. In blended families, it's important to make new members feel welcome. Your parents or guardian can help make the change smoother by talking with you about what to expect when adjusting to new family members.

▼ The addition of a newborn baby brings added responsibilities to all family members.

 How might a family adjust to a new family member?

A66

Set Health Goals

Everyone in a family has responsibilities. Think of three chores you can do at home on a regular basis. Make a poster to remind you of your chores.

1 **Write the health goal you want to set.** For example, it might be "I will work to have healthful family relationships."

2 **Explain how your goal might affect your health.** Working with your family will help build healthful family relationships. This improves family and social health. How might this affect your mental and physical health?

3 **Describe a plan you will follow to reach your goal. Keep track of your progress.** Make a Health Behavior Contract. You might want to use a calendar to keep track of the chores you do. Each time you do a chore, put a smiley face next to that chore under the day you completed it.

4 **Evaluate how your plan worked.** At the end of the week, add up the smiley faces. How many chores did you do? Which chores did you not do? Share this calendar with your parents or guardian. Hang the completed health behavior contract on the refrigerator. This will remind you to continue to do your chores on time.

LESSON REVIEW

Review Concepts

1. **Describe** ways family members work together.

2. **Explain** how family members might adjust after a parent loses a job.

3. **Explain** the difference between separation and divorce.

4. **List** four ways a family might get new family members.

Critical Thinking

5. **Analyze** What could a child do to adjust to the divorce or separation of his or her parents?

6. **LIFE SKILLS** **Set Healthy Goals** How might you reach this health goal: "I will adjust to family changes in healthful ways"?

Healthful Friendships

You will learn . . .

- how a true friend acts.
- how to use resistance skills.
- how peers show good character.
- what to look for when making new friends.

Vocabulary

- **friend**, *A69*
- **peer**, *A71*
- **peer pressure**, *A71*

You will meet many people in your lifetime. Some of these people will become very important to you. You will form close relationships with them. These people will become your friends.

How True Friends Act

A **friend** is a person who likes and supports you. You have friends you go to school with, friends you play with, and friends you really like to talk to. Friends that you do almost everything with are called your best friends.

Everyone has friends, but not all people make true friends. A true friend is a person who is responsible and caring. A true friend thinks about your feelings, not just his or her own.

Suppose that a person calls you a friend but tries to get you to act in wrong ways. This person isn't a true friend. A true friend wants you to be responsible. Or maybe a person calls you a friend but treats you badly. This person also isn't a true friend. A true friend cares about you.

A Want Ad Write and design a want ad for a true friend. Include a job description. Post the want ad in the classroom.

 What is a friend?

A True Friend

- stands by you
- tells you the truth
- respects your family's guidelines
- wants you to spend time with your family
- lets you have other friends
- does not tell other people things about you
- does not put you down
- wants you to make responsible decisions
- wants you to take care of your health
- wants you to have good character

▲ A true friend cares about you.

How to Use Resistance Skills

You may discover that one of your friends practices risk behaviors. If you are a true friend, encourage responsible behavior. If your friend pressures you to choose risk behaviors, then he or she isn't a true friend. Use resistance skills to say "no."

Steps for using resistance skills:

1. **Look at the person. Say "no" in a firm voice.** Make eye contact. Speak in a confident way.

2. **Give reasons for saying "no."** Explain why the risk behavior is not responsible.

3. **Match your behavior to your words.** Stay away from situations in which peers might try to talk you into risk behaviors and unwise decisions. Offer other ideas. Walk away if the pressure continues.

4. **Ask an adult for help if you need it.** Talk with your parents, guardian, or other responsible adult. The adult may need to get involved if your peer's behavior could put others at risk.

Friends who respect you will take "no" for an answer. If a friend continues to pressure you to do a wrong act or make an unwise decision, you may need to end the relationship.

 What should you do if a friend tries to pressure you into doing something wrong?

Use Resistance Skills

- **Look at the person. Say "no" in a firm voice.**
- **Give reasons for saying "no."**
- **Match your behavior to your words.**
- **Ask an adult for help if you need it.**

Peers and Character

The people you spend most of your time with are your peers. A **peer** is someone who is about the same age as you, but may or may not be your friend. Peers may dress, talk, or act alike. You may fit in with some peers, but not others. When people your own age try to influence you, they are using **peer pressure**. Sometimes peers try to get you to do something wrong, such as breaking class rules. These peers are not true friends.

True friends influence each other in healthful ways. They encourage each other to follow rules and make responsible decisions. True friends have good character. They want you to have good character.

 What is a peer?

Art LINK

Make a Card

Design a greeting card for a friend. Draw a picture on the front illustrating friendship. Write a 4-line poem about friendship inside the card.

 ACTIVITY LIFE SKILLS

CRITICAL THINKING

Use Resistance Skills

A peer pressures you to leave school early. What should you do? Pair up with a classmate and take turns using resistance skills.

1. **Look at the person. Say "no" in a firm voice.** Look at your partner. Make eye contact and say "no" in a firm voice.

2. **Give reasons for saying "no."** Tell reasons why you will not leave school early.

3. **Match your behavior to your words.** Use body language that sends a "no" message clearly. What is one other thing you can do?

4. **Ask an adult for help if you need it.** Involve your teacher in your role-play. Who else might be able to help?

A71

Character

Interview Friends

Caring When you care about others, you are interested in them. You care about how they feel and what they think. Make a list of your friends. For each one, write down what you know about their feelings and opinions. Think of one word that you would use to describe each friend to someone who doesn't know them.

Making Friends

Most of your friends might be the same age as you. But age isn't what determines who becomes your friend. Having at least one thing in common helps you become friends with someone.

Finding Things in Common

Friendship is built on having something in common. One of the easiest ways to make new friends is to get involved in new activities, such as a school club or a new sports team. Spending time with people in these types of groups helps you get to know other people. Here's what to look for when making new friends.

Similar interests You may enjoy the same hobbies, sports, or other activities.

Similar values You may follow the same guidelines for behavior. You may share the same beliefs.

Enjoy each other's company You like doing things together.

Belong to the same groups You may go to school together or play the same sports. You may be in the same school clubs.

◀ Friends share common interests.

When choosing a new group to get involved with, think about the kind of people who make up the group. Groups organized by responsible adults, such as scout troops and sports teams, are best. They provide a safe environment where you can make new friends.

When making new friends, avoid people who make fun of you or say negative comments about other people. Beware of gangs who break laws and take unnecessary risks. These groups are not respectful of others. These groups might try to persuade you to do things you don't want to do. They might pressure you to choose illegal actions and can be dangerous.

 **Why do friendships form?**

On Your Own

FOR SCHOOL OR HOME

Form Your Own Group

Start a club for classmates with the same interests. Place a notice at school emphasizing a special interest such as reading, listening to a certain kind of music, writing stories and so on.

LESSON REVIEW

Review Concepts

1. **List** three actions that show a true friend.

2. **List** resistance skills to use if pressured to do a wrong act.

3. **Define** peer pressure.

4. **Describe** three things to look for when making new friends.

Critical Thinking

5. **Conclude** What should you do if a peer pressures you to help him break a classroom rule?

6. **LIFE SKILLS** **Use Resistance Skills** You are with a friend at the skating rink. You run into a group of peers who pressure you to leave with them. You are supposed to stay at the rink until your older sister picks you up. Write four reasons you would give for saying "no."

When Others Are Unkind

You will learn . . .

- what to do when you feel left out.
- what to do when others try to harm you.

Vocabulary

- **clique**, *A75*
- **abuse**, *A76*
- **bully**, *A76*

You may try really hard to have healthful relationships. But some of the people you have relationships with may not show good character. They may not be honest. They may not be trustworthy. They may be unkind.

When You Feel Left Out

There will be times when you feel left out. A friend may pay less attention to you after meeting someone new. A group of your friends may go to a movie without you. Friends usually don't leave you out on purpose. When you feel left out you may have hurt feelings. Here are some different actions you can take when you feel left out.

- **Share your feelings.** Talk about how you feel. Be honest with your friends.

- **Call another friend.** You might have many different friends. You can make plans to do something together or just talk.

- **Talk to your parents or guardian.** Everyone has felt left out at times. Your parents or guardians can help you handle hurt feelings.

- **Say nothing.** Sometimes even true friends need space and time for other things and other friends.

▲ When you feel left out, make plans of your own with other friends.

Cliques

Some people may become friends with others who are in a clique. A **clique** (KLEEK) is a group of people who keep others out of their group. People who belong to a clique may reject you. You may feel disappointed. At times like this, you might ask yourself, are these people respectful of others? Would they make true friends?

 In what way are people in a clique hurtful to others?

When Others Try to Harm You

Some people may show unkind behavior toward you. Such behavior is called abuse. **Abuse** is rough or harsh treatment. It is unkind, hurtful behavior done on purpose. Tell a responsible adult about unkind behavior or abuse. There are three types of abuse.

Emotional Abuse Some people tease others. Maybe someone has called you names. Maybe someone treated you differently from the way they treated others. This is emotional abuse. It is harmful to your mental and emotional health.

Physical Abuse A person may hit, shove, or trip you on purpose. A person may throw things at you. This is physical abuse. Physical abuse can cause injury.

Bullying A person who threatens or frightens you is a **bully**. Bullies may harm others emotionally or physically. A person who is harmed by a bully often feels alone, sad, and confused. That person may build up anger inside.

Protecting Yourself Against Abuse

- **Do not allow abuse.**

- **Do not keep abuse a secret.** Tell a responsible adult.

- **Find help.** Go to a parent, guardian, teacher, or other responsible adult when you have private time. Tell the adult that you need to talk. Know where and how to find help if it is ever needed again.

- **Spend time with friends.** Friends give you support in hard times.

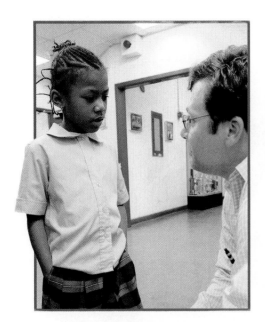

▲ Choose a time and place to talk about a problem where you won't be interrupted.

- **Leave the situation if you are in danger of harm.** If a bully tries to abuse you, there are different choices you can make. Look the bully in the eye and say, "I expect you to treat me with respect. I will not be bullied."

- **Be aware of your surroundings.** Change your routes or the times you do things. Try to stay around a group of safe people when possible.

 What is abuse?

Practice Healthful Behaviors

A classmate is treating you in an unkind manner. How can you protect yourself from abuse?

1. **Learn about a healthful behavior.** Work with a small group of classmates. List five examples of unkind behavior that you would report to your teacher.

2. **Practice the behavior.** Take turns and act out how you would protect yourself.

3. **Ask for help if you need it.** Role-play telling a responsible adult about the abuse.

4. **Make the behavior a habit.** Continue to practice what you might say and do until it becomes a habit.

◀ How are these students role-playing an unkind behavior?

LESSON REVIEW

Review Concepts

1. **Recall** what to do when you feel left out.

2. **Explain** the differences among the three types of abuse.

Critical Thinking

3. **Analyze** What should you do if a bully tries to harm you?

4. **LIFE SKILLS** **Practice Healthful Behaviors** Someone shoves you on the playground. The next day, this person shoves you again. What healthful behaviors would you practice to protect yourself from abuse?

5. **LIFE SKILLS** **Access Health Facts, Products, and Services** You are being emotionally abused by a school bully. You need help. Name two adults who might help you in school.

CHAPTER 2 REVIEW

Use Vocabulary

clique, *A75*

conflict, *A53*

environment, *A60*

family guidelines, *A59*

friend, *A69*

respect, *A45*

separation, *A65*

Choose the correct term from the list to complete each sentence. Write the word on a separate sheet of paper.

1. Treating others as you want to be treated is called ___?___.

2. A strong disagreement or a fight is called a ___?___.

3. Rules set by your parents or guardian are called ___?___.

4. When a couple is still married but not living together in the same house, it is called a(n) ___?___.

5. A person who likes and supports you is a(n) ___?___.

6. A group of people who reject others is called a(n) ___?___.

7. Everything around you is your ___?___.

Review Concepts

Answer each question in a complete sentence.

8. List four steps to follow to improve communication skills.

9. Describe healthful ways to manage anger.

10. Identify three different types of families. List family members in each type.

11. List four ways family members work together.

12. What is a true friend?

13. What is a clique?

Reading Comprehension

Answer each question in a complete sentence.

Family members also follow family guidelines, or rules set by parents or guardians that tell children how to act. Family guidelines can help you resolve conflicts and get along with other family members. By following family guidelines, you show that you respect your parents or guardian. You stay healthy and safe, and form healthful habits.

14. What are family guidelines?

15. Who sets family guidelines?

16. Who follows family guidelines?

Critical Thinking/Problem Solving

Answer each question in a complete sentence.

Analyze Concepts

17. Your friends have been arguing. They can't come to a solution that makes both of them happy. What steps can they follow to resolve conflict?

18. You have been feeling angry all day. When you get home from school, you find your younger brother in your room. How can using self-control help you stay calm?

19. Your best friend is moving to another city. You feel sad and lonely. How can you adjust to this change?

20. A friend is teased on the playground every day. Some of his peers laugh at him. What kind of abuse is this? How can this friend protect him- or herself?

21. Your friend's family has invited a foster child to stay with them. What does this mean?

Practice Life Skills

22. **Use Resistance Skills** At recess you see a group of friends sneaking into the school through the back door. They wave to you to join them. What should you do?

23. **Make Responsible Decisions** Your friend has invited you over to her house to play. You already promised your sister that you'd help with her chores. What should you do? Use the *Guidelines for Making Responsible Decisions™*.

Read Graphics

Review the chart that shows Kyle's household chores for a week.

Kyle's Household Chores Chart		
Day	**Daily Chores**	**Weekly Chores**
Monday	Make bed ✔ Walk dog ✔	Take out trash ✔
Tuesday	Make bed ✔ Walk dog ✔	
Wednesday	Make bed Walk dog ✔	Wash dishes ✔
Thursday	Make bed Walk dog ✔	
Friday	Make bed Walk dog ✔	Clean room
Saturday	Make bed Walk dog ✔	Put away clean clothes

24. On which days did Kyle complete all his chores?

25. How well did Kyle do at completing his chores? Explain your answer.

 LOG ON www.mmhhealth.com
Find out how much you know about family and social health.

Effective Communication

Make a Collage

Draw a series of pictures illustrating emotions. Think about scenes or colors for emotions such as joy, anger, surprise, sadness, worry, happiness and so on. Combine the drawings in a collage.

Self-Directed Learning

Write a Paragraph

Find pictures of family members. Write each person's name on a sheet of paper. Then write paragraphs telling the traits that you share with each person. Include any health habits that you may have learned from them.

Critical Thinking and Problem Solving

Make a Game

Work with a partner. Write down four family guidelines on index cards. Determine what might happen if each guideline is broken and write these on another set of index cards. Mix up the cards and match them up.

Responsible Citizenship

"Adopt" a Senior Citizen

With your teacher's permission, plan a class project to "adopt" an older adult who cannot get around. Visit the person twice a month. Make a list of what your adopted senior citizen might need. Think about activities you can do with your new friend.

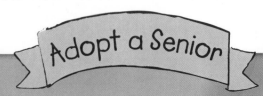

Adopt a Senior

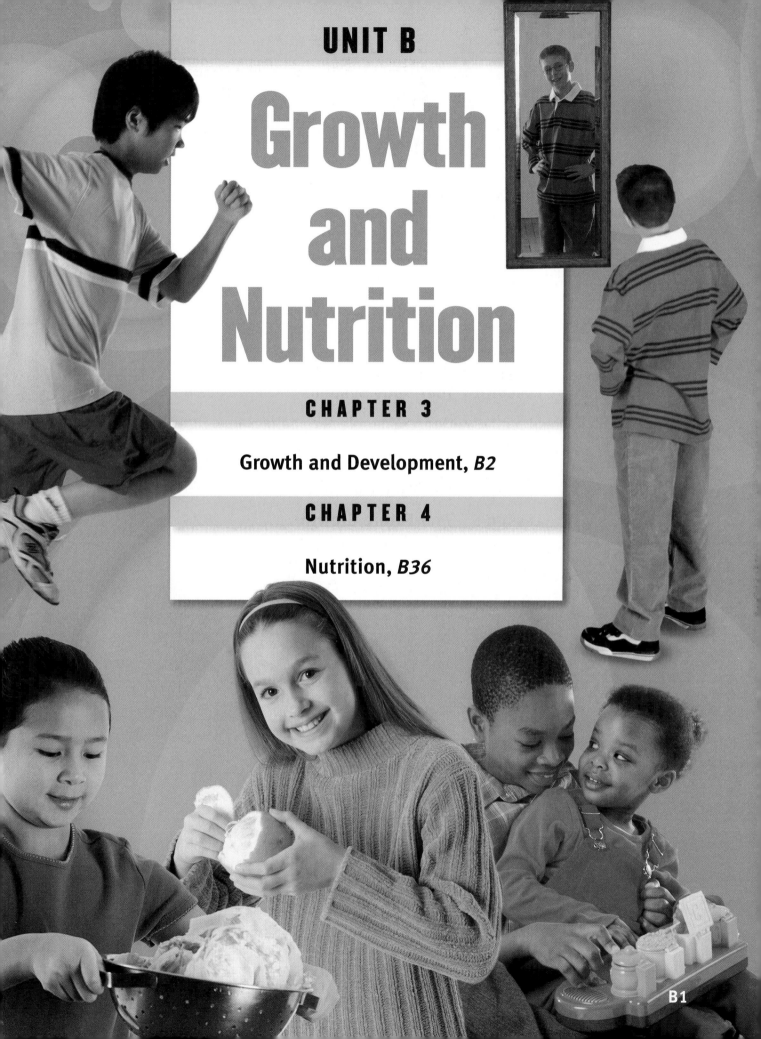

UNIT B

Growth and Nutrition

CHAPTER 3

Growth and Development, *B2*

CHAPTER 4

Nutrition, *B36*

CHAPTER 3
Growth and Development

What Do You Know?

How much do you know about your body? On a separate piece of paper, match each healthful habit with a body system. Some systems may be used more than once.

Healthful Habit

1. ___?___ Eating foods high in calcium

2. ___?___ Wearing sunscreen, even in winter

3. ___?___ Chewing food well

4. ___?___ Avoiding tobacco smoke

5. ___?___ Exercising 30 to 60 minutes a day

6. ___?___ Wearing a helmet when riding a bike

7. ___?___ Avoiding high-fat foods

System

a. Circulatory system

b. Digestive system

c. Muscular system

d. Nervous system

e. Respiratory system

f. Skeletal system

g. Skin

Practicing healthful behaviors benefits your body systems. Read **Growth and Development** to find out how.

LOG ON www.mmhhealth.com Find out more about growth and development.

Your Body Systems

You will learn . . .

- how your body is organized.
- how body systems work together.

Vocabulary

- **cell**, *B5*
- **tissue**, *B5*
- **organ**, *B5*
- **body system**, *B5*

A house is built on a framework and has many systems including a heating system, air conditioning, wiring, and plumbing. If something happens to the wiring system of a house, all the other systems are affected and may stop working. Your body is similar. It is built on a framework (your skeletal system) and has many systems that interact with each other.

How Your Body Is Organized

Your body is made of cells. A **cell** is the smallest working part of a living thing. Cells have different shapes and sizes. Each kind of cell has a different job.

A group of the same kind of cells forms a **tissue** (TISH•ew). Cells in a tissue work together to do a specific job. Muscle cells form muscle tissue. Bone cells form bone tissue.

An **organ** is a body part made of different kinds of tissues. Your eye is an organ. It is made up of nerve tissue, muscle tissue, and other materials. Organs form body systems. A **body system** is a group of organs that work together to do a certain job. Your circulatory system is a body system. The bones in your body are parts of your skeletal system.

What is the smallest working unit of your body?

Before a child is born, his or her skeleton is made up of a soft, flexible material called cartilage. Then bone cells begin to replace most cartilage cells. Eventually cartilage only remains at the ends of certain bones.

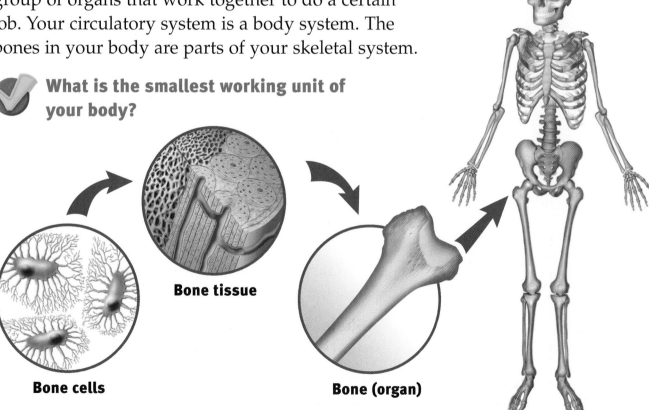

Bone cells

Bone tissue

Bone (organ)

▲ The bones in your body are organs. Together they form the skeletal system.

Skeletal system

Body Systems Work Together

Your body systems work together. For example, your circulatory system works with your respiratory system. When you breathe in, air enters your nose. The air goes through the nasal passages to your lungs, which are part of your respiratory system. The air contains oxygen. Blood in the circulatory system picks up the oxygen in your lungs. Your blood then takes the oxygen to other parts of your body.

Anything that affects one body system can affect the other body systems. Suppose you are standing next to an adult who is smoking. The smoke from the cigarette is in the air you breathe. When you take a breath, you breathe in the cigarette smoke. The smoke enters your respiratory system. The harmful materials in the smoke enter your blood. Your circulatory system carries those harmful materials to your body's cells.

The Body Systems

The body has seven systems. Each has a specific job to do.

Skeletal system Your skeletal system is made of bones. It supports your body and protects other organs.

Muscular system Your muscles help you move.

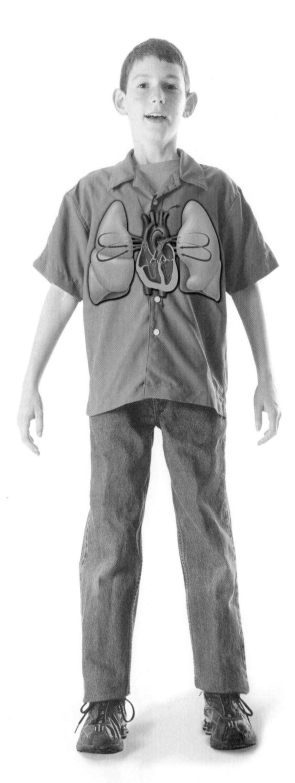

▲ Your respiratory and circulatory systems work together to move oxygen-rich blood throughout the body.

Skin Your skin covers your body. It protects your other body systems from germs and from losing water.

Nervous system Your nervous system controls other body systems.

Digestive system Your digestive system changes food into substances your body can use.

Circulatory system Your circulatory system moves oxygen and other substances to all body cells.

Respiratory system Your respiratory system takes in oxygen and releases carbon dioxide.

 List the seven body systems.

Access Health Facts

Make a poster about how to access health facts about exercise.

1 **Identify when you might need health facts.** Work with a small group. Tell when you might need information about the benefits of physical activity.

2 **Identify where you might find health facts.** List places to look for information. You might talk with your physical education teacher. What other sources might you use?

3 **Find the health facts you need.** Research the sources you identified.

4 **Evaluate the health facts.** Make the poster using the best information you found.

LESSON REVIEW

Review Concepts

1. **Explain** how the body is organized.

2. **Describe** how the body systems affect one another.

3. **Explain** how cells are important to tissues.

Critical Thinking

4. **Synthesize** How might the digestive system and the circulatory system work together?

5. **Compare** Explain how tissues and organs differ from one another.

6. **LIFE SKILLS** **Access Health Facts, Products, and Services** Choose one of the body systems. Write three questions asking health facts about that system. Explain where to find information about the system. How would you evaluate health facts about that system?

Bones, Muscles, and Skin

You will learn . . .

- the structure and function of the skeletal system.
- the structure and function of the muscular system.
- the structure and function of skin.

Vocabulary

- **posture**, *B9*
- **joint**, *B9*
- **bone marrow**, *B9*
- **epidermis**, *B12*
- **dermis**, *B12*

Healthful behaviors affect your body. When you take care of your body, you feel good. Your body works well. Healthful behaviors keep your body healthy and safe.

Skeletal System

You have more than 200 bones in your body. These bones form a frame that supports your body and protects softer organs. Together, all your bones form your skeletal (SKEL•ut•ul) system. Your skeletal system affects your **posture**, which is how a person sits, stands, or moves. Exercising and eating foods with calcium helps strengthen bones.

The place where two or more bones meet is called a **joint**. Joints at your knees, elbows, wrists, hips, and neck help your body to move in different ways.

Some bones make blood cells in bone marrow. **Bone marrow** is a soft tissue in the center of many bones, such as those in your arms and legs.

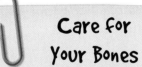 **What is a joint?**

Care for Your Bones

- Eat foods high in calcium.
- Exercise regularly.
- Have good posture.
- Wear gear that protects you from injury.

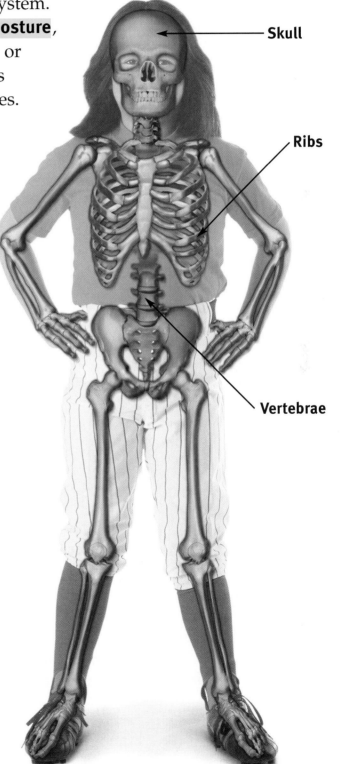

The Skeletal System

Skull

Ribs

Vertebrae

Muscular System

ACTIVITY

Health Online

Rest your Muscles!

Research the proper way to rest muscles after physical exercise. Use the e-Journal writing tool to write a report on your findings. Visit **www.mmhhealth.com** and click on the ⒺJournal.

The Muscular System

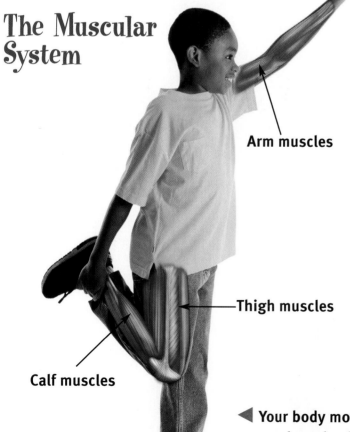

Arm muscles

Thigh muscles

Calf muscles

◄ **Your body moves easily when you have healthy muscles.**

All muscles in the body are a part of the muscular system. Muscles help you make different movements. Some of these are movements you choose to make. For example, you might choose to raise your hand. Your brain sends a message to your arm muscles telling them what you want to do. Muscles that help you make movements you control are called *voluntary muscles*. Muscles that move your bones are voluntary muscles.

Parts of your body move without your thinking about it. Food moves through your digestive system with the help of muscles that you do not control. The muscles of your digestive system are involuntary muscles. *Involuntary muscles* make movements that you cannot control.

Caring for Your Muscles

It is important to develop habits that keep your muscles strong and flexible.

- **Exercise regularly.** Walk, run, ride a bike, jump, skip, play on a sports team—do activities that get you moving.

- **Stretch.** Stretching keeps your muscles flexible.

- **Warm up before exercising. Cool down after exercising.** Warm-up and cool-down stretches help prevent injury.

- **Sit and stand straight.** Having good posture prevents you from slouching. When you slouch, your chest muscles get short and tight.

- **Eat healthful foods.** Healthful foods help build and strengthen your muscles.

What are three ways to keep muscles healthy?

CAREERS

Occupational Therapist

Occupational therapists are trained to work with people who have disabilities. Sometimes these people have had a serious accident or have been ill for a long time. Occupational therapists help people with disabilities find new ways to do things on their own. They prepare them to work again.

LOG ON www.mmhhealth.com Find out more about health careers.

◄ **The way you sit at a computer affects how well you work and how you feel.**

B11

Skin

Your skin is made of two layers of skin cells. The **epidermis** is the outer layer of skin cells. The **dermis** is a thick layer of cells below the epidermis. The diagram below shows the structure of skin.

Skin is the largest organ in your body. It holds your body together. Skin acts like a shield, protecting you from germs and the harmful effects of the sun. Skin also helps control body temperature. Water is lost through your skin in the form of sweat when you are warm. As sweat evaporates, excess heat is given off and your body cools. You sweat less when your body is cool. Less heat is released through your skin.

Wear skin protection when you are in the sun. Without protection, you have an increased risk of skin cancer when you are older.

The Parts of Skin

The **epidermis** makes new skin cells and sheds old skin cells.
The **dermis** contains sweat glands, hair follicles, oil glands, blood vessels, and nerves.
Nerves carry messages to the brain.
Oil glands make oils that help protect your skin.
Blood vessels carry oxygen to the skin cells and carry away carbon dioxide.
Sweat glands release sweat. Sweat helps cool the body.
A **hair follicle** is the place from which a hair grows.

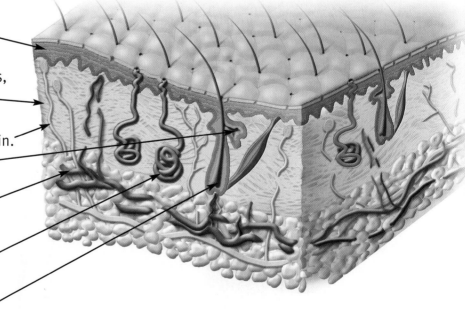

Caring for Your Skin

Practice healthful behaviors to protect your skin.

- **Stay out of the sun.** The sun's rays are strongest between the hours of 10:00 A.M. and 4:00 P.M.

- **Wear sunscreen.** Wear sunscreen with a sun protection factor (SPF) of 15 or higher.

- **Cover up.** Wear a hat and protective clothing when out in the sun.

- **Avoid risk behaviors.** Stay away from tanning booths and lamps.

- **Keep your skin clean.** Wash daily.

✓ **List three ways to care for skin.**

ACTIVITY — LIFE SKILLS

CRITICAL THINKING

Set Health Goals

Your skin is a very important body system. It protects you against germs and the harmful effects of the sun.

1 **Write the health goal you want to keep.** Set the health goal "I will care for my skin."

2 **Explain how your goal might affect your health.** When you take care of your skin you are helping your body stay healthy.

3 **Describe a plan you will follow to reach your goal. Keep track of your progress.** Write a daily skin-care routine you will follow. Make a Health Behavior Contract to help you keep track of your skin-care routine.

4 **Evaluate how your plan worked.** Has your skin remained healthy? Did you protect your skin from the sun? How might you improve your Health Behavior Contract to track your progress better?

LESSON REVIEW

Review Concepts

1. **Explain** the structure and function of bones.

2. **Describe** the function of the muscular system.

3. **Tell** how you can take care of your bones, muscles, and skin.

Critical Thinking

4. **Analyze** How can taking care of a cut help protect other body systems?

5. **LIFE SKILLS** **Set Health Goals** You know that regular exercise is important for bone health. Use the four steps for setting health goals to show how you can include regular exercise in your weekly routine.

B13

More Body Systems

You will learn . . .

- the structure and function of the digestive system.
- the structure and function of the circulatory system.
- the structure and function of the respiratory system.
- the structure and function of the nervous system.

You may think that what you eat affects only your digestive system. However, the foods you eat affect all of your body systems. You can care for your body systems by following a healthful diet. Make it a habit to choose healthful foods.

Vocabulary

- **digested**, *B15*
- **circulation**, *B16*
- **respiration**, *B17*
- **neuron**, *B18*

Digestive System

The food you eat is not used directly by cells. Food must be **digested** (digh•JES•tid), or changed into a form your body can use.

In your digestive system, food is changed into substances that can enter your bloodstream. Blood then carries the digested substances to your body cells. The cells get energy from some of the substances. Other substances are used to build, repair, and maintain tissues.

Protect Your Digestive System

- Take small bites.
- Chew your food well.
- Drink water.
- Eat healthful foods.

 What happens to food during digestion?

The Digestive System

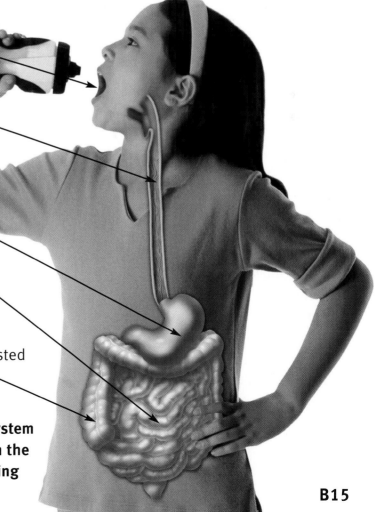

Digestion starts in the **mouth** with chewing. Chewing breaks up food and mixes it with saliva.

The muscles in the **esophagus** move food down to the stomach.

Food gets churned in the **stomach**. Stomach acid and other liquids prepare food to be broken down.

Food moves to the **small intestine,** where it *breaks down* into substances the body can use and is *absorbed* into the bloodstream.

The **large intestine** removes water from digested food. It also removes waste from the body.

▶ **The parts of the digestive system work together to break down the food you eat into fuel. Drinking water helps digestion.**

Circulatory System

The heart and blood vessels make up your circulatory system. The heart is a muscle that pumps blood throughout the body. It is the main organ of circulation. **Circulation** (sur•kyuh•LAY•shuhn) is the movement of blood throughout the body. Blood flows throughout your body in blood vessels.

There are three kinds of blood vessels—arteries, capillaries, and veins. *Arteries* (AHR•tuh•reez) are blood vessels that carry blood away from the heart. *Capillaries* (KAP•uh•layr•eez) are very small blood vessels that connect arteries to veins. *Veins* (VAYNZ) are blood vessels that return blood to the heart.

What are three kinds of blood vessels?

Protect Your Circulatory System

- Eat healthful foods.
- Limit fats.
- Exercise 30 minutes per day.
- Avoid tobacco smoke.
- Manage stress.

The Circulatory System

The **heart** is a muscle that pumps blood throughout the body. Exercise strengthens your heart muscle.

Arteries (red) are blood vessels that carry blood away from the heart. Healthful foods help prevent excess fat from narrowing your arteries. Stress and high fat foods can narrow arteries and restrict blood flow.

Veins (blue) are blood vessels that return blood to the heart.

Capillaries are very small blood vessels that connect arteries to veins.

▶ Blood moves away from your heart through arteries. Blood moves toward your heart through veins.

Respiratory System

Every time you inhale, your body takes in air that contains oxygen. Cells need oxygen to live. *Breathing* is the movement of air into the lungs and waste gases out of the lungs. **Respiration** (RES•puh•RAY•shuhn) is the process by which cells use oxygen to obtain energy from the break down of food.

Your circulatory system helps with respiration. Blood picks up oxygen in the lungs and carries it to cells throughout your body. As your body cells use oxygen, they release a waste gas called carbon dioxide (di•AHK•seyd). Carbon dioxide is carried by the blood in veins back to your heart and then to your lungs. Carbon dioxide leaves your body when you exhale.

 Why is oxygen important to your body?

The **trachea** is divided into smaller and smaller air ways that carry air into the lungs.

▶ **Exercise makes the heart and lungs stronger. Smoking damages lung tissue. Avoid tobacco smoke and places where strong fumes are present.**

> ## Protect Your Respiratory System
> - **Exercise regularly.**
> - **Stay away from tobacco smoke.**
> - **Stay away from dangerous fumes.**

The Respiratory System

Air enters and leaves through the **nose** and the **mouth**.

Oxygen enters the blood in the lungs. Veins bring carbon dioxide back to the lungs where it is released from the body.

Nervous System

The Nervous System

The **brain** is the main organ of the nervous system. It sends messages to and receives messages from all parts of the body.

Your body has billions of neurons. A **neuron** (NOO•rahn) is a nerve cell. Neurons make up the nervous (NUR•vuhs) system.

The human brain is a mass of neurons protected by the skull. The spinal cord is a long column of neurons that extends down the back from the base of the brain. Your spinal cord is protected by the bones of the vertebral column.

Sense Organs

Sense organs are also part of the nervous system. Sense organs help you get information about your environment. There are five sense organs. They are your eyes (vision), ears (hearing), nose (smell), tongue (taste), and skin (touch). Messages travel through neurons from the sense organs to the brain. The brain processes the information and sends out the correct response through other neurons.

The **spinal cord** is a long column of neurons. It extends down the back from the base of the brain.

Nerves carry information from the sense organs to the brain, where it is processed.

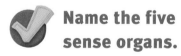
Name the five sense organs.

◀ Your nervous system controls how your body reacts to changes around you.

B18

Protect Your Nervous System

Protect your brain and spinal cord by following healthful habits.

- **Get plenty of sleep and rest.** Sleep restores energy to your nervous system.

- **Wear your seat belt when you ride in a car.** Car accidents often cause brain and spinal cord injuries.

- **Wear a helmet when you skate or ride a bike, skateboard, or scooter.** The helmet protects your skull and brain from injury in case you fall.

- **Avoid alcohol and other harmful drugs.** Alcohol and drugs affect your senses. You are at a greater risk of injury when your senses aren't sharp.

ACTIVITY LIFE SKILLS

CRITICAL THINKING

Be a Health Advocate

Make a poster to promote the use of safety helmets to protect the nervous system.

1. **Choose a healthful action to communicate.** You want to tell people to wear a safety helmet while riding a bike.

2. **Collect information about the action.** Research reasons why it is important to wear a safety helmet. Record what you find.

3. **Decide how to communicate this information.** What will you put on your poster? How will you get the attention of others?

4. **Communicate your message to others.** Make your poster. Hang it where others can see it.

LESSON REVIEW

Review Concepts

1. **List** the organs that make up the digestive system.

2. **Describe** the function of the circulatory system.

3. **List** the organs that make up the respiratory system.

4. **List** the organs that make up the nervous system.

Critical Thinking

5. **Evaluate** Write three interview questions that someone could ask a family member about what they do to take care of their health.

6. **(LIFE SKILLS) Be a Health Advocate** February is Heart Awareness Month. Write a letter to the editor of your newspaper telling ways that people can improve their heart health.

The Stages of the Life Cycle

You will learn . . .

- the factors that affect your growth.
- ways that you have changed since birth.
- ways that you are changing during childhood.

Vocabulary

- **heredity**, *B21*
- **hormone**, *B21*
- **life cycle**, *B22*
- **infancy**, *B22*
- **childhood**, *B24*
- **learning disability**, *B25*

Think about ways that you have changed since you were a baby. You have grown taller. You have more teeth and hair. You learned to tie your shoes. You learned how to ride a bike. You will continue to change and learn your whole life.

Factors That Affect Growth

Many factors affect growth. You can control some, but not all, of these factors. Your heredity is one factor that you can't control. **Heredity** refers to the traits passed to you from your birth parents. The color of your eyes, hair, and skin are traits you inherited from your birth parents. Heredity also affects how you grow. If both of your parents are tall, it is likely that you also will be tall.

Other factors that you can't control are hormones. A **hormone** (HOR•mohn) is a chemical produced by the body that controls certain body processes. For example, human growth hormone helps your body grow and develop.

Your *environment* is everything around you. It includes other people, the air you breathe, the food you eat, and where you live. You may have little control over your environment.

Factors that you have some control over are your habits and how healthy you keep yourself. Your *habits* are your usual ways of doing things. Practicing healthful habits helps your body to grow. Staying in good health helps your body grow.

 What are hormones, and how do they affect growth?

▶ **You can control the habits you practice. How does wearing a mouthguard help protect your health?**

Infancy

Every living organism has a life cycle. The **life cycle** is the order of change each living organism passes through during its life. The life cycle of some insects lasts only a few days. The life cycle of some tortoises lasts more than 100 years. The life cycle of a human is about 78 years. In humans, the first stage of life is called **infancy**. Infancy is the period of growth from birth to one year. When you were an infant, your body went through many changes.

▲ **During the first year after birth, an infant goes through many changes.**

Physical Changes

You probably grew about an inch per month until you were six months old. Then you probably grew about one-half inch per month until you were one year old. Teeth usually begin to develop before the end of the first year. You gained weight quickly as you grew longer. Most babies double their weight in just a few months after birth. Your senses of sight, smell, and taste improved as you grew. Your heredity, nutrition, and health affected how fast you grew.

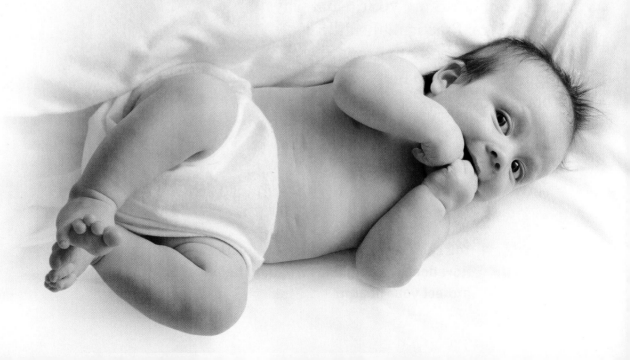

Mental and Emotional Changes

You learned many actions as an infant. You may have learned to cry to get attention or when you heard a loud sound that startled you. Later you learned to express different emotions through sound. You probably said your first words before you turned one year old.

Family and Social Changes

You developed feelings of closeness with your family and caregivers when you were an infant. This is called bonding. *Bonding* made you feel safe and secure.

You began to recognize the voices and smells of your parents or guardian. You might have cried if someone other than your parents or guardian tried to hold you. Later, you began to respond to people around you. You might have smiled when you recognized someone. You might have giggled when someone made a funny sound or showed you a soft toy.

 Name three changes that occur during the first year of life.

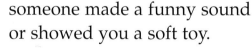

On Your Own
FOR SCHOOL OR HOME

Classify Changes

Ask your parents or guardian about how you or someone else in your family changed during infancy. Perhaps there is a photo album or book of the changes. Make a chart of the changes. Classify each change as physical, mental, and emotional, or family and social.

Consumer Wise

How Much Does It Cost?

A new infant might use 11 diapers a day for the first three months. How many disposable diapers would be used in 90 days? Find out how much they would cost.

Childhood

Childhood is the stage of growth from 1 to 12 years. Many changes take place during childhood.

Physical Changes

You grow steadily during this period. Your muscles develop and you gain more control over them. You now have some teeth that will last your whole life.

Mental and Emotional Changes

As you got older you used language to talk about ideas. You used words to communicate what you wanted and needed. Now you are learning to organize ideas and to understand time and numbers.

You are beginning to understand your own feelings. You know how happiness and sadness feel inside. This knowledge helps you understand how other people feel, too.

You are also beginning to make responsible decisions with your parents or guardians. You feel proud when you learn new tasks.

Family and Social Changes

You also change socially during childhood. You make friends. You learn to share with others. You learn to accept that people are different from one another.

Your parents or guardian start allowing you to do more activities on your own during this time. You gain more independence when you show that you are responsible. *Independence* (in•duh•PEN•duhns) is the ability to do tasks without the help of others.

 List three changes you go through in childhood.

Write About It!

Expository Writing
Make a list of changes someone your age might expect. Write a paragraph describing how these changes might make you feel. Share your paragraph with a parent or guardian.

▲ **You begin to help your family during childhood.**

Learning Styles

Everyone learns best in a certain way. Perhaps you take notes or draw pictures to refresh your memory later. You might act out scenes to remember ideas. Or maybe you make up questions and write out the answers.

Some people learn in special ways. A **learning disability** (DI•suh•BI•luh•tee) is a difference that causes a person to have trouble learning. He or she might need to study in certain ways or take special classes. Or maybe he or she needs extra time to do work. People with learning disabilities also have to find the best ways to learn.

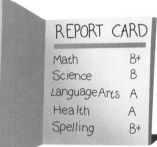

REPORT CARD

Math	B+
Science	B
Language Arts	A
Health	A
Spelling	B+

Set Health Goals

You decide that you want to get better grades in school this year. You can set a health goal.

1 **Write the health goal you want to set.** Your goal is: I will discover my learning style.

2 **Explain how your goal might affect your health.** Doing well in school will affect your health positively. Your emotional and mental health will improve. What other effects on health might occur?

3 **Describe a plan you will follow to reach your goal. Keep track of your progress.** Write a Health Behavior Contract to help you.

4 **Evaluate how your plan worked.** If your plan fails, talk to your parents or guardian. How might you change your plan to do better?

LESSON REVIEW

Review Concepts

1. **Recall** the five factors that affect growth.

2. **Name** three ways you've changed since birth.

3. **List** three ways you are changing during childhood.

4. **Describe** two different types of learning styles.

Critical Thinking

5. **Predict** You visit your friend's new baby brother. What might you expect the baby to be able to do?

6. **LIFE SKILLS** **Set Health Goals** Set a health goal: "I will learn the stages of the human life cycle." Line up photographs of yourself as an infant through the age you are now. Describe how your face has changed from infancy through early childhood.

Your Future Growth

You will learn . . .

- about changes that will occur in adolescence.
- about changes that will occur in adulthood.
- habits to practice for healthful growth and aging.
- the final stage of the life cycle.

As your older brothers, sisters, or cousins grew, you may have noticed how they became taller. They took on more responsibilities. They have grown in other ways, too. Like them, you will continue to change.

Vocabulary

- **adolescence**, *B27*
- **puberty**, *B27*
- **adulthood**, *B28*
- **death**, *B30*

Adolescence

Adolescence (AD•uhl•ES•uhns) is the stage of growth from 12 to 18 years. Puberty usually occurs during this stage of the life cycle. **Puberty** (PYOO•buhr•tee) is the time when a person's body changes and becomes able to reproduce. Most girls reach puberty between the ages of 8 and 13. Boys reach puberty between the ages of 10 and 15.

Physical Changes

Most adolescents have a *growth spurt* when they grow very quickly. You could grow four inches in a year. You might develop acne. You also may start to sweat more. You might start to use deodorant under your arms. Girls and boys begin to develop adult bodies during adolescence. People grow at different rates.

Mental and Emotional Changes

You will become more independent during adolescence. You will be able to understand more complex ideas. You will begin to make plans for the future by thinking about a future career and how you will prepare for it.

Family and Social Changes

During adolescence, you might change the way you get along with friends. You might begin to care more about what your friends and others think of you. You might become more involved in activities after school.

▲ During adolescence, you may grow several inches in a year. This is called a growth spurt.

 List three changes that occur during adolescence.

Write
About It!

Write a Narrative Paragraph Write a paragraph describing how you might look as an adult. Tell what you might do for a job. Describe how you might have changed over the years. Share your writings with your parents or guardian.

▲ Many adults exercise, play games, and continue to work as they age.

Adulthood

You will become a young adult after adolescence. **Adulthood** is the stage of growth from 18 to 70 years and beyond. A teacher, a parent or guardian, or a principal could all be adult role-models. They can be models for you throughout your years as an adult.

Physical Changes

Your body may continue to develop during early adulthood. You may grow a bit taller. You become more physically mature. Your eyesight might begin to change. You may need glasses. Your hair may change in color. To maintain your best physical health, eat healthful foods and get physical activity.

Mental and Emotional Changes

As an adult you will be busy taking on new responsibilities. You will need to work to take care of yourself. You may set new goals. You may decide to continue your education and learn new skills. Reading books and learning new skills help keep your mind active throughout adulthood.

Family and Social Changes

During this stage you might get married and start a family. As your children become adults, you may feel sad as they become more independent. You may be happy because you are proud of them. You may make new friends and find new occupations.

 List three changes that can occur during adulthood.

Healthful Aging

Your body will change throughout your life. Practicing healthful behaviors now will help keep you healthy longer. Following a healthful diet will give your body the energy to make those changes. It will help you stay healthy and live longer.

Physical activity improves your physical, mental, and emotional health. It also keeps your heart, muscles, and bones strong. As you age, you may be active in different ways. Maybe you will swim instead of run.

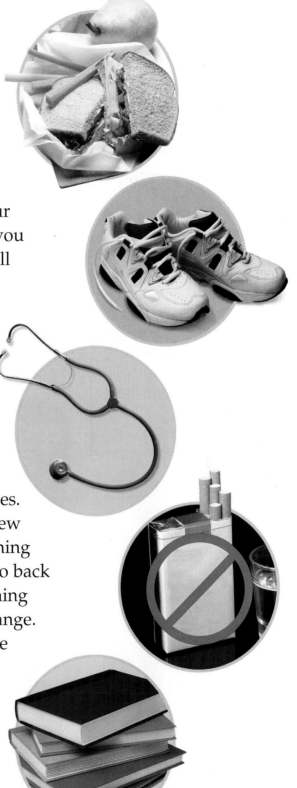

Having regular checkups improves your health. You and the physician treating you can watch for changes in your health needs.

Not smoking helps you age healthfully. Smoking increases the risk of health problems. It can harm your health and the health of people around you. Alcohol and other illegal drugs have harmful effects on your body, too. Drinking alcohol can cause accidents and diseases.

As you age, keep your mind active. Learn new skills. You will never be too old to learn something new. You might want to continue working or go back to school. You may take up a new hobby. Learning challenges your mind and body to adapt to change. Keeping your mind active makes your life more enjoyable, too.

 Name three ways to age healthfully.

Death and the Life Cycle

Death is the end of the life cycle. For humans, death occurs when a person's heart and brain no longer work. The heart stops beating. The person stops breathing.

Sometimes people die without warning. They might have a heart attack or an accident. Sometimes people are ill for a period of time before they die. Family members might care for them at home. They might need care in a hospital or nursing home.

When people are ill for a long time, you might know that they are going to die. You have time to tell them good-bye. You have time to tell them that you love them.

It is hard to lose people you love. You might feel very sad or angry because you will not see them again. You miss them being in your life. It is normal to feel like this.

ACTIVITY BUILD Character

Good Memories

Respect Your are never too young to show respect for someone when a person close to them has died. Make a card and write a short note telling the family about a good memory you have of time spent with that person. Decorate your card in bright colors. Have your parents or guardian read the note and mail it.

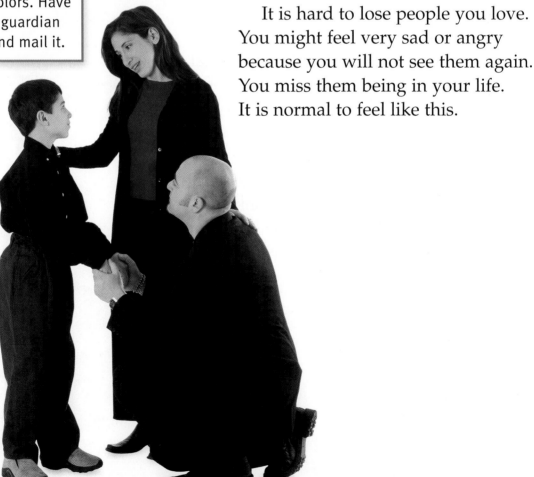

You need support when someone you care about dies. It is important to talk about your feelings. This is a good time to recall your memories of the person. With time, you will feel better.

Some people become ill after they lose a loved one. Take extra care of your health. Eat healthful foods, exercise regularly, get plenty of rest and sleep and stay in touch with family and friends.

List two ways to take care of your health after a loved one dies.

ACTIVITY

LIFE SKILLS

CRITICAL THINKING

Use Communication Skills

The family pet has died. How would you communicate to your parents or guardian how you are feeling? Role-play with a partner what you could do.

1. **Choose the best way to communicate.** How can you communicate how you feel? You could talk to your parents or guardian. What else might you do?

2. **Send a clear message. Be polite.** Tell your parents or guardian how you feel. Talk about the family pet. How else might you get your message across? What might you say in this situation?

3. **Listen to each other.** Listen carefully to your parents' or guardian's advice. They have experienced a loss, too. Let them express their feelings.

4. **Make sure you understand each other.** Ask questions if you do not understand what happens when a family pet dies. What else might you do?

LESSON REVIEW

Review Concepts

1. **Explain** how your body changes during adolescence.

2. **List** three ways you might change as an adult.

3. **Name** three ways to age healthfully.

4. **Tell** why it is important to talk about your feelings when a loved one dies.

Critical Thinking

5. **Describe** What is important about the changes that take place during puberty?

6. **LIFE SKILLS** **Use Communication Skills** How can you communicate to your parents, guardians or grandparents ways to stay healthy? What should you tell them?

Practice Healthful Behaviors

Problem Jamal wants to be more active after school.
He often plays video games or watches television.
How can Jamal break his old habits?

"Aren't you going to play video games today?"

"No thanks. I'm going to start exercising after school. Do you want to join me?"

"I always watch my favorite shows on TV after school. Come on!"

Solution Sometimes habits are hard to change.
The steps on the next page can help Jamal practice
a healthful behavior and make it a habit.

B32

Learn This Life Skill

Follow these steps to practice healthful behaviors. The Foldables™ can help you.

1 **Learn about a healthful behavior.**

Jamal has decided to play basketball for 30 minutes after school. How can he learn more about the healthful behavior? How can he benefit from this activity?

2 **Practice the behavior.**

After Jamal learns how he can benefit from playing basketball, he starts the activity. What can he do to get the most out of this activity?

3 **Ask for help if you need it.**

Jamal wants to get more exercise than he would by just shooting hoops. He asks his friends to join him in a game.

4 **Make the behavior a habit.**

The decision to involve his friends helps Jamal stick to the behavior. What else might he do if he needed help?

Practice Healthful Behaviors

1. I learned to...

2. Practice the behavior.

3. Ask for help if you need it.

4. Make the behavior a habit.

Practice Healthful Behaviors

Practice This Life Skill

Would you get tired of basketball as your form of physical activity? What can you do to remain active all year long? Make a plan that involves a variety of physical activities.

CHAPTER 3 REVIEW

Use Vocabulary

body system, *B5*

circulation, *B16*

dermis, *B12*

heredity, *B21*

joint, *B9*

puberty, *B27*

Choose the correct term from the list to complete each sentence. Write the word on a separate sheet of paper.

1. The time when a person's body changes and becomes able to reproduce is called __?__.

2. The layer of skin that contains sweat glands, hair follicles, oil glands, blood vessels, and nerves is the __?__.

3. The traits passed on to you from your parents is called your __?__.

4. Cells, tissues, and organs make up a __?__.

5. The transport of blood throughout the body is called __?__.

6. The place where two or more bones meet is a __?__.

Review Concepts

Answer each question in complete sentences.

7. List the four main stages of the life cycle. Then list a feature of each stage.

8. How does exercise affect your muscles?

9. Why does your body need to digest food?

10. How does liquid help digest food?

11. Name three things your skeletal system does.

12. What does the respiratory system take in and what does it release?

Reading Comprehension

Answer each question in complete sentences.

Your circulatory system helps with respiration. Blood picks up oxygen in the lungs and carries it to cells throughout your body. As your body cells use oxygen, they release a waste gas called carbon dioxide (di•AHK•seyd). Carbon dioxide is carried by the blood in veins back to your heart and then to your lungs. Carbon dioxide leaves your body when you exhale.

13. What does blood pick up in the lungs?

14. Where does oxygen go after it enters the lungs?

15. When does carbon dioxide leave the body?

Critical Thinking/Problem Solving

Answer each question in complete sentences.

Analyze Concepts

16. Give an example of a habit that is healthful to more than one body system. Explain how this habit can help keep you healthy.

17. You've been working at the computer all afternoon. How might this affect your posture?

18. You start to think about how your lungs move when you are breathing. Do you control that movement by thinking about it? Why or why not?

19. What effect do the foods you eat have on the health of body systems?

20. What in your environment affects your health? How can you control it?

Practice Life Skills

21. **Practice Healthful Behaviors** It is important to keep your respiratory system healthy. Physical activity helps keep your respiratory system working correctly. Name two activities that help keep your respiratory system healthy. How can you make these physical activities a habit?

22. **Make Responsible Decisions** You are fixing your bike in the garage when your father pulls the family car in and closes the door down. You smell fumes. What should you do? Why?

Read Graphics

Use the chart to answer questions 23–25.

My Healthful Habits

Skeletal System	Nervous System	Skin
• I will eat foods high in calcium. • I will exercise every day.	• I will wear a seat belt in a car. • I will wear a helmet when I ride my bike.	• I will wear sunscreen with an SPF of 15. • I will wash daily.

23. Which body system can riding a bike help you to keep healthy?

24. What should you do to protect your nervous system when you're on your bike?

25. What should you do to protect your skin when you're on your bike?

 LOG ON www.mmhhealth.com
Find out how much you know about how your body grows and changes.

CHAPTER 4

Nutrition

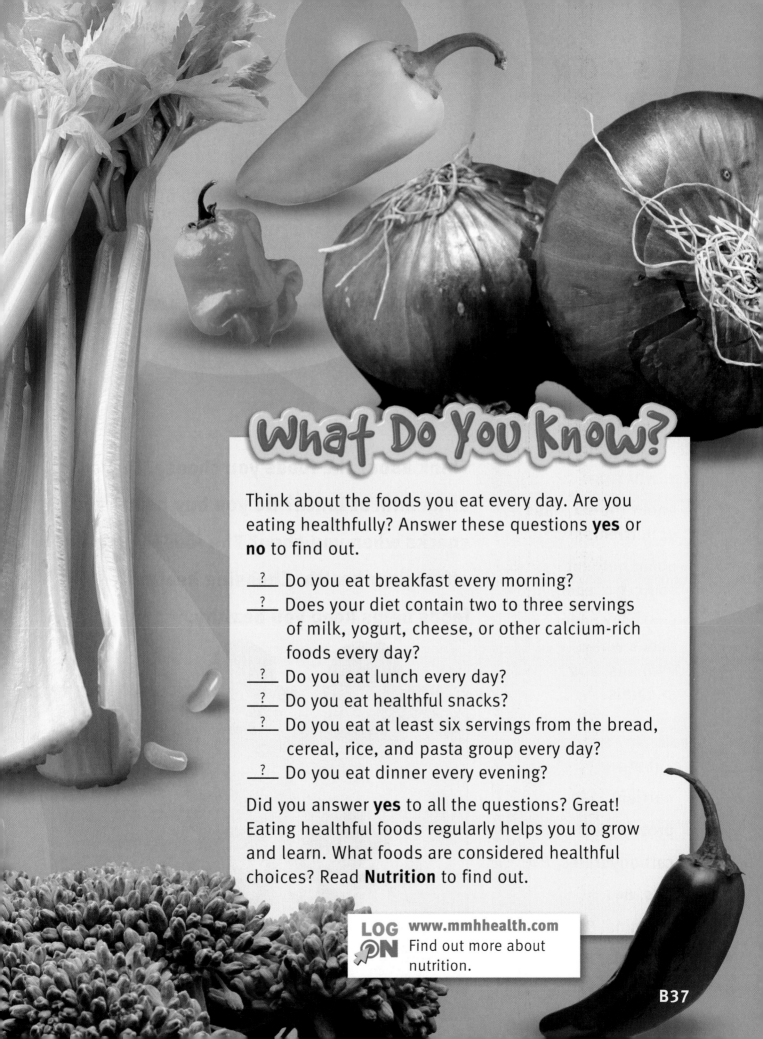

What Do You Know?

Think about the foods you eat every day. Are you eating healthfully? Answer these questions **yes** or **no** to find out.

__?__ Do you eat breakfast every morning?

__?__ Does your diet contain two to three servings of milk, yogurt, cheese, or other calcium-rich foods every day?

__?__ Do you eat lunch every day?

__?__ Do you eat healthful snacks?

__?__ Do you eat at least six servings from the bread, cereal, rice, and pasta group every day?

__?__ Do you eat dinner every evening?

Did you answer **yes** to all the questions? Great! Eating healthful foods regularly helps you to grow and learn. What foods are considered healthful choices? Read **Nutrition** to find out.

LOG ON **www.mmhhealth.com**
Find out more about nutrition.

Getting the Nutrients Your Body Needs

You will learn . . .

- about the six kinds of nutrients.
- about nutrient sources of energy.
- why your body needs water, vitamins, and minerals.

Vocabulary

- **nutrient**, *B39*
- **protein**, *B39*
- **carbohydrates**, *B40*
- **fats**, *B41*
- **vitamins**, *B42*
- **minerals**, *B42*

Think about the foods you choose. Do you drink milk at lunch? Do you buy healthful snacks when you shop? The foods you eat affect your health. Choosing healthful foods helps keep you healthy.

Nutrients

A **nutrient** (NOO•tree•uhnt) is a substance in a food that is used by the body. Some nutrients give you energy. Some nutrients are used for growth. Others are used to repair tissues.

There are six kinds of nutrients: proteins, carbohydrates, fats, water, vitamins, and minerals. You need different amounts of each kind of nutrient every day.

Protein Builds Bodies

Protein is a nutrient that is needed to build, grow, and repair body cells. Your body contains a large amount of this nutrient. Protein is the main nutrient that makes up the cells of your body. Meat, fish, eggs, and dairy foods such as milk and cheese are good sources of protein. You also can get protein from nuts and beans.

 How does your body use protein?

To stay healthy you need to include fiber in your diet. Fiber is the part of grains and plant foods that your body doesn't digest. It passes through your digestive system and leaves the body as solid waste. Bran cereals, whole-wheat bread, brown rice, fruits, and vegetables contain fiber.

▶ **Peanut butter is a good source of protein.**

Your Main Energy Sources

Your body needs a constant supply of energy. You use energy to move around. You also use energy to stay warm, breathe, think, and grow. Your main energy sources are carbohydrates and fats.

Carbohydrates

Carbohydrates (kar•boh•HY•drayts) are nutrients that supply the main source of energy for your body. There are two kinds of carbohydrates—starches and sugars. Breads, cereal, rice, and pasta contain starches. Some vegetables, such as potatoes and beans, also have starches. Starches provide long-lasting energy.

Sugars are found naturally in foods such as milk and fruit. Sugars also are added to many foods. Syrup, jellies, soft drinks, and candies are made mostly of sugar. These foods provide energy that does not last. They supply few of the other nutrients your body needs.

◀ The sugars in milk are a source of carbohydrates. Why does your body need carbohydrates?

Facts About Fat

Fats are nutrients that provide energy and give foods flavor. Fats come from both plants and animals. There are three kinds of fats: saturated, unsaturated, and trans fats.

Saturated (SA•chuh•RAY•tuhd) *fats* are fats found mostly in foods that come from animals. Examples include fats from meat, butter, and eggs. Coconut and palm oil also have saturated fats. Fats from vegetables, nuts, seeds, and fish are mostly *unsaturated fats. Trans fats* are unsaturated fats that are changed into saturated fats. They are used to keep packaged foods from spoiling. Margarine and cookies contain trans fats. Saturated fats and trans fats increase the risk of heart disease.

You need some fat in your diet. However, too much fat can cause you to gain more weight than you should. Being overweight increases the risk of type 2 diabetes, heart disease, and some cancers. To stay healthy, eat less fat, especially saturated fats and trans fats.

 Why do you need fats in your diet?

► **These foods are low in fat. What other foods might be low in fat?**

Water, Vitamins, and Minerals

Water is a nutrient that keeps your body temperature normal. It helps remove waste. Water surrounds your joints and helps protect them from injury. If you don't get enough water, you may feel tired, dizzy, or weak. You cannot live very long without water.

You need about six to eight glasses of water every day. You can get this by drinking water and other beverages, and by eating fruits and vegetables.

Vitamins (VY•tuh•muhnz) are nutrients that help your body use carbohydrates, proteins, and fats. They protect you from illness. Some vitamins keep your eyes and skin healthy. **Minerals** are nutrients that help chemical processes in the body. Minerals help muscles and nerves work. Some minerals also help your body use vitamins.

 Why does your body need water?

Some Important Vitamins

Name	What It Does	Food Sources
Vitamin A	Keeps eyes, teeth, gums, skin, and hair healthy	Milk, eggs, red peppers, spinach, carrots, sweet potatoes, cantaloupe
Vitamin B^1	Helps the body use energy; helps the nervous system	Whole-grain breads and cereal, tortillas, eggs, pasta, rice
Vitamin B^2	Helps cells get energy; helps nerve cells work	Milk, yogurt, eggs, whole-grain bread, green vegetables, beans, nuts
Vitamin B^{12}	Helps make red blood cells	Meat, fish, poultry, milk, eggs
Vitamin C	Helps the heart, cells, and muscles function	Citrus fruits, green peppers, tomatoes, strawberries, broccoli
Vitamin D	Helps build strong teeth and bones	Milk, fish, liver, tuna, eggs

Some Important Minerals

Name	What It Does	Food Sources
Calcium	Builds strong bones and teeth	Yogurt, milk, cheese, beans, tofu, salmon, green vegetables
Potassium	Helps your body get energy; helps the heart, muscles, and nerves; keeps water balance in cells	Bananas, oranges, peanut butter, potatoes, meat, vegetables
Iron	Helps red blood cells	Liver, meat, chicken, beans, fish, eggs, whole-grain cereals
Phosphorus	Builds bones, teeth, and cells	Milk, eggs, whole-grain cereals, meat, poultry, beans, cheese, nuts, seeds
Sodium	Keeps water balance in cells; helps muscles work	Table salt, soy sauce, most foods
Zinc	Helps you grow; helps wounds heal	Milk, eggs, fish, poultry, seafood, whole-grain bread and cereal

LESSON REVIEW

Review Concepts

1. **Recall** six kinds of nutrients your body needs.

2. **Identify** two nutrients that are sources of energy.

3. **Explain** how to give your body enough water every day.

4. **Explain** the functions of vitamins and minerals for your body.

Critical Thinking

5. **Synthesize** Suppose you are unable to drink milk. List four nutrients you may miss. What other foods can you eat to get these nutrients?

6. **LIFE SKILLS** **Practice Healthful Behaviors** You often get tired about an hour after breakfast. You know that protein provides lasting energy. What could you do to make sure you eat foods with protein for breakfast?

Making Healthful Food Choices

You will learn . . .

- how to use the Food Guide Pyramid.
- how to follow the Dietary Guidelines.
- ways to keep nutrients in foods
- why table manners are important.

Vocabulary

- **food group**, *B45*
- **Food Guide Pyramid**, *B45*
- **Dietary Guidelines**, *B46*

To stay healthy, you need to eat healthful foods. You can choose foods that provide the nutrients you need to reduce the risk of disease. You can make healthful food choices.

The Food Guide Pyramid

The **Food Guide Pyramid** is a guide that shows the number of servings from each food group that you need each day. Foods that contain many of the same types of nutrients make up a **food group**. A serving is an amount of food.

✓ **What is the Food Guide Pyramid?**

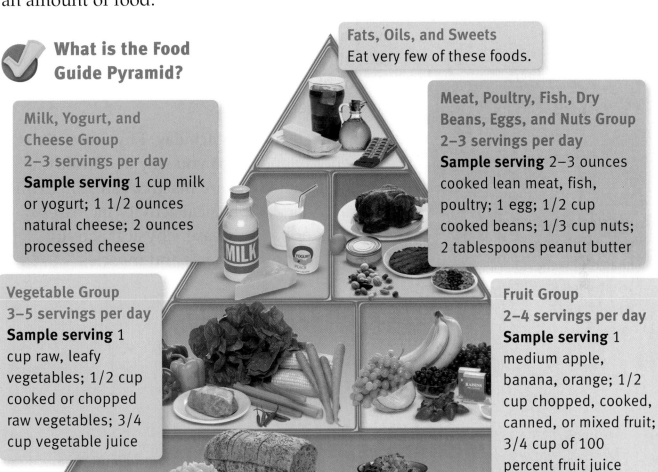

Fats, Oils, and Sweets
Eat very few of these foods.

Milk, Yogurt, and Cheese Group
2–3 servings per day
Sample serving 1 cup milk or yogurt; 1 1/2 ounces natural cheese; 2 ounces processed cheese

Meat, Poultry, Fish, Dry Beans, Eggs, and Nuts Group
2–3 servings per day
Sample serving 2–3 ounces cooked lean meat, fish, poultry; 1 egg; 1/2 cup cooked beans; 1/3 cup nuts; 2 tablespoons peanut butter

Vegetable Group
3–5 servings per day
Sample serving 1 cup raw, leafy vegetables; 1/2 cup cooked or chopped raw vegetables; 3/4 cup vegetable juice

Fruit Group
2–4 servings per day
Sample serving 1 medium apple, banana, orange; 1/2 cup chopped, cooked, canned, or mixed fruit; 3/4 cup of 100 percent fruit juice

Bread, Cereal, Rice, and Pasta Group
6–11 servings per day
Sample serving 1 slice bread; 1/2 bagel or English muffin; 1 ounce ready-to-eat cereal; 1/2 cup cooked cereal, rice, pasta; 5–6 small crackers

The Food Guide Pyramid
A Daily Guide

The Dietary Guidelines

The **Dietary Guidelines** are suggested goals for eating that help you stay healthy and live longer. Use these goals to make healthful food choices and prevent disease.

1. **Aim for a healthful weight.** Your healthful weight is the weight that is just right for you. Staying at your healthful weight decreases your risk of high blood pressure, type 2 diabetes, and some cancers.

2. **Be physically active each day.** Physical activity uses energy and helps you stay at a healthful weight. People who are inactive can gain extra weight. A lack of physical activity increases your risk of heart disease. Physical activity helps to strengthen bones and muscles.

▼ Physical activity helps you maintain a healthful weight. What does *healthful weight* mean?

3. Use the Food Guide Pyramid to make food choices. Eat at least the smallest number of servings from each food group every day. Are you very active? Then you may need to eat more servings for extra energy. Eat only small amounts of the foods at the top of the pyramid.

4. Eat a variety of grains. Eat whole grains every day. Grains are low in fat. They also are high in starch and fiber. Eating fiber helps reduce the risk of heart disease and colon cancer.

5. Eat a variety of fruits and vegetables every day. Fruits and vegetables have the vitamins, minerals, and fiber that you need.

6. Keep food safe to eat. Sometimes germs get into foods. They can cause people to become ill.

7. Eat foods that are low in saturated fat and not too high in unsaturated fat. Eating foods that have saturated fat increases the risk of heart disease and certain cancers.

8. Limit how much sugar you eat. Sugar combines with plaque and causes tooth decay. Too much sugar can cause weight gain.

9. Use little salt. You need less than a teaspoon of salt every day. Too much salt might raise blood pressure. Packaged foods such as chips and hot dogs contain added salt.

10. Do not drink alcohol. Alcohol can harm the liver and affect how you think. It is against the law for people your age to drink alcohol.

 What are the Dietary Guidelines?

Rice is the primary food for half of the world's population. In many places, it is eaten with every meal. Rice can be used to make many different foods, including cooked rice, breakfast cereals, desserts, and rice flour.

On Your Own

FOR SCHOOL OR HOME

Taste Test

Ask your parents or guardian for permission to try this. Fill a glass with 12 ounces of water. Add 7 teaspoons of sugar and mix. Take a small taste. What does it taste like? One can of regular soda contains about 7 teaspoons of sugar.

Use Communication Skills

Your younger sister does not eat vegetables. How might you convince her to do so? Pair up with a classmate and role-play using communication skills.

1 **Choose the best way to communicate.** You could talk to her. What else might you do to communicate with her?

2 **Send a clear message. Be polite.** Explain why it's important to eat vegetables. Offer to find recipes for vegetable dishes. What else might you do?

3 **Listen to each other.** Listen as your partner responds to reasons you gave for eating vegetables.

4 **Make sure you understand each other.** Ask if your partner understands the reasons for eating vegetables. Ask if she or he understood your offer to find recipes. Tell what you heard. Then, switch roles.

Keeping Nutrients in Food

Some actions and conditions reduce the amount of nutrients in foods. There are ways to keep nutrients in foods. Here's how.

- **Store meats, dairy foods, fruits, and vegetables at cool or cold temperatures.** This helps keep these foods from spoiling. When food spoils, vitamins and minerals are lost. Germs can grow in spoiled food and make you ill.

- **Keep dairy foods away from light.** Light destroys nutrients in dairy products.

- **Eat fresh foods soon after you buy or pick them.** The amount of nutrients in fresh foods decreases over time. Don't keep fresh foods for too long before you eat them.

- **Do not overcook vegetables.** Eat vegetables raw whenever possible. If you steam them, do so only for a short time. Avoid boiling vegetables because boiling removes many nutrients.

Table Manners

Suppose that you are sitting across the table from your friend, who is talking with his mouth full. You might find it hard to enjoy your meal. Talking while you chew or eating with your mouth open shows disrespect and may be unsafe because you could choke.

Table manners are polite ways to eat. They are important because they help make meals pleasant for everyone and help keep you and others safe.

- **Wash your hands before eating.** Dirt and germs can make you ill.

- **Use a napkin.** Place your napkin across your lap. Use it to wipe your hands and mouth.

- **Do not rush.** You might choke.

- **Keep used utensils on your plate.** Germs spread easily when the table becomes dirty.

- **Clean up spilled foods or drinks.** Someone might slip and be injured.

 Why should you use table manners?

LESSON REVIEW

Review Concepts

1. **Assess** how many servings you should eat daily from each food group in the Food Guide Pyramid.

2. **List** five Dietary Guidelines.

3. **List** three ways to keep nutrients in foods.

4. **Name** three table manners.

Critical Thinking

5. **Infer** Placing a napkin on your lap when you eat shows good table manners. Why is this so?

6. **LIFE SKILLS** **Use Communication Skills** The doctor has told a family member to eat foods that are low in saturated fats. You have suggestions for this family member. How can you communicate these suggestions?

Food Labels and Food Ads

You will learn . . .

- how to read a food label.
- to identify appeals that are found in food and beverage ads.
- how to order healthful foods at a fast-food restaurant.

Vocabulary

- **food label,** *B51*
- **additive,** *B51*
- **preservative,** *B51*
- **calorie,** *B51*
- **advertisement,** *B52*
- **commercial,** *B52*
- **fast-food restaurant,** *B53*

Many foods come in packages. The food labels on these packages provide information about the food that is inside. This information can be used to help you follow the Dietary Guidelines.

Food Labels

A **food label** is nutrition information printed on a food container. A food label lists ingredients. It also tells how much of each nutrient is in each serving in the form of a Nutrition Facts label. Food labels list ingredients in order from those present in the greatest amount to those in the least amount. If sugar is listed as the first ingredient, then there is more sugar in one serving of the food than any other ingredient.

A food label also will tell you what has been added to the food. An **additive** (A•duh•tiv) is anything that has been added to make the food look or taste better or be more healthful. Some additives are vitamins. Others are preservatives. A **preservative** (pri•ZUHR•vuh•tiv) is something that is added to a food to keep it from spoiling too fast.

You can use the Nutrition Facts part of a food label to find out how much fat, sugar, or salt there is in a serving. A sample Nutrition Facts label is shown on this page.

Serving Size is the amount of food in a serving. **Servings Per Container** is the number of servings in the package. A package may contain more than one serving.

Tells the number of calories in one serving of the food. A **calorie** is a unit used to measure the energy produced by food in the body. **Calories from Fat** tells how many calories in one serving of the food come from fat.

The **Percent Daily Value** tells the percentage of each kind of nutrient in one serving.

Tells which vitamins and minerals are present.

Tells how much or how little you need of certain nutrients. The information is given for persons on a 2,000-calorie a day diet and persons on a 2,500-calorie a day diet.

 **What is a food label?**

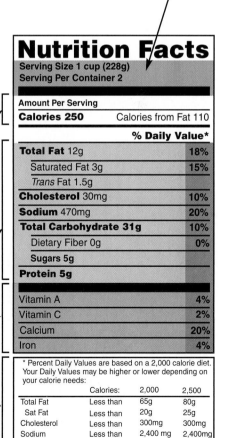

Nutrition Facts

Serving Size 1 cup (228g)
Serving Per Container 2

Amount Per Serving	
Calories 250	Calories from Fat 110

	% Daily Value*
Total Fat 12g	18%
Saturated Fat 3g	15%
Trans Fat 1.5g	
Cholesterol 30mg	10%
Sodium 470mg	20%
Total Carbohydrate 31g	10%
Dietary Fiber 0g	0%
Sugars 5g	
Protein 5g	

Vitamin A	4%
Vitamin C	2%
Calcium	20%
Iron	4%

* Percent Daily Values are based on a 2,000 calorie diet. Your Daily Values may be higher or lower depending on your calorie needs:			
	Calories:	2,000	2,500
Total Fat	Less than	65g	80g
Sat Fat	Less than	20g	25g
Cholesterol	Less than	300mg	300mg
Sodium	Less than	2,400 mg	2,400mg
Total Carbohydrate		300g	375g
Dietary Fiber		25g	30g

B51

Food Ads

An ad, or **advertisement**, is an announcement that tells people about a product or an event. You might see ads in magazines. Some are on billboards or buses. A **commercial** is an ad on television or radio. A song or a famous person might be used in a commercial. Each time you hear the song or see the person, you think of the food or drink.

Influences at the Store

Stores also try to influence your food choices. Store owners place foods meant to appeal to you at your eye level. They want you to ask your parents or guardian to buy the product for you.

The next time you are in a food store, look at the cereals on the shelves at your eye level. Most of them have a lot of sugar. You may get used to eating sweet cereals and want to buy more. Healthful cereals have little sugar. These are often on the top or bottom shelves.

 What is an advertisement?

Appeals Found in Food and Beverage Ads

The ad shows people having fun. The message is that if you drink or eat the product, you'll have fun, too.

The ad includes a gimmick, such as a prize or free offer. The ad offers you a reward for trying the product.

The ad uses cartoon characters or famous people. A spokesperson tells you that the food tastes great or that it is healthful. The company hopes you will copy the spokesperson and buy the product.

The ad says that you deserve the best. The ad tries to convince you that you are "worth" using this product.

Fast Food

A **fast-food restaurant** is a place that serves food quickly. To persuade you to eat there, some fast-food restaurants offer toys or games with certain meals. Here's how you can eat healthfully at fast-food restaurants.

- **Use the Dietary Guidelines** to make healthful food choices.

- **Use the Food Guide Pyramid** to get the servings you need from the five food groups.

- **Ask to see nutrition information** for the foods and beverages you order.

 Why might fast-food restaurants include toys with their meals?

ACTIVITY **LIFE SKILLS** **CRITICAL THINKING**

Use Resistance Skills

Companies make commercials to influence your choices. Role-play. Have a friend pretend to be in a TV commercial for a new kind of soda pop. Resist the commercial's appeals, and make healthful food choices.

1. **Look at the person. Say "no" in a firm voice.** What else could you do?

2. **Give reasons for saying "no."** You might say, "Soda pop is not healthful. It contains too much sugar." What might you choose instead?

3. **Match your behavior to your words.** When you are at the store, you may be tempted to buy the soda pop. How might you resist?

4. **Ask an adult for help if you need it.** Who might help you?

LESSON REVIEW

Review Concepts

1. **Explain** how to read a food label.

2. **Recall** three appeals that are found in food and beverage ads.

3. **Explain** how to order healthful foods at a fast-food restaurant.

Critical Thinking

4. **Analyze** Use the Dietary Guidelines to analyze the Nutrition Facts on page B51. Is this a healthful food choice? Explain.

5. **LIFE SKILLS** **Use Resistance Skills** Your friends want to buy candy and chips to eat while watching a video. Tell how you can use resistance skills and choose healthful foods.

Eating Healthful Meals and Snacks

You will learn . . .

- what a balanced diet is.
- how to choose healthful meals and snacks.
- how to use the Dietary Guidelines to plan a healthful breakfast.
- ways to compare meals at restaurants.

Vocabulary

- **balanced diet**, *B55*
- **snacks**, *B55*
- **empty-calorie food**, *B56*

You make food choices every day. Maybe you choose what to eat for breakfast, lunch, or snacks. How can you make sure that you get all the nutrients you need?

A Balanced Diet

A **balanced diet** is a daily eating plan. It includes eating the correct servings from each of the five food groups. Eating too few servings from a food group may mean that you do not get the right amounts of some nutrients. This might affect your growth.

You can have a balanced diet in several ways. You might eat three main meals a day and some snacks. **Snacks** are foods that you eat between meals. Some people like to eat four or five smaller meals each day without snacking between meals. Either way is fine, as long as the foods that are eaten are healthful.

Snacks give you energy to do your homework and other activities. Snacks can help you get the servings you need from the food groups. For example, you could have half a bagel after school to get one of the nine servings you need from the bread group. Or you could have celery sticks with peanut butter to get an extra serving from the vegetable group. You would also get a serving from the meat, poultry, fish, dry beans, eggs, and nuts group. What other snacks could you include in a balanced diet?

What is a balanced diet?

CAREERS
Nutritionist

A nutritionist is a person who helps others learn about healthful eating. Many nutritionists work in schools and hospitals. Some work in nursing homes. Nutritionists also help individuals learn how to eat. They teach people how to treat or reduce the risk of illness by eating healthful foods.

LOG ON **www.mmhhealth.com** Find out more about other careers in health.

▲ A nutritionist may counsel a person on how to eat healthfully for maintaining a weight loss.

How to Choose Healthful Meals and Snacks

These guidelines can help you choose healthful meals and snacks.

- **Plan your meals and snacks for the day.** Planning ahead helps you include all of the healthful food groups.

- **Use the Food Guide Pyramid.** Start at the bottom of the pyramid. The numbers 6-3-2-2-2 tell you the fewest number of servings you need from each group.

- **Eat a variety of foods.** If you have a banana for breakfast, try an orange at lunch and some watermelon after dinner. Variety helps you get the nutrients you need.

- **Avoid empty-calorie foods.** An **empty-calorie food** is a food that is low in vitamins and minerals but high in calories. These foods often contain sugar, salt, or saturated fats. Empty-calorie foods can cause weight gain. Those with sugar can cause tooth decay. Candy, cupcakes, chips, and salted pretzels are empty-calorie foods.

▼ **The meals shown give you the correct number of servings from the Food Guide Pyramid.**

Breakfast	Lunch	Dinner

3 bread, 1 milk, 2 fruit	1 meat, 2 bread, 1 milk, 2 vegetable, 1 fruit	2 bread, 2 vegetable, 1 meat, 1 fats, 1 milk

A Healthful Breakfast

While you sleep, your body is fasting. To break the fast, you need to eat a healthful breakfast. The Dietary Guidelines help you to make choices.

- **Use the Food Guide Pyramid to make food choices.** Breakfast should supply some of the servings you need from the five food groups. Then you will get a variety of nutrients. Be certain to have protein.

- **Eat a variety of grains, including whole grains.** You might eat whole-grain cereal, oatmeal, or a bran muffin.

- **Eat a variety of fruits.** You might choose fresh fruit or fruit juice, such as orange or apple juice.

- **Eat foods that are low in saturated fat and not too high in unsaturated fat.** Eat a slice of low-fat bread rather than a donut.

- **Limit how much sugar you eat.** Avoid sugar-coated cereal, soda, and pastries.

- **Use little salt.** Read labels to be certain you don't get much salt.

 Why do you need to eat a healthful breakfast?

Health Online

Analyze Fast-Food Breakfasts

Many fast-food restaurants serve breakfast. Research the nutrition facts for breakfasts served at two fast-food restaurants. Use the e-Journal writing tool to write a report comparing your findings. Visit **www.mmhhealth.com** and click on e-Journal.

 Write About It!

Expository Writing Plan a different breakfast menu for each day of the week. Try to include a variety of foods from as many of the different food groups as possible. Don't forget to include foods that are high in protein. Share your menus with your classmates.

Comparing Meals

When you eat at a restaurant, make wise choices when you order. A well-balanced meal includes foods from different food groups and provides you with a variety of nutrients. A well-balanced meal is low in fat and salt. It also contains fiber and vitamins.

How to Compare Meals at a Restaurant

Here are two guidelines to help you compare meals.

- **Analyze the foods in the meal** to see how many servings there are from the five food groups. For example, suppose you order a double cheeseburger on a whole-wheat bun, a glass of milk, and fruit. This meal has two servings from the meat group, two from the bread group, three from the milk group, and one from the fruit group.

- **Think about how foods are prepared.** Suppose you decide to order broiled chicken served on a whole-wheat bun. The chicken is not fried. It is a more healthful choice. Foods that are steamed, broiled, or grilled are more healthful than fried foods.

✓ **Describe a well-balanced meal at a restaurant.**

MAKE a Difference

Human Food Chain

Each November, the school children of Boothbay Harbor Elementary School in Maine and other community members collect food to feed the hungry. They form a Human Food Chain, lining up side-by-side holding hands. The half-mile-long chain begins at the school and ends at a food pantry.

Meal 1

Happy's Place

Double cheeseburger, with lettuce, tomato, Ketchup and mustard on a whole-wheat bun

French fries

Ice cream

Soda

FINE FAMILY DINER

Meal 2

Broiled chicken breast on a whole-wheat bun

Green salad with fat-free dressing

Banana

Skim milk

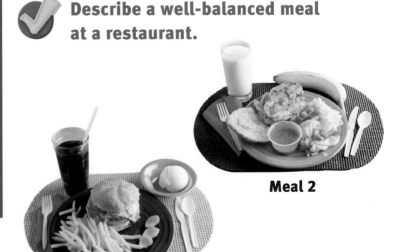

Meal 2

Meal 1

Make Responsible Decisions

You are at a fast-food restaurant and want to eat a healthful meal. You can choose to eat one of the two meals shown on page B58. What should you do?

1 **Identify your choices. Check them out with your parent or trusted adult.** Use the menus and photos on page B58 to help you compare the foods included in each.

2 **Evaluate each choice. Use the *Guidelines for Making Responsible Decisions™*.** Answer the questions that apply to the situation.

3 **Identify the responsible decision. Check this out with your parent or trusted adult.** Decide which meal contains the most healthful choices.

4 **Evaluate your decision.** Which choice did you make? Is it a responsible decision? How will this decision help you stay healthy?

Guidelines for Making Responsible Decisions™

- Is it healthful?
- Is it safe?
- Does it follow rules and laws?
- Does it show respect for myself and others?
- Does it follow family guidelines?
- Does it show good character?

LESSON REVIEW

Review Concepts

1. **Identify** two eating plans that can help you achieve a balanced diet.

2. **Name** three guidelines to help you choose healthful meals and snacks.

3. **List** foods you might eat for a healthful breakfast.

4. **Explain** two ways to compare meals at restaurants.

Critical Thinking

5. **Apply** Make an eating plan for one day that includes meals and snacks and follows the Dietary Guidelines.

6. **LIFE SKILLS** **Make Responsible Decisions** It's time for breakfast. You can have a bowl of whole-grain cereal or a doughnut. What should you do? Use the *Guidelines for Making Responsible Decisions™* to help you make your choice.

Analyze What Influences Your Health

Problem You are shopping for food with your family and see lunch foods in brightly colored packages. The package is cool, but is the food healthful?

We should think about this before we buy it.

GREAT NEW TASTE!

Wow! This package is cool. Can we buy it for lunch?

That does look tasty!

Solution Before you buy, use the steps on the next page to figure out what is influencing your choices.

B60

Learn This Life Skill

Follow these steps to help you analyze what influences your health. Use the Foldables™ to help.

1 **Identify people and things that can influence your health.**

In this situation, what has the company that produced the food done to influence your food choices?

2 **Evaluate how these people and things can influence your health.**

The company wants you to buy this food. Will you allow the brightly colored package to influence you? Reading the label is a better way to make healthful food choices.

3 **Choose healthful influences.**

Read the food label and use the Dietary Guidelines to make food choices. Ask your parents or guardian for suggestions.

4 **Protect yourself against harmful influences.**

Don't be tempted to buy a food because you like the food package.

Practice This Life Skill

Look at the packaging of three foods. Follow the four steps above to analyze how companies try to influence your choices. Discuss your ideas with a classmate.

Preventing Foodborne Illness

You will learn . . .

- the ways people react to foods.
- how to prevent foodborne illness.

Vocabulary

- **food allergy**, *B63*
- **food intolerance**, *B63*
- **lactose**, *B63*
- **MSG**, *B63*
- **foodborne illness**, *B64*

Everyone needs food. However, some people react to certain foods. Some people become ill after eating foods or drinking beverages that have germs in them. To prevent this, you need to make sure that your food is safe.

Reactions to Foods

Some people sneeze, itch, or get an upset stomach after eating certain foods. These people may have a food allergy or a food intolerance. A **food allergy** is a reaction to a food that is caused by the immune system. Peanuts, milk, shrimp, and eggs are common triggers of food allergies. Food allergies can be life threatening. They can cause breathing problems and even death.

A **food intolerance** is a reaction of the body to a food or something in a food. For example, some people cannot digest **lactose**, the sugar in milk. These people may get cramps, gas, and a stomachache when they eat dairy products.

Another substance that can cause a reaction in people is MSG. **MSG** (also called monosodium glutamate) is used to flavor meats, seafood, and soups. People who are sensitive to MSG might get a headache, have trouble breathing, feel pressure around their heart, or feel warm after eating a food that contains MSG.

People who have a food allergy or food intolerance must avoid certain foods. They must check the ingredients in food. They must ask about ingredients before ordering at a restaurant. If you notice changes in your body each time you eat a certain food, tell your parents or guardian. A doctor can test you for a food allergy or food intolerance.

 What are some common causes of food allergies?

▶ **The proteins in these foods cause 90 percent of serious food allergies. What is a food allergy?**

Foodborne Illness

A **foodborne illness** is a sickness caused by eating food or drinking beverages that contain harmful germs. Symptoms include stomachache, headache, fatigue, dizziness, cramps, diarrhea, and vomiting.

Ways to Prevent Foodborne Illness

- **Keep hands clean.** Wash your hands before and after handling food, after using the restroom, and after handling pets. When washing your hands, use warm, soapy water.

- **Keep food clean.** Wash raw fruits and vegetables before you eat or cook them.

- **Keep kitchen surfaces clean.** Scrub cutting boards and utensils before you use them. Use different utensils and cutting boards for different foods, especially for raw foods such as meat and eggs.

- **Keep hot foods hot.** Eat meat or poultry that is well cooked. Cooking kills most germs. Meat that looks pink inside may not be completely cooked.

- **Keep cold foods cold.** Germs grow more slowly at cold temperatures. Refrigerate cold foods soon after you buy them. Wrap and put leftover food in the refrigerator. If you forget to refrigerate a food after dinner, throw it away the next morning. The food may have spoiled.

- **Do not eat uncooked cookie dough.** Raw eggs in cookie dough may contain germs.

- **Do not share utensils, cups, or straws.** This can spread germs.

▲ **Wash raw fruits before eating or preparing them.**

- **Do not buy dented, leaking, or bulging cans.** They may contain germs.

- **Check dates on foods and beverages.** Milk, yogurt, and other foods have "sell by" dates on their packages. The dates tell the last date that a store can safely sell these foods. Consumers should use the food within a week of its sell-by date. Other foods have "use by" dates. These tell when the foods are likely to become unsafe to eat. Check the date at the store before you buy these foods.

 List three ways you can prevent foodborne illnesses.

CRITICAL THINKING

Be a Health Advocate

You want to keep foods safe to eat. How can you encourage others to do the same?

1. **Choose a healthful action to communicate.** You want to keep foods safe to eat.

2. **Collect information about the action.** Visit the library. Collect information on ways to keep food safe to eat. Where else might you find information about food safety?

3. **Decide how to communicate this information.** Suppose you decide to make a poster. Show one or more ways to keep food safe to eat.

4. **Communicate your message to others.** Where might you put your poster for others to see?

LESSON REVIEW

Review Concepts

1. **Identify** two ways people might react to foods.

2. **Define** the phrase *foodborne illness*.

Critical Thinking

3. **Apply** Your family has been away for the day. When you get home, you see that the milk has been left out. Why should you throw it away?

4. **LIFE SKILLS** **Be a Health Advocate** Collect food labels from foods with ingredients that may cause allergic reactions. Use the food labels to make a poster highlighting the ingredients.

5. **LIFE SKILLS** **Use Communication Skills** You are out with friends. You want to wash your hands before eating, but no one else does. Use communication skills to role-play why it is important to wash your hands before eating.

A Healthful Weight

You will learn . . .

- how to balance food intake with physical activity.
- ways to maintain a healthful weight.

Vocabulary

- **healthful weight,** *B67*
- **body image,** *B68*
- **underweight,** *B68*
- **overweight,** *B68*

Everyone has a healthful weight. Staying at a healthful weight is one goal of following the Dietary Guidelines. Finding a balance between the foods you eat and the energy you use is the key to achieving this goal.

Balancing Food Intake and Physical Activity

Your **healthful weight** is the weight that is suggested for your age and size. You feel your best when you are at a healthful weight.

To stay at a healthful weight, you need to use as much energy as you take in from food. Energy from food is measured in calories. You use calories when you breathe, sleep, and digest food. You also use calories when you walk, watch television, and clean your room. To stay at a healthful weight, you need to use about the same number of calories that you take in; added calories are needed for growth. The calories you take in is your *caloric input*. The calories you use is your *caloric output*.

 How do calories affect your healthful weight?

Math LINK
Calorie Count

Your friend wants to lose weight by getting plenty of physical activity. He will swim for one hour each day after school. Look at the chart below. How many calories will he use while swimming each day? How many calories will he use if he swims each day after school for one week?

Calories in food (Caloric Intake)		
Food	**Portion**	**Calories**
Egg	1 large	75
Blueberries	1 cup	80
Whole-wheat bread	1 slice	80
Low-fat milk	1 cup	100
Chicken breast (skinless)	3 ounces	140

Calories Used in Physical Activity (Caloric Output)	
Activity	**Calories/Hour**
Washing dishes	51
Dancing	114
Bicycling	147
In-line or roller skating	159
Swimming	201

Ways to Maintain a Healthful Weight

Body image is the way you feel about how your body looks. When you like and accept your body, you have a positive body image. A positive body image helps you feel good about who you are.

Ads can make you think you have to look a certain way or be as thin as a model. Instead of comparing yourself to others, remember that people have different shapes. Everyone has his or her own healthful weight.

Being Underweight or Overweight

Some people may not be at a healthful weight. Instead, they may be underweight or overweight.

Being **underweight** is having a weight below your healthful weight. Some people are underweight because they eat less food than their body uses or have gone through a growth spurt. To gain weight, eat more servings from the Food Guide Pyramid and exercise to build muscle.

Being **overweight** is having a weight above your healthful weight. Some people are overweight because they take in more calories than they use over time. To lose weight, be more active. Eat plenty of fruits and vegetables. Avoid high-calorie and high-fat foods.

 What does it mean to be overweight or underweight?

▼ **You can gain weight by building muscle.**

B68

Access Health Facts, Products, and Services

You hear about an exercise that is supposed to help people lose weight in a healthful way. How can you learn more about it?

1 **Identify when you might need health facts, products, and services.** Work with a small group. Choose an exercise and learn something about it. Is it safe? Is it good for people your age? What else might you need to know?

2 **Identify where you might find health facts, products, and services.** Where might you get more information about this exercise? Consider talking with your parents or guardian about researching online to look for information. Ask your school nurse or physical education teacher for help.

3 **Find the health facts, products, and services you need.** Assign each person in the group a different source to research. Decide whether each source of information is reliable.

4 **Evaluate the health facts, products, and services.** What did your group conclude? Is the exercise safe?

▶ **Exercise helps you burn calories and lose weight.**

LESSON REVIEW

Review Concepts

1. **Identify** how to balance food intake with physical activity.

2. **Tell** ways to gain weight.

Critical Thinking

3. **Infer** Why is it important to have a positive body image?

4. **LIFE SKILLS** **Access Health Facts, Products, and Services** You overeat when you feel bored. How might you find information on the connection between boredom and overeating?

5. **LIFE SKILLS** **Set Health Goals** Set a health goal to stay at a healthful weight. What are four steps to follow to reach your health goal?

Use Vocabulary

additive, *B51*

body image, *B68*

food group, *B45*

healthful weight,
  B67

lactose, *B63*

nutrient, *B39*

preservative, *B51*

snacks, *B55*

Choose the correct term from the list to complete each sentence. Write the word on a separate sheet of paper.

1. A(n) __?__ is the weight suggested for your age and size.

2. Foods you eat between meals are called __?__.

3. A substance in food that your body uses to keep you healthy is a(n) __?__.

4. The way you feel about how your body looks is __?__.

5. The sugar in milk is called __?__.

6. A substance that helps foods look or taste good is called a(n) __?__.

7. A substance that keeps foods from spoiling is __?__.

8. Foods that contain many of the same types of nutrients are called a __?__.

Review Concepts

Answer each question in complete sentences.

9. Why does your body need protein? Name three foods that provide protein.

10. Name two reasons that your body needs water.

11. Why is it important to read food labels?

12. List three symptoms a person with a food intolerance may have.

13. Why is it important to keep cold foods cold?

Reading Comprehension

Answer each question in complete sentences.

The Food Guide Pyramid is a guide that shows the number of servings from each food group that you need each day. A serving is an amount of food. The food group at the bottom of the pyramid has the greatest number of servings needed.

14. What is the Food Guide Pyramid?

15. What does the Food Guide Pyramid show you besides the number of servings you need?

16. How might you use the Food Guide Pyramid?

Critical Thinking/Problem Solving

Answer each question in complete sentences.

Analyze Concepts

17. You want to reduce the amount of fat you eat. Which types of fats would you reduce?

18. What guide might you use to get the correct amount of servings from the food groups?

19. You try to use table manners at all times. Name three table manners. Tell why each is important.

20. At the grocery store, you see a new brand of cereal for children on a shelf at eye level. Why is it placed on this shelf?

21. Suppose you are helping to make dinner. You sneeze, but forget to cover your mouth. How might this spread foodborne illness?

Practice Life Skills

22. **Analyze What Influences Your Health** You see your favorite sports star advertising a new sports drink. Use the four steps to analyze how this might influence you.

23. **Make Responsible Decisions** In the morning, you can stay at home and eat a healthful breakfast, or you can rush off to school. Use the *Guidelines for Making Responsible Decisions*™ to decide which one is the more healthful choice.

Read Graphics

Use the charts to answer the questions.

Calories in Food (Caloric Intake)

Food	Portion	Calories/Hour
Egg	1 large	75
Blueberries	1 cup	80
Whole-wheat bread	1 slice	80
Low-fat milk	1 cup	100
Chicken breast (skinless)	3 ounces	140

Calories Used In Physical Activity (caloric output)

Activity	Calories/Hour
Washing dishes	51
Dancing	114
Bicycling	147
In-line or roller skating	159
Swimming	201

24. Suppose you ate 3 ounces of chicken breast (skinless) and 1 cup of low-fat milk. How many calories would you consume?

25. Using the answer in number 24, what are two physical activities that you could do to burn off the same number of calories?

 LOG ON www.mmhhealth.com
Find out how much you know about nutrition.

Effective Communication

Write a Script

In small groups, write a skit about nutrition and a balance diet to present to younger students in your school. Demonstrate how to choose healthful foods and give examples of healthful snacks.

Self-Directed Learning

Make a Chart

List your five favorite foods in a chart. Add information about the serving size of each food, how many calories are in a single serving, and what the fat and fiber counts are in each. Decide which of the foods is most healthful.

Favorite food	Serving Size	Calories per serving	How much fat?	How much fiber?
Hamburger sandwich	quarter pound sandwich	420	20 g	2 g
Happy oats cereal	¾ cup cereal	110	6 g	
Fat-free milk	1 cup	40	0	
Baked beans	About 1 cup	123		
Noodle soup	cup			

My Favorite Foods

Critical Thinking and Problem Solving

Design an Ad

Make an advertisement that promotes a healthful food such as oatmeal. Think about what information should be in your ad. What might your ad say or show that would make people want to eat oatmeal?

Responsible Citizenship

Write a Guidebook

Choose a food group. In small groups design two pages describing the food group. Show examples of food in that group and identify how the food group fits into the Food Guide Pyramid. Compile the pages into the book and photocopy the guide.

food Guide Pyramid

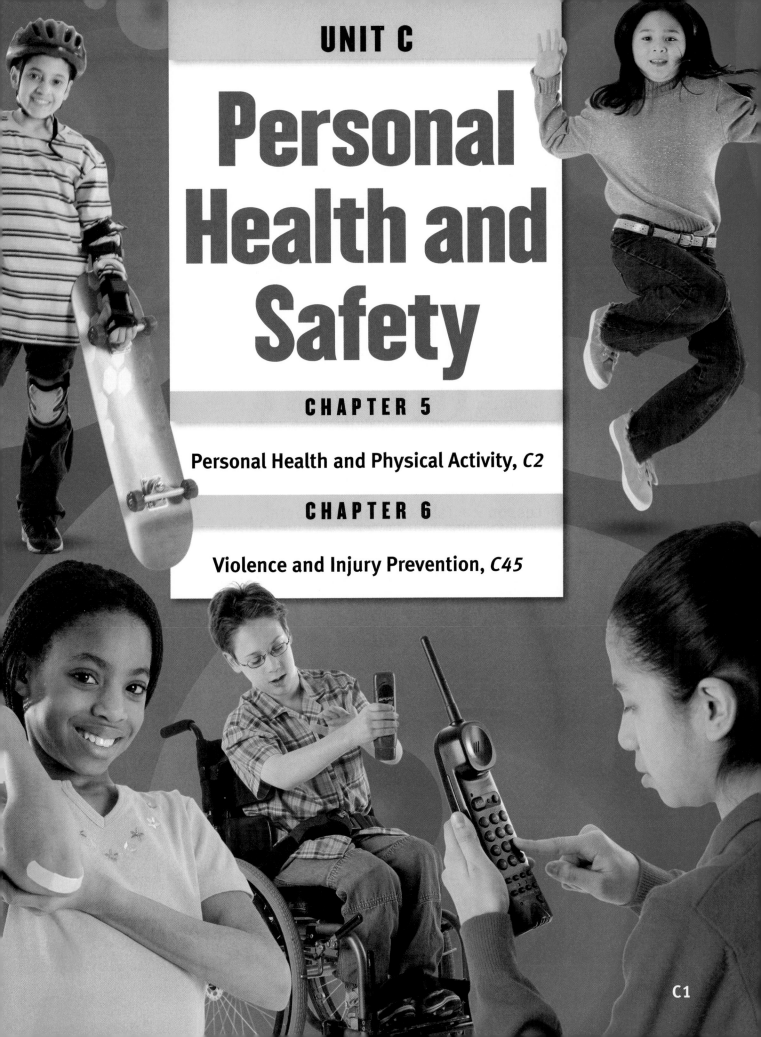

UNIT C

Personal Health and Safety

CHAPTER 5

Personal Health and Physical Activity, *C2*

CHAPTER 6

Violence and Injury Prevention, *C45*

CHAPTER 5

Personal Health and Physical Activity

20/200

20/100

20/70

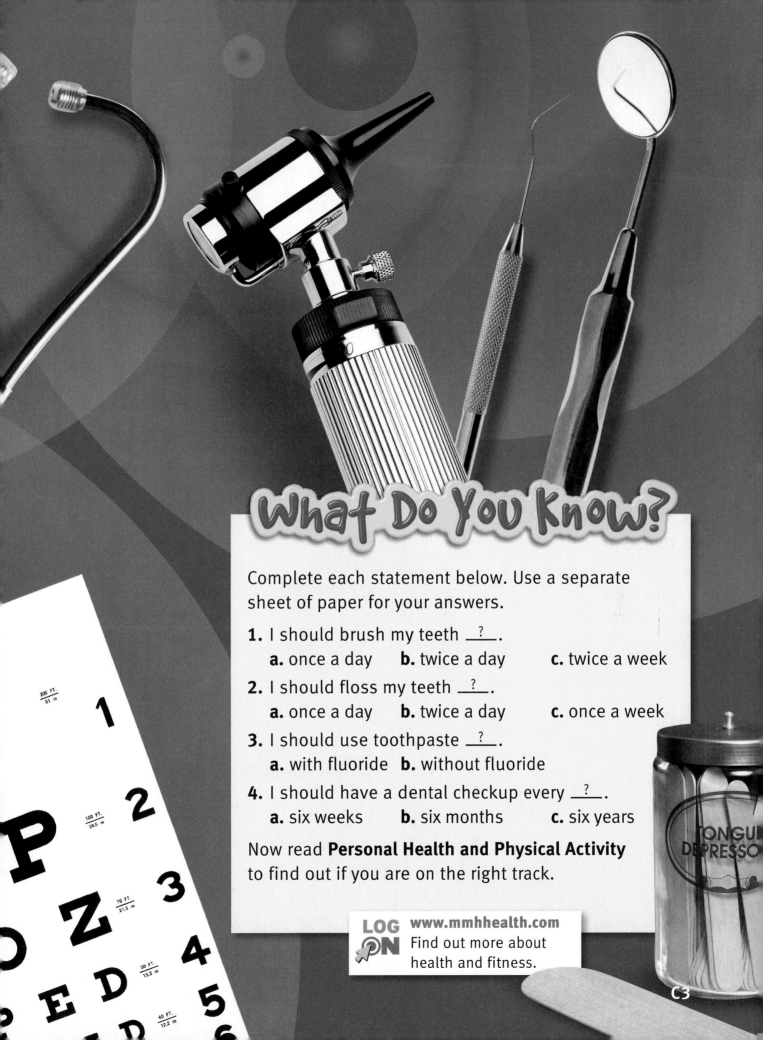

What Do You Know?

Complete each statement below. Use a separate sheet of paper for your answers.

1. I should brush my teeth __?__.
   a. once a day   **b.** twice a day   **c.** twice a week

2. I should floss my teeth __?__.
   a. once a day   **b.** twice a day   **c.** once a week

3. I should use toothpaste __?__.
   a. with fluoride   **b.** without fluoride

4. I should have a dental checkup every __?__.
   a. six weeks   **b.** six months   **c.** six years

Now read **Personal Health and Physical Activity** to find out if you are on the right track.

LOG ON   www.mmhhealth.com
Find out more about health and fitness.

C3

Take Care of Your Health

You will learn . . .

- what role each member of your health-care team plays in your health.
- ways to take care of your eyes.
- ways to take care of your ears.

Vocabulary

- **nearsighted**, *C6*
- **farsighted**, *C6*
- **hearing loss**, *C8*

Many people help keep you healthy. These people make up your personal health-care team. Each member of your health-care team has a certain job to do.

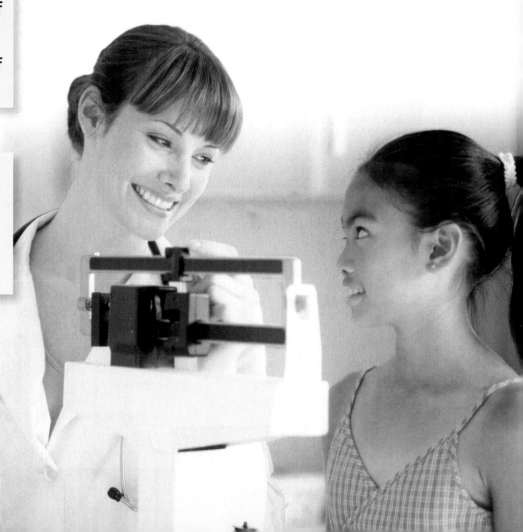

Your Health-Care Team

The members of your health-care team may include the following people.

- **Your parents or guardian** care about your health. They see that you have medical and dental care.

- **Your doctor** examines you during a checkup and when you show symptoms of illness. He or she records your visits and keeps notes on your health.

- **Your dentist** examines your teeth and gums during a checkup. If needed, he or she will fill a cavity, apply a sealant, treat gum disease, or recommend braces.

- **Your teacher** sends you to the school nurse when you are ill or injured.

- **Your school nurse** communicates with parents or guardians, doctors, teachers and counselors about each student's health-care needs. He or she may dispense prescribed medicines and watches for health conditions that keep students from learning.

- **You** also are a member of your health-care team. You can develop habits that help you stay healthy.

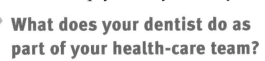 **What does your dentist do as part of your health-care team?**

ACTIVITY

On Your Own

FOR SCHOOL OR HOME

Make a Personal Health Record

Work with your parents or guardian to compile your own personal health record. A personal health record is written information about your health history. It includes information such as your date of birth, weight and length at birth, family history of disease, dates of checkups and vaccinations, medicines taken regularly, allergies, surgeries, and major illnesses.

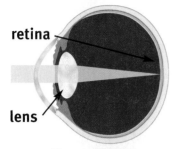

retina

lens

Normal eye

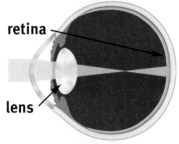

retina

lens

Nearsighted eye

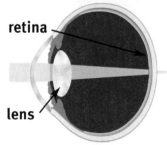

retina

lens

Farsighted eye

▲ **The shape of the eyeball affects how you see.**

Your Eyes

Your eyes, ears, and nose help you sense the world around you. You are able to see because light bounces off of objects and enters your eye. There the lens bends the light and focuses it onto a layer called the retina (RE•ti•nuh). The light causes the retina to send nerve impulses to the brain. In the brain, these impulses are interpreted as the images of the objects that you see.

Vision Problems

People with normal vision see objects clearly whether the objects are close or far away. People who are **nearsighted** see close-by objects clearly. Objects that are far away from them look blurry. To be nearsighted means that the lens focuses light rays in front of the retina.

Other people are farsighted. People who are **farsighted** see far away objects clearly, but objects that are nearby look blurry. To be farsighted means that the lens focuses light rays behind the retina. Glasses or contact lenses can help correct these vision problems.

Parts of the Eye

Iris Adjusts the size of the pupil.

Pupil Allows different amounts of light to enter the eye.

Lens Focuses light rays on the retina.

Retina Changes light into nerve signals and sends them to the optic nerve.

Optic nerve Sends signals to the brain.

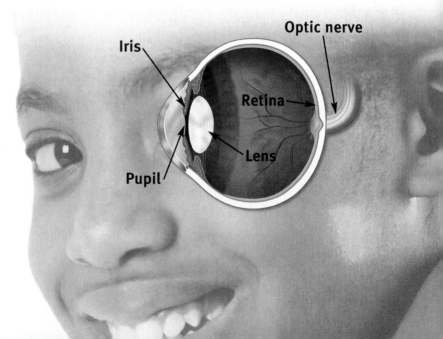

Common Eye Infections and Injuries

When a person gets *pinkeye*, the inside of the eyelid becomes infected. The eyes look red and swollen. There is medicine for pinkeye. A *sty* is an infection in the glands of the eyelid. A red bump with a yellow center appears. Do not touch a sty.

A *black eye* is a common eye injury. It is bruised tissue around the eye. The tissue looks deep blue or black, then turns yellow and greenish as it heals.

Take Care of Your Eyes

- **Get treatment** for an eye injury or infection. Tell an adult if you have symptoms of any eye problem.

- **Avoid eyestrain.** Read in well-lighted areas. Rest your eyes every 20 minutes when at a computer.

- **Wear a face shield** or a facemask when playing contact sports or safety glasses when working in a science lab.

- **Wear sunglasses** to protect against the sun's ultraviolet (UV) rays.

- **Have regular eye exams.** During the exam, the doctor looks inside your eyes and checks your vision.

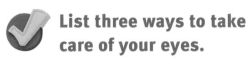 **List three ways to take care of your eyes.**

Make Responsible Decisions

You are having trouble reading words written on the chalkboard at school. You do not want to wear glasses. What should you do? Write a skit that shows the responsible decision. Include the four steps below in your skit.

1 **Identify your choices.** You could keep it to yourself or tell a parent or guardian.

2 **Evaluate each choice.** Use the *Guidelines for Making Responsible Decisions™*.

Guidelines for Making Responsible Decisions™

- **Is it healthful?**
- **Is it safe?**
- **Does it follow rules and laws?**
- **Does it show respect for myself and others?**
- **Does it follow family guidelines?**
- **Does it show good character?**

3 **Identify the responsible decision.** Explain why your decision is responsible. Check it out with your parent or a trusted adult.

4 **Evaluate your decision.** How does your decision help your health?

Your Ears

Your ears allow you to hear a wide range of sound, from the crash of thunder to the whisper of the wind blowing through the branches of a tree. Hearing sound helps you in many of your daily activities and can give you pleasure.

Hearing Problems

Hearing loss is a problem in one or both ears that prevents a person from hearing properly. People who have hearing loss often turn an ear toward the sound to hear it better. They might speak loudly, mispronounce words, ask you to repeat what you have said, or turn up the volume of the TV or radio.

A special machine is used to test for hearing loss. The machine plays different sounds into a set of earphones placed over the ears. The person being tested raises a hand when he or she hears a sound.

ACTIVITY

Science
LINK

Compare Sounds

Collect four unbreakable objects. Drop each object and compare the sound that each makes. Rate the loudness of each sound. The loudness of sound is measured in decibels (dB). An airplane taking off measures about 120 dB. A purring cat measures only about 25 dB.

Parts of the Ear

Ear Canal Directs sound waves to your eardrum.

Eardrum Vibrates when struck by sound waves.

Cochlea (KO•klee•uh) Contains a fluid and hairs that vibrate and send signals to the auditory nerve.

Auditory nerve Sends signals to the brain. The brain identifies the sound.

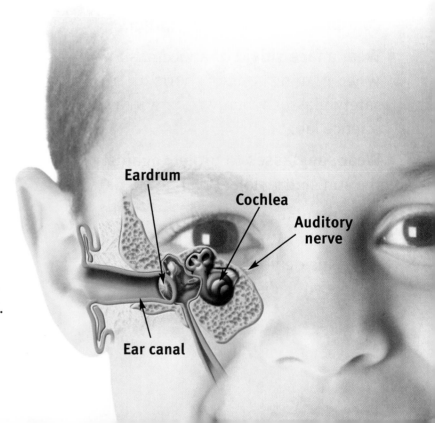

Eardrum

Cochlea

Auditory nerve

Ear canal

Protect Your Ears

- **Get treatment** for an ear injury or infection. Ears can become infected when you have a cold or flu. If left untreated, some ear infections may cause hearing loss.

- **Wear a helmet** to protect your ears when playing certain sports, such as baseball and football.

- **Never put objects in your ear.** Cleaning inside your ear with a cotton swab can damage the eardrum.

- **Turn down the volume.** Loud sounds can destroy the tiny nerve endings in the inner ear. This can cause hearing loss.

- **Have regular hearing tests.** These tests can detect hearing problems early so that they can be treated.

- **Wear earplugs or noise reducing earmuffs** when you will be around loud noises.

 List three ways to take care of your ears.

Test Sounds

Cover your ears with your hands. How does this change how well you hear? Try covering your ears with other materials, such as gloves, paper, and foam. How did the sounds change? Hearing protectors, such as ear plugs, do the same thing. Find out what types of ear protection are available for purchase in a store.

◄ **Keep the volume on a headset low to be safe.**

LESSON REVIEW

Review Concepts

1. **List** three members of your health-care team. Tell what each member does.

2. **Describe** ways you can take care of your eyes.

3. **Explain** ways you can protect your ears.

Critical Thinking

4. **Infer** Some baseball players would rather not wear helmets. What would you say to those players?

5. **LIFE SKILLS Make Responsible Decisions** When watching TV, you often turn up the volume. The other people who are watching complain that the volume is too loud. What might be the problem? What should you do?

Take Care of Your Teeth

You will learn . . .

- about the structure and function of teeth.
- ways to care for your teeth and gums.
- ways to protect your teeth against injury.

Taking care of your teeth is important to your health. Teeth are essential to eating and speaking. They help you look your best. They give shape to your mouth and light up your smile.

Vocabulary

- **primary teeth**, *C11*
- **permanent teeth**, *C11*
- **dental plaque**, *C12*
- **cavity**, *C12*
- **fluoride**, *C12*
- **sealant**, *C14*

Kinds of Teeth

People grow two sets of teeth, primary ("baby") and permanent. **Primary teeth** grow in first. Primary teeth begin cutting through a baby's gums between the ages of 6 and 14 months. A baby will get 20 primary teeth. It's important to keep primary teeth healthy. They help a child to develop speech. They also hold the place where permanent teeth will grow. At around age 6, primary teeth begin to fall out, making way for the permanent teeth. **Permanent teeth** are teeth that, with care, should last a lifetime.

Right now, you probably have some primary and some permanent teeth. In about 10 years, you should have all 32 of your permanent teeth. This will include four large molars called wisdom teeth.

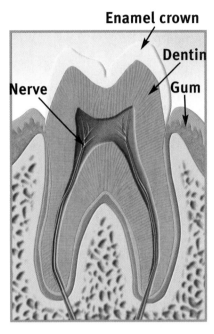

▲ The parts of a tooth

 How do the four kinds of teeth help you eat?

Kinds of Teeth

Incisors (8 in all) have flat, sharp edges. They bite into and cut food.

Bicuspids (8 in all) crush and grind food.

Cuspids (4 in all) tear food apart.

Molars (eventually 12 in all) crush and grind food.

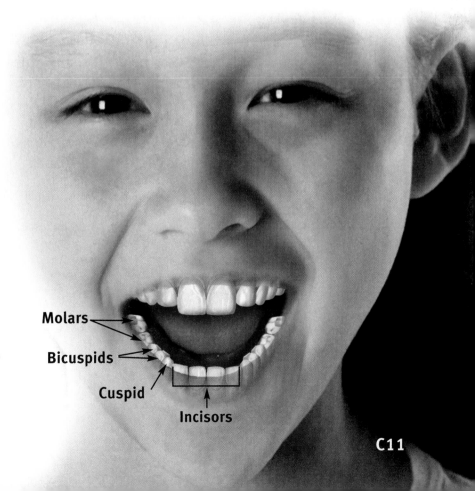

Caring for Your Teeth and Gums

Do You Know?

Dental plaque also collects on the tongue. Often bad breath comes from bacteria in dental plaque that coats the back of the tongue. Brushing the tongue helps cut down on bad breath.

On a daily basis, teeth become coated with a sticky film called **dental plaque** (PLAK). Bacteria that live in dental plaque break down sugars and starches in food and make an acid. This acid can wear away tooth enamel, causing a **cavity**, or hole, to form. If you don't brush every day, dental plaque can harden into a crust called *tartar*. Tartar can damage your gums. You can slow dental plaque and tartar from building up on teeth. Brush them at least twice a day.

Regular dental care includes daily brushing and flossing. Brushing with a toothpaste that has fluoride (FLOOR•ide) cleans teeth and helps prevent tooth decay. **Fluoride** is a mineral that hardens tooth enamel. Dental floss is a string made to clean between the teeth. Some floss is waxed. Some brands are flavored. The photographs below show you how to use dental floss.

How to Floss

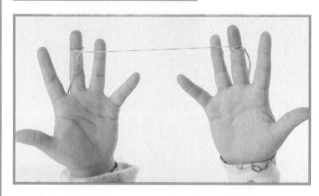

▲ Break off about 18 inches of dental floss. Wind some of it around the middle finger of each hand.

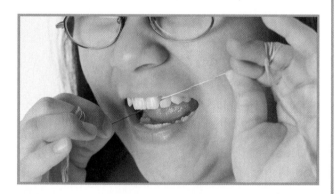

▲ Insert floss between two teeth. Gently move it up to the gum line and down the sides of your teeth. Unwind a clean length from your fingers for the next two teeth.

Choose the Right Dental-Care Products

Using the right dental care products can protect your teeth against decay. But it's not easy to know which products to choose because there are so many brands of toothpaste, dental floss, and toothbrushes available.

Talking to your dentist can help you learn what to look for in a dental-care product. Dentists often recommend using a toothbrush with soft bristles and toothpaste with fluoride. They may recommend different types of floss depending on how your teeth are spaced.

Many dental products carry the American Dental Association (ADA) Seal of Acceptance. A product with this seal meets the ADA's requirements for effectiveness. Look for this seal on any dental-care product you purchase.

 How does a cavity form?

ACTIVITY

Health Online

Compare Toothbrushes

Toothbrushes come in different shapes and sizes. Research different toothbrush designs. Use the e-Journal writing tool to report on your findings. Visit **www.mmhhealth.com** and click on *e-Journal*.

How to Brush

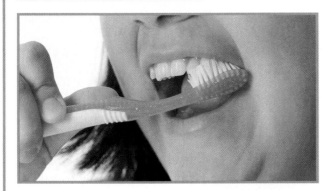

▲ Use a soft-bristle toothbrush. Start at the gum line. Use circular strokes for the front and side of each tooth. Brush the chewing surfaces of your back teeth.

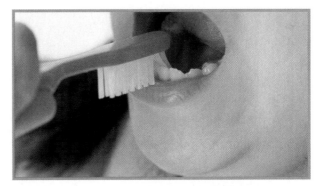

▲ Use the tip of your toothbrush to brush the inner part of your front teeth. Brush your gums and tongue, too.

Have Dental Checkups

Have a dental checkup every six months. During a checkup, your teeth are cleaned and flossed by a dental hygienist (HI•gen•est). The dentist will check your teeth for cavities. The dental hygienist might take X-rays of your teeth. An X-ray can show whether your teeth are coming in straight. It also might show some cavities. Sometimes a sealant is put on the back teeth if they have no decay. A **sealant** is a thin layer of plastic-like material painted on healthy molars. A sealant keeps plaque away from tooth enamel. It protects teeth from acids that cause decay.

Choose a Healthful Diet

Your teeth also benefit from a healthful diet that is low in sugar. Foods and beverages with lots of sugar help bacteria cause tooth decay. The bacteria use this sugar to form the acids that attack your teeth. Choose snack foods low in sugar such as vegetable sticks. Drink water instead of soft drinks and fruit punch. Eat cereal that is not sugar-coated.

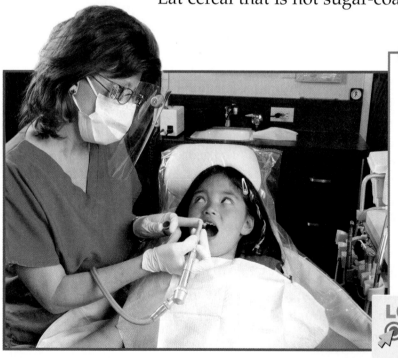

CAREERS

Dental Hygienist

Dental hygienists work with dentists. They clean and polish your teeth. They take X-rays of your teeth. Dental hygienists also tell you how to take better care of your teeth.

LOG ON www.mmhhealth.com
Find out more about health careers.

Protect Teeth From Injury

You can protect your teeth against damage and injury. Here are some do's and don'ts.

- **DO** wear a seat belt with a shoulder strap when riding in a car.
- **DO** wear a mouth guard when playing contact sports.
- **DON'T** hold objects between your teeth. This includes hair clips, safety pins, pencils, and paper clips.
- **DON'T** use your teeth as a cutting or opening tool.

 List three ways to protect your teeth.

CRITICAL THINKING

Access Health Products

Your dentist suggests that you should floss more regularly. You decide to look at types of floss and to make a chart to compare them.

1 **Identify when you might need health products.** You need to floss everyday. How many times should you floss daily?

2 **Identify where you might find health products.** Where does your family buy dental care products? Do you buy them at a grocery store or at a drug store?

3 **Find the health products you need.** Find different types of dental floss. You can visit a drug store with your parents or guardian. Or you can look in your home medicine cabinet.

4 **Evaluate the health products.** Do any of the different types of floss carry the ADA seal of acceptance? What does this seal tell you about the floss? Make a chart comparing different types of floss.

LESSON REVIEW

Review Concepts

1. **Explain** the difference between primary and permanent teeth.

2. **List** three ways to care for your teeth and gums.

3. **List** ways to protect your teeth from injury.

Critical Thinking

4. **Analyze** How are plaque and daily flossing related?

5. **LIFE SKILLS** **Access Health Products** You are shopping for toothpaste. There are many brands from which to choose. What should you think about in making your choice?

Good Grooming

You will learn . . .

- how to choose grooming products.
- ways the media tries to influence your choice of grooming products.
- ways to care for skin, hair, and nails.

Vocabulary

- **grooming,** *C17*
- **ringworm,** *C18*

As you get ready for school in the morning, you brush your teeth, wash your face, and comb your hair. Do you use any grooming products in this process? How do these products promote health?

Choosing Grooming Products

Grooming is taking care of your body and appearance. Grooming includes keeping your teeth, skin, hair, and nails clean and healthy. To do this, use grooming products such as toothpaste, soap, and shampoo.

Before choosing a grooming product, read the label carefully. The label tells you what is in the product and how to use it safely. The label also might have a list of side effects. A *side effect* is an unwanted feeling or response after taking a drug or using a product. Examples of side effects are a rash or dizziness.

Media Influences

An *advertisement*, or *ad*, is a paid announcement. Many ads for grooming products appear in magazines and on television. What is there about an ad that might cause you to ask your parents or guardian to buy the product?

- Is it trying to make you think that you will be more popular or attractive if you use this product?

- Is an athlete or actor advertising the product?

- Does it offer a bonus, such as "Buy one, get one free?"

- Does it suggest that everyone chooses this product?

 **What is grooming?**

Read the Label

Select two different shampoo products that treat dandruff, a flaking condition of the scalp. Read the labels for cautions about side effects. Compare the kinds of side effects that are listed on the two products. Compare the action you are to take in case such side effects appear.

Skin, Hair, and Nails

Your skin, hair, and nails protect your body. By keeping them clean and by eating a healthful diet, you help keep your body healthy.

Skin

Your skin blocks germs from getting inside your body. It protects the tissues and organs inside your body. Keep your skin healthy.

- **Keep skin clean** by bathing or showering regularly. To keep your skin clean, use soap and water each day to remove dirt, germs, sweat, and oil from your skin. Keeping your skin clean and dry helps prevent skin diseases, such as ringworm. **Ringworm** is caused by a fungus. Symptoms of ringworm include red patches on the skin with ring-like, itchy, painful sores.

- **Wear sunscreen** with SPF 15 or higher. To guard against the sun's harmful rays, use sunscreen with a *Sun Protection Factor* (SPF) of 15 or higher. Put sunscreen on about 30 minutes before going outside. Wear a long-sleeved shirt and a hat.

Hair

Keep your hair healthy with a few simple activities.

- **Brush and comb** your hair every day.

- **Wash your hair** with shampoo regularly to keep it clean.

- **Get treatment** for any scalp infections. You can get head lice by sharing hats, combs, or brushes with people who have head lice. You can get rid of head lice by using shampoos that kill lice and their eggs.

▼ **Protect against the sun's rays using the American Cancer Society's "slip, slop, slap" method. *Slip* on a long-sleeved shirt. *Slop* on sunscreen of SPF 15 or higher. *Slap* on a hat and sunglasses to protect your eyes.**

Nails

Nails help you scratch and help you pick up small objects. Nails can tell something about your health. Choose habits to keep nails healthy.

- **Keep nails clean** with a nailbrush.

- **Trim nails** by cutting straight across with nail clippers. Smooth rough edges with a nail file.

- **Do not bite your nails.** Biting your nails can cause the skin around them to break, letting germs in.

 How should nails be trimmed?

ACTIVITY

LIFE SKILLS

CRITICAL THINKING

Analyze What Influences Your Health

Magazine ads for hair care products try to influence you to buy the product.

1 **Identify people and things that can influence your health.** What ads influenced your choice of a hair-care product?

2 **Evaluate how these people or things can affect your health.** What did the ad show or say? Did it provide health related information?

3 **Choose healthful influences.** Read the information on the label of a hair-care product.

4 **Protect yourself against harmful influences.** Compare the information in the ads you've seen with those on product labels. Which contains information you can trust?

CONDITIONER

LESSON REVIEW

Review Concepts

1. **Explain** how to choose grooming products wisely.

2. **List** three influences that ads for grooming products might use to get a person to buy a product.

3. **List** three ways to keep your skin healthy.

Critical Thinking

4. **Analyze** How does taking a shower or bath each day protect your health?

5. **LIFE SKILLS** **Analyze What Influences Your Health** You see an ad for a skin-care product that promises to clear up all blemishes. What should you do before you buy the product?

Be Physically Active

You will learn . . .

- the benefits of physical activity.
- why you need each of the five kinds of health-related fitness.
- what fitness skills you can develop.

Vocabulary

- **physical fitness,** *C22*
- **muscular strength,** *C22*
- **muscular endurance,** *C22*
- **flexibility,** *C23*
- **heart and lung endurance,** *C23*
- **healthful body composition,** *C23*

Do you like to play sports? Perhaps you enjoy swimming or biking. Physical activity improves health in many ways.

The Benefits of Physical Activity

Regular physical activity has many benefits. It improves your total health. You keep a healthful weight. You build strong muscles. When you have been active during the day, you sleep better and wake up refreshed. By being active now, you also reduce your risk of heart disease, diabetes, and high blood pressure.

Physical activity can benefit you mentally and emotionally. When you walk, swim, or play tag with friends, you have fun. You spend less time thinking about things that bother you. Being physically active can help you pay attention. You do better in school.

When you are physically active, your family and social health also benefit. New relationships can be built. If you clean out the basement with your family, you have a chance to make your family stronger. If you are on a sports team or sing in a school choir, you meet people who like to do some of the same things that you like to do.

 How does physical activity improve physical health?

ACTIVITY

Math LINK

Favorite Sports

Take a survey to find out which team sport students in your class like. Use the information to make a graph. Which was the most popular sport? Which sport was least popular? Share and display your graph with your class.

◀ **Participating in a community run is a great way to spend time with others.**

C21

Five Kinds of Health-Related Fitness

Do You Know

The world record for non-stop push-ups is held by Minoru Yoshida of Japan who did 10,507 push-ups non-stop in October 1980.

Physical fitness means having your heart, lungs, muscles, and joints in good condition. The five areas of health-related fitness are muscular strength, muscular endurance, flexibility, heart and lung endurance, and healthful body composition.

Muscular Strength

Muscular strength is the ability to use your muscles to push, pull, lift, throw, or kick. When you lift a heavy box, play tug-of-war, or do push-ups, you need muscular strength. Doing pull-ups or quickly going up a flight of stairs helps improve muscular strength.

Muscular Endurance

Can you walk or bicycle for 30 minutes without getting tired? If so, you have muscular endurance. **Muscular endurance** is the ability to use your muscles for a long time without stopping. Pulling a person or a pile of newspapers in a wagon for 30 minutes can improve muscular endurance.

Flexibility

Can you touch your toes with your fingers while bending your knees only slightly? If you can, then you have flexibility (flek•suh•BIL•uh•tee). **Flexibility** is the ability to bend and move your body. Having flexibility helps protect your joints from injury. Stretching, dancing, and gymnastics are physical activities that improve flexibility.

Heart and Lung Endurance

Heart and lung endurance is the ability to stay active without getting tired. Activities that make your heart beat faster for a period of time improve heart and lung endurance. Swimming, bicycling, jogging, shoveling snow, or mowing grass for 30 minutes without stopping all help keep your heart and lungs healthy.

Healthful Body Composition

A **healthful body composition** means having a lean body without too much fat. A certain amount of fat is important for health. Your body uses fat as a source of energy. Fat also protects internal organs. However, too much fat can harm health. The proper balance of lean muscle tissue and fat tissue helps maintain health.

 List two activities that you can do to improve heart and lung endurance.

Skill-Related Fitness

Skill-related fitness refers to the skills you use in physical activity. There are six fitness skills. They improve with practice. When you dribble a basketball or jump rope, you use fitness skills.

- **Agility** (uh•JIL•uh•tee) is the ability to move quickly and easily. You are agile when you change positions quickly, such as when you play baseball, basketball, and soccer. Moving a soccer ball away from an opponent takes agility.

- **Coordination** is the ability to use body parts and senses together for movement. You are coordinated when you can run and dribble a basketball at the same time. You show coordination when you step quickly in the right direction to hit a moving tennis ball.

- **Balance** is the ability to keep from falling. Keeping your balance is important for many activities. When you in-line skate or walk on a balance beam without falling, you use balance skills.

- **Speed** is the ability to move quickly. When you run fast to reach home plate or to hit a tennis ball, you use speed.

C24

- **Power** is the ability to combine strength and speed. You need power to hit a baseball or to kick a soccer ball far.

- **Reaction time** is the time that it takes you to respond to something. For example, the time it takes you to move after you realize a softball is coming toward you in the outfield is your reaction time. Good reaction time is important in games that involve catching, throwing, or hitting objects.

 List two sports that use agility.

Set Health Goals

You want to improve your fitness skills so that you can be on the school track team this year. You decide to set a goal to help you meet this outcome.

1 **Identify the health goal you want to set.** Health Goal: I will get plenty of physical activity.

2 **Tell how your goal will affect your health.** Make a list of fitness skills used in track. Write a benefit for each fitness skill you use in track.

3 **Describe a plan you will follow. Keep track of your progress.** Use a Health Behavior Contract to record which fitness skills you practice and when you practice them. Tell who will help you to stay on task.

4 **Evaluate how your plan worked.** How will you tell if your level of skill-related fitness increases?

LESSON REVIEW

Review Concepts

1. **Describe** ways that physical activity can improve mental and emotional health.

2. **List** five kinds of health-related fitness.

3. **List** the six fitness skills.

Critical Thinking

4. **Apply** Give an example of a sport that requires muscular strength and muscular endurance.

5. **Apply** You are recovering from a broken arm. The doctor sends you to a physical therapist to improve flexibility and muscular strength. Name two activities the therapist might have you practice. Explain your choices.

6. **LIFE SKILLS** **Set Health Goals** You set a health goal to get plenty of physical activity. Name one physical activity that you can do for each of the five kinds of health-related fitness.

C25

Be Physically Fit

You will learn . . .

- about a test that measures health-related fitness.

- about five exercises involved in a fitness test.

In school you may take tests in reading and math to see how well you know these subjects. Did you know that there are tests that measure your physical fitness?

Vocabulary

- **sit-ups or curl ups,** *C28*

- **pull-ups,** *C28*

- **sit-and-reach or V-sit and reach,** *C28*

- **shuttle run,** *C28*

- **one-mile walk/run,** *C28*

- **percent body fat pinch,** *C29*

Fitness Tests

Do you know how physically fit you are? There are several different tests to measure your level of physical fitness, including your muscular strength, muscular endurance, flexibility, heart and lung endurance, and body composition. *The President's Challenge* is a test that measures your level of health-related fitness. The table below lists the specific tests and the scores needed to complete the highest level of the *President's Challenge*.

 What is the purpose of a fitness test?

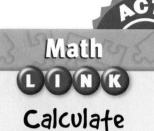

Math LINK

Calculate Percents

You would like to improve your time in the one-mile run/walk test. Your time now is 20 minutes. What will your time be after you improve by 10 percent?

	Age	V-sit Reach or Sit and Reach (inches)	Pull-Ups	Curl-Ups (timed one minute)	Shuttle Run (seconds)	One-Mile Run (minutes: seconds)
Boys						
	8	+3.0	5	40	11.1	8:48
	9	+3.0	5	41	10.9	8:31
	10	+4.0	6	45	10.3	7:57
	11	+4.0	6	47	10.0	7:32
Girls						
	8	+4.5	2	38	11.8	10:02
	9	+5.5	2	39	11.1	9:30
	10	+6.0	3	40	10.8	9:19
	11	+6.5	3	42	10.5	9:02

THE PRESIDENTIAL PHYSICAL FITNESS AWARD

Source: U.S. Department of Health and Human Services

▲ Each of the five tests in the *President's Challenge* measure a specific part of fitness in inches, repetitions, or time. See page C28 for more about the tests.

Health Fitness Tests

How do you get ready for a math test or a spelling test? Do you practice doing problems? Do you practice spelling words that you will be tested on? Practice is something you do to become better at a skill. You can practice for health-related fitness tests too. When you perform the skills shown on these pages over and over, you will become better at doing them. You also will benefit because your overall health will improve.

▲ **Shuttle Run** The **shuttle run** measures total body coordination.

▶ **Pull-Ups** **Pull-ups** test upper body strength and endurance. Your arm and shoulder muscles will work hard when you do pull-ups.

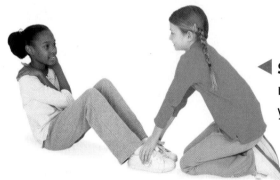

◀ **Sit-Ups or Curl-Ups** **Sit-ups or curl-ups** measure the strength and endurance of your abdominal muscles.

▶ **V-Sit and Reach** The **V-sit and reach** or *sit and reach* measures the flexibility of the muscles in your back and legs.

◀ **One-Mile Walk/Run** The **one-mile run/walk** measures your heart and lung endurance. Complete the one-mile walk/run as fast as you can.

Measuring Your Body Fat

Some body fat is needed for keeping your body warm, for protection, and as an energy reserve. The **percent body fat pinch** is a test to measure the amount of body fat you have. The thickness of the pinch tells whether you have too much, too little, or just enough body fat.

▶ **The thickness of the fold of skin on your upper arm is measured.**

ACTIVITY

LIFE SKILLS

CRITICAL THINKING

Use Communication Skills

After school you want to practice the fitness test activities. Your friends want to watch television. You want them to see how the activities will keep them healthy.

1. **Choose the best way to communicate.** Write a list of three ways to communicate with your friends about the need to practice for fitness tests.

2. **Send a clear message. Be polite.** Draw or record the message that you want to communicate.

3. **Listen to each other.** Pair up with a classmate and share your message.

4. **Make sure you understand each other.** Ask your classmate to repeat the reasons you gave for practicing for the fitness tests. Did he or she understand? What can you do to improve how your message was delivered?

 What do pull-ups measure?

LESSON REVIEW

Review Concepts

1. **Describe** the purpose of fitness tests.

2. **Name** the kind of health-related fitness that the one-mile walk/run measures.

3. **Identify** Which fitness test measures abdominal muscle strength? Which test measures the flexibility of muscles in the back and legs?

Critical Thinking

4. **Analyze** Why is the one-mile walk/run used to measure your heart and lung endurance?

5. **LIFE SKILLS** **Use Communication Skills** You need to practice for the upcoming President's Challenge. Identify a person you can ask for help. Explain how you will communicate with that person.

Set Up a Personal Fitness Plan

You will learn . . .

- the difference between aerobic and anaerobic exercise.
- lifetime sports you can enjoy now.
- the importance of taking responsibility for developing and maintaining a personal fitness plan.

Vocabulary

- **aerobic exercise,** *C31*
- **anaerobic exercise,** *C31*
- **lifetime sport,** *C32*

A personal fitness plan requires planning.

Choose physical activities that you enjoy.

That will make it easier to stick to your plan.

It will be more fun, too.

Aerobic and Anaerobic Exercise

No matter what kind of physical activity you take part in, your cells need oxygen. **Aerobic** (ay•ROH•bik) **exercise** is exercise that uses a lot of oxygen at a steady pace over a long period of time. When you ride a bike for a half hour or more, your heart beats at a steady rate and supplies a steady flow of oxygen to cells in your body. **Anaerobic** (ann•uh•ROH•bik) **exercise** is exercise that uses a lot of oxygen in a short period of time and faster than your body can supply. If you run sprints, you move fast. You breathe hard and fast and deep in an effort to supply your cells with oxygen.

 Compare aerobic and anaerobic exercise.

Aerobic Exercise	Anaerobic Exercise

Examples swimming, jogging, and bicycling at a steady pace	**Examples** push ups, sit ups, pull-ups, soccer, basketball, and sprints
Benefits improves heart and lung endurance and body composition	**Benefits** builds muscle strength; improves flexibility

Lifetime Sports

Social Studies
L I N K

Worldwide Workout

Research dance from other cultures. Physical activities that have their origin in other countries and cultures can be healthful and fun. Irish step dancing provides aerobic exercise and increases coordination. Native American dances, such as the women's traditional dance or the men's grass dance, increase heart and lung endurance. Then teach the class a dance from another culture.

A **lifetime sport** is a sport that you can enjoy throughout your life. Suppose you enjoy taking walks. You can take walks with your family right now. When you become older, you will still be able to take walks. Suppose you enjoy swimming. Do you enjoy the benefits of swimming now? When you are older, you will still be able to swim and have benefits from this physical activity.

Some sports are not lifetime sports. You may play football or soccer now, but you probably will not play these sports for your entire life. Most people do not play strenuous sports for their entire lives. However, there are many physical activities that people enjoy and benefit from later in life. You can start doing some of these activities now. Make a goal to participate in lifetime sports. The chart on the next page shows some lifetime sports and their health fitness benefits. Other lifetime sports might be bowling, softball, tennis, golf, dancing, weight training, biking, and skating.

▶ **An afternoon of biking with your family has many health benefits. List two of them.**

Lifetime Sports

The Physical Activity	Equipment and Safety	What Benefits
Walking Slow or fast movement on foot, but not to the point of running. 	• Comfortable shoes with support • Smooth surface with up and down inclines • Walk with a partner • Wear reflective clothing after dark	• Increases heart and lung endurance. • Improves muscular endurance. • Improves body composition.
Swimming Movement through water using one of several strokes 	• Swimsuit • Goggles • Earplugs • Safe place to swim • Don't swim in unsafe weather conditions • Swim with a partner	• Good for all parts of the body. • Builds muscular strength, heart and lung endurance, and flexibility. • Improves body composition.
Jogging Running slowly	• Jogging shoes • Running track or smooth surface • Run with a partner • Don't run in unsafe weather conditions • Wear reflective clothing after dark	• Builds flexibility, muscular endurance, heart and lung endurance. • Improves body composition.
Bicycling Pedaling a bike 	• A bike in good condition • Safety helmet • Water bottle • Smooth surface • Bike path or bike lane	• Improves body composition. • Builds muscular endurance and heart and lung endurance.

 What is a lifetime sport?

Taking Responsibility

By now, you probably realize that it is important to be physically active throughout life. You can make a personal physical fitness plan for yourself. A personal *physical fitness plan* is a plan you make to improve your level of fitness. You know which physical activities you like to do. Maybe you have figured out areas of health fitness that you want to improve, such as heart and lung endurance. If you make a plan and carry it out, you will be taking responsibility for your own fitness.

One student's plan is shown below.

 Who should see your personal physical fitness plan before you begin?

My Personal Physical Fitness Plan

I will keep a diary about my physical fitness plan.

I will write a Health Behavior Contract.

I will attach my Health Behavior Contract to eight sheets of paper in a folder.

I will write a day of the week at the top of each of seven sheets of paper. On each, I will write exercises that I did that day. I will write "How My Plan Worked" on the eighth sheet.

I will write a paragraph on the last sheet of my physical activity diary. I will tell if I did the activities that I promised to do. If I did not, I will say why.

I will explain how I can change my plan to make it better.

▲ **Use a calendar to make your physical activity schedule.**

Set Health Goals

You have learned that staying fit with lifetime sports can reduce the risk of many diseases. But it requires planning to succeed.

1 **Write the health goal you want to set.** Health Goal: I will get plenty of physical activity.

2 **Explain how your goal might affect your health.** Physical activity will reduce your risk of heart disease and other diseases. What other ways will it benefit health?

3 **Describe a plan you will follow to reach your goal. Keep track of your progress.** Write a Health Behavior Contract. Your plan should include a lifetime sport.

4 **Evaluate how your plan worked.** Mark a time on your calendar to discuss your progress with your parents or a physical fitness instructor especially if you have trouble setting aside time to reach your goal.

Health Behavior Contract

Name _____ Date _____

1 **Health Goal** | I will get plenty of physical activity.

2 **Effect on My Health** | Physical activity will make my heart and other muscles strong. It will reduce my risk of having certain diseases when I am older.

3 **My Plan** | I will plan the following workouts:

Exercise	Goal	How often
Stretch	Increase flexibility	Two to three days a week
Lift one pound weights	Build muscular strength	Two to four days a week
Run	Increase heart and lung endurance	Three to five days a week

LESSON REVIEW

Review Concepts

1. **Explain** how to take responsibility for your physical fitness.

2. **List** four examples of lifetime sports.

3. **Compare and Contrast** How are aerobic and anaerobic exercise alike? How are they different?

Critical Thinking

4. **Analyze** What are some long-term health benefits that might come from participating in lifetime sports?

5. **LIFE SKILLS** **Set Health Goals** Write a Health Behavior Contract in which you do aerobic exercises and anaerobic exercises three times a week.

Be Fair and Be Safe

You will learn . . .

- how you can be a good sport and a good teammate.
- ways to prevent injuries when you exercise and play sports.
- how sleep affects performance.

Vocabulary

- **compete**, *C37*
- **warm-up**, *C38*
- **cool-down**, *C38*
- **safety equipment**, *C38*

When you participate in sports and games, you want to be a good sport and an enthusiastic teammate. You want to play fair and follow rules that keep you and all your teammates safe. You want to choose actions to prevent injuries.

Be a Good Teammate and Sport

Being a good teammate is an important part of playing sports and other games. When you play any sports, you cooperate with your teammates to score points. To *cooperate* is to work well with others toward a common goal. You pass or kick the ball to your teammate who is open. You guard the other team's players so that your team can get in the best position to score.

When you play against another team, you **compete** (kum•PEET), or play to win. When you compete, you still have to play safe and fair. Even though you are trying to win the game, show respect for other players. Never tease, shove, hit, or kick another player. Always play by the rules of the game.

 What does it mean to cooperate?

▲ Respecting players from the other team is an important part of being a good sport. In what other ways can you show good sportsmanship?

BUILD Character
Make a Poster

Trustworthiness Being trustworthy means that you do what is right. For example, when playing a game that uses school equipment, you need to return the equipment to its proper place. You also have to report any damage to the equipment. Make a poster that shows how you and your classmates can be trustworthy when using school sports equipment.

Stay Safe When Active

There are several precautions you can take to get fit safely. A **warm-up** is five minutes or more of easy physical activity done before you exercise. Warming up helps raise your heart rate and warms up your muscles. Gentle jogging followed by stretching is a useful warm-up.

A **cool-down** is five to ten minutes of easy physical activity done after exercising that cools your muscles and gradually lets your heart rate return to normal. A cool-down can include stretching and walking at a slower pace.

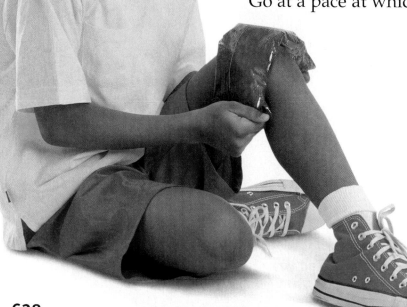

▼ **If you become injured during physical activity, stop and get help.**

Ways to Prevent Injuries

These behaviors can help you prevent injuries.

- **Know your limits.** A *limit* is a point at which you must stop. If you try to do more than you are able, you risk injuring yourself. Take rests.

- **Go at a safe pace.** People have different abilities. Go at a pace at which you feel comfortable.

- **Use correct form.** Correct posture and body movement reduce your risk of injury.

- **Use approved safety equipment. Safety equipment** is the approved helmets, padding, and mouth guards that you wear to keep from getting injured.

Sleep and Performance

Being tired can lead to injuries and can affect how well you do in school. *Rest* is a period of relaxation or a stopping of activity. *Sleep* is a deep relaxation in which you are not aware of what is happening around you. Children your age need between 10 and 12 hours of sleep each night. How well you sleep affects how you perform in school. Being well rested also reduces accidents among children.

✓ **What is sleep?**

LIFE SKILLS · CRITICAL THINKING

Be a Health Advocate

Josie notices that some of her volleyball teammates warm up and cool down at practice, but forget to cool down after games. How can she promote the use of warm-up and cool-down activities?

1. **Choose a healthful action to communicate.** Josie's concern is to help her teammates make warm-up and cool-down a regular part of exercise, even on game day.

2. **Collect information about the action.** Where can you get information about warm-up and cool-down exercises?

3. **Decide how to communicate this information.** Josie decides that drawings of cool-down exercises would help her volleyball teammates.

4. **Communicate your message to others.** Make a booklet that explains the importance of warm-up and cool-down exercises. Distribute the booklet to your classmates.

LESSON REVIEW

Review Concepts

1. **List** three ways you can stay safe when you exercise and play sports.

2. **Explain** why warm-up and cool-down exercises help prevent injury.

3. **Explain** how you can be a good team player and a good teammate.

Critical Thinking

4. **Analyze** How might getting a good night's sleep on Monday affect your performance during a test on Tuesday?

5. **LIFE SKILLS** **Be a Health Advocate** Plan an article for the local newspaper that advocates ways to stay safe when exercising and playing sports.

Access Health Facts, Products, and Services

Problem Jack needs running shoes for cross-country training. There are so many styles to choose from that he is confused. How can Jack know which running shoes are right for him?

"The **Z99 SuperFlash** is very popular."

"Which running shoes should we buy?"

"That's true. It's popular, but there is another brand that has better support and costs less."

Solution Jack decides to collect information about cross-country running shoes and take the information with him when he and his parent or guardian go to buy the shoes.

Learn This Life Skill

Follow these steps to access health facts, products, and services.

1 **Identify when you might need health facts, products, and services.**

Jack writes down what he needs to find out about running shoes. He includes cost and quality in his list. What else might Jack need to know?

2 **Identify where you might find health facts, products, and services.**

Where might Jack find the information he is looking for? He might read articles in running magazines. He could get advice from a coach. What else might he do?

3 **Find the health facts, products, and services you need.**

Jack writes down the facts he finds. He shares it with his parents.

4 **Evaluate the health facts, products, and services.**

At the store, Jack works with his parents to evaluate the running shoes based on the facts he's gathered.

Practice This Life Skill

Use the steps that Jack used to select running shoes. Write a plan for finding a pair of inline skates.

Use Vocabulary

aerobic exercise, C31

farsighted, C6

grooming, C17

heart and lung endurance, C23

dental plaque, C12

warm-up, C38

Choose the correct term from the list to complete each sentence. Write the word on a separate sheet of paper.

1. When you can exercise for a long time without getting out of breath, you have __?__.

2. People who see distant objects well but have a hard time seeing things up close are __?__.

3. Several minutes of easy exercise at the beginning of a workout is called a __?__.

4. An exercise that uses oxygen at a steady pace over a long period of time is a(n) __?__.

5. A sticky substance that coats teeth and that contains bacteria is called __?__.

6. Taking care of your appearance is called __?__.

Review Concepts

Answer each question in complete sentences.

7. What is tooth enamel, and what does it do?

8. How can you take care of your vision and hearing?

9. Describe the correct way to floss and brush your teeth.

10. List the five areas of health-related fitness.

11. List an activity that improves each area of health-related fitness.

12. Explain the benefits of playing lifetime sports now.

Reading Comprehension

Answer each question in complete sentences.

On a daily basis, teeth become coated with a sticky film called **dental plaque** (PLAK). Bacteria that live in dental plaque break down sugars and starches in food and make an acid. This acid can wear away tooth enamel, causing a **cavity**, or hole, to form.

13. What is dental plaque?

14. Why do you need to remove dental plaque from teeth?

15. How is the acid that causes tooth decay formed?

Critical Thinking/Problem Solving

Answer each question in complete sentences.

Analyze Concepts

16. How might an ad influence your choice of grooming products?

17. Explain how getting enough sleep helps you throughout your day.

18. You're at the beach. You have left your hat at home. A friend offers to share an extra hat with you. What should you do? Explain your choice.

19. List the six fitness skills. Which fitness skills are used when you play soccer? Which fitness skills are used when you bowl?

20. Give an example of a grooming habit. Explain how this habit protects health.

Practice Life Skills

21. **Access Health Facts, Products, and Services** You have seen advertisements for teeth whiteners on television and in magazines. You are considering using one of these products, but don't know if it is safe. How could you find out?

22. **Make Responsible Decisions** Your friend is sleeping over at your home. Your friend wants to stay up late and watch a movie. You have a soccer game the next morning. What should you do? Use the *Guidelines for Making Responsible Decisions*™ to help you decide.

Read Graphics

The table shows Emily's physical activity plan for one week. Use it to answer questions 23–25.

Day of the Week	Easy Physical Activity	Challenging Physical Activity
Sunday	Walked the dog for 30 minutes	
Monday		Soccer practice, 1 hour
Tuesday	Rode my bike for 30 minutes	
Wednesday	Played tag with my friends for 1 hour	Soccer practice, 1 hour
Thursday	Played tag with my friends for 1 hour	
Friday		
Saturday	Went swimming with friends for 2 hours	

23. On which day(s) did Emily spend the most time doing physical activity?

24. How much time did Emily spend on physical activity during the week?

25. Why do you think that Emily classified swimming with friends as easy physical activity?

LOG ON www.mmhhealth.com
Find out how much you know about physical activity.

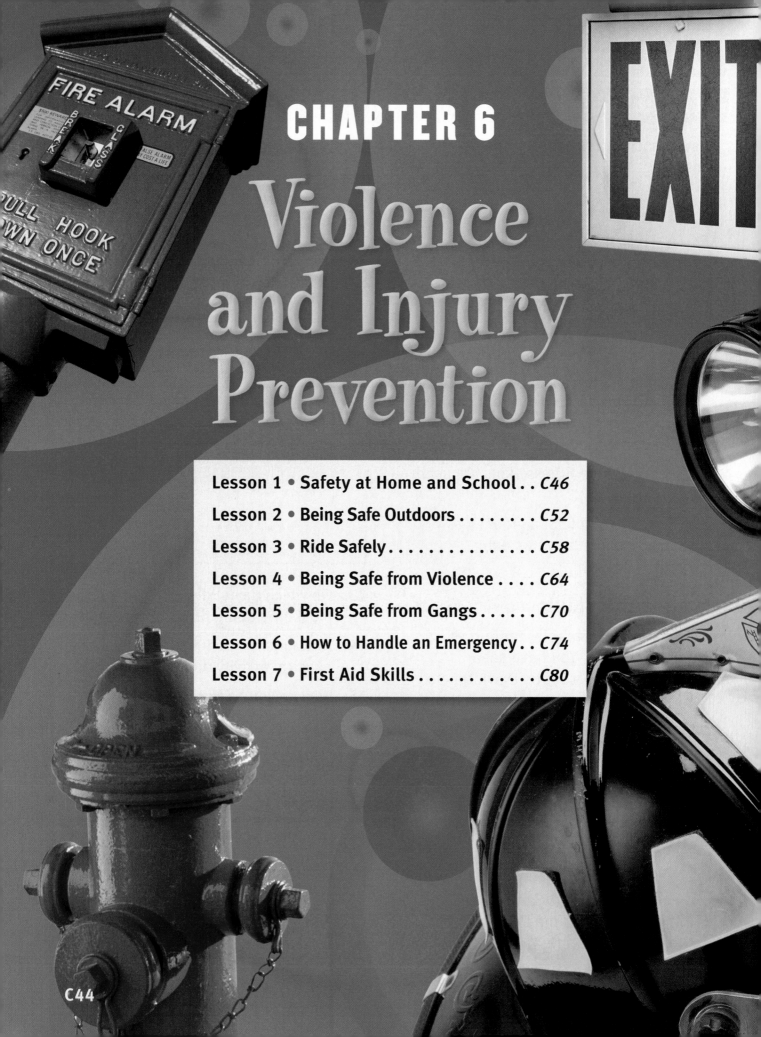

CHAPTER 6

Violence and Injury Prevention

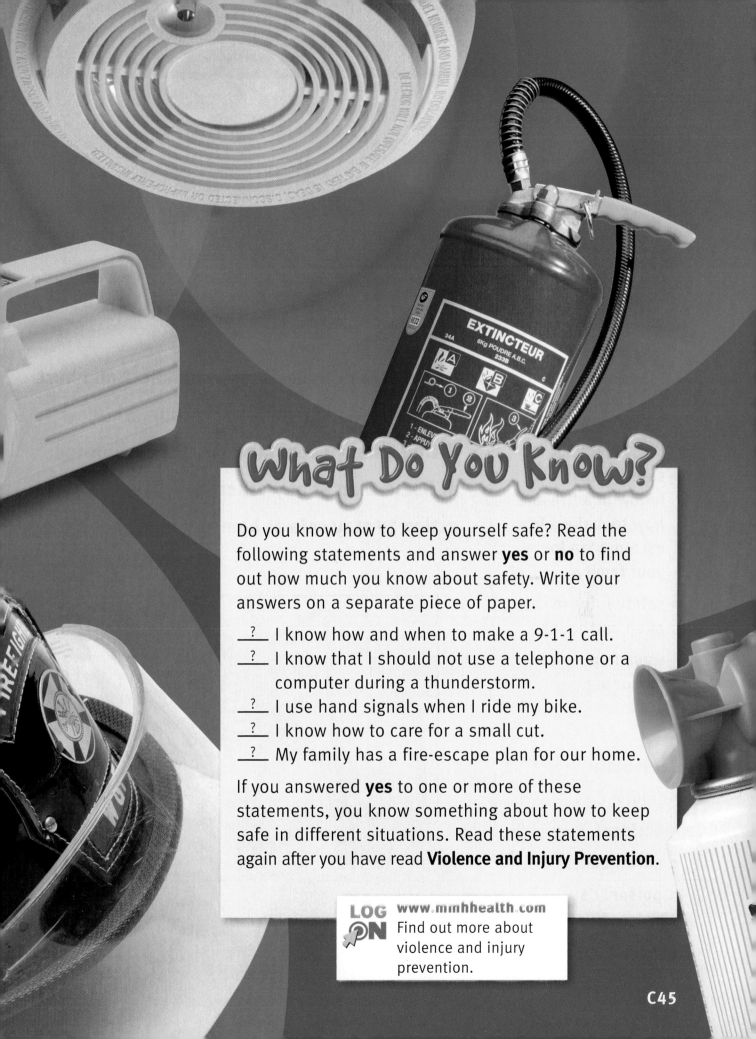

What Do You Know?

Do you know how to keep yourself safe? Read the following statements and answer **yes** or **no** to find out how much you know about safety. Write your answers on a separate piece of paper.

 _?_ I know how and when to make a 9-1-1 call.

 _?_ I know that I should not use a telephone or a computer during a thunderstorm.

 _?_ I use hand signals when I ride my bike.

 _?_ I know how to care for a small cut.

 _?_ My family has a fire-escape plan for our home.

If you answered **yes** to one or more of these statements, you know something about how to keep safe in different situations. Read these statements again after you have read **Violence and Injury Prevention**.

LOG ON www.mmhhealth.com
Find out more about violence and injury prevention.

Safety at Home and School

You will learn . . .

- safety rules to prevent falls.
- safety rules to follow in a fire and how to make a fire escape plan for your family.
- safety rules in case of an earthquake.
- ways to prevent poisoning.

Vocabulary

- **injury**, *C47*
- **accident**, *C47*
- **earthquake**, *C49*
- **poison**, *C50*

Have you ever tripped over an object and hurt yourself? Maybe you've been hurt while lifting a heavy box. More people are injured at home than at any other place. You can take action to stay safe at home and at school, too.

Prevent Falls

Suppose you step on a toy that has been left on the stairs or slip on a wet spot on the kitchen floor. You could fall and be injured. An **injury** is harm done to a person. Injuries are often the result of accidents. An **accident** is an unexpected event. Many accidents can be prevented. Learn to prevent falls at home and at school.

At Home

- Keep stairs and floors clear of objects.

- Keep electric cords close to walls, not out where people can trip over them.

- Put non-slip mats in the bathtub and shower.

- Turn on the lights before you enter a room or climb a stairway.

- Do not stand on a chair to reach high objects.

- Don't lean against window screens or windows.

- Ask your parents or guardian to fasten loose rugs to the floor with carpet tape.

At School

- Walk in the halls, don't run.

- Keep halls and classroom aisles free of objects.

- Report a wet floor, or other dangerous conditions, to a teacher.

- Follow playground rules, and use equipment safely.

 **What is an injury?**

Physical Education
L I N K

How Athletes Fall

Watch a professional sporting event on TV to see how athletes fall, to make injuries less likely. For example, a soccer player rolls into a fall instead of onto an outstretched arm. Rolling may help make a fall softer and may help prevent broken bones. Describe how the athletes that you observe fall safely.

ACTIVITY

On Your Own

FOR SCHOOL OR HOME

Develop a Family Fire Escape Plan

Make a fire escape plan for your home. Share it with all family members.

1. Make a map of your home. Draw two ways to escape from each room. Memorize each escape plan.

2. Plan where to meet outside your home.

3. Practice the plan.

▼ **STOP where you are.**

▼ **DROP to the ground.**

▲ **ROLL to put out any flames. Cover your face.**

Fire Safety

Fire in a home can destroy property and sometimes kill. Some common causes of fire in the home are burning candles, bad electric cords, matches, smoking, and space heaters. All homes need a smoke alarm for every floor and a fire extinguisher in the kitchen and in the garage. In case of fire, use the following tips to keep safe.

At Home

- Yell loudly to others in the house. Get out fast! Don't pick up anything. Don't go back inside.

- Feel a door if it is closed. If a door feels hot, do not open it. There is probably fire on the other side. Find another way out.

- Close the door when you leave a room.

- Crawl on your hands and knees to keep below the level of the smoke.

- Stop, Drop, and Roll if your clothes catch fire. The pictures show you how.

- Close the door and place a towel or clothing against the bottom of the door if you get trapped inside. Bang on or open a window and yell "Fire."

- Plan ahead where to meet outside.

At School

- Stay in line and stay quiet.

- Stay outside.

- Stay with your class so that your teacher knows that you are safe.

 What should you do if your clothes catch fire?

Earthquake Safety

An **earthquake** is the movement of a part of Earth's surface caused by sudden shifting of rock along a fault. A fault is a crack in Earth's crust. Homes in earthquake areas are bolted to the foundation to keep them from shifting when the ground shakes.

Before an Earthquake

Inside the house, tall, heavy furniture and water heaters can be bolted to the walls. Safety latches can be installed on cabinets to keep dishes and other items from falling out. Keep heavy items on lower shelves.

During an Earthquake

DROP and COVER. Drop to the floor and get under something sturdy or stand in a doorframe. Stay away from glass doors, windows, and bookcases. Keep away from trees, buildings, streetlights, and electric wires if you are outside. If you are in a car, the driver of the car should pull over, away from buildings, bridges, and overpasses. Do not get out of the car.

After an Earthquake

Ground movements that occur after an earthquake are called *aftershocks*. Stay away from structures that might have been weakened and could fall during an aftershock. Get out of the building or area if you smell gas. Report the leak to an adult. Wear shoes. There might be broken glass on the ground.

▲ During an earthquake, stand in a doorway. The doorframe can protect you from things that fall.

 What are three ways to be safe before, during, and after earthquakes?

Avoid Poisons

Many products used at home contain chemicals that dissolve grease and kill germs. These products can be harmful to humans and pets if they are swallowed, inhaled, or splashed into eyes or onto skin. Many of these products are poisonous. A **poison** is a substance that can harm you if it is swallowed or gets on your skin. Some causes of poisoning at home include cleaning products, plants, pesticides, paints, and solvents. Misuse of medicines and cosmetics also cause poisonings. You can be safe from poisons by following some simple rules.

Prevent Poisonings

- Never eat or drink anything unless you are certain that it is food or drink.

- Do not eat spoiled food.

- Do not eat any mushrooms or berries unless you are told by a responsible adult that they are safe to eat.

- Ask a responsible adult when you are not sure whether something is poisonous.

- Keep small children and pets away from houseplants. Parts of many houseplants are poisonous.

- Keep windows open when you are using products that give off strong odors or vapors.

- Wear gloves or goggles if the label on the product tells you to do so.

ACTIVITY

Science
L I N K

Are These Plants Poisonous?

Investigate why you should be careful with poinsettias, daffodils, and holly berries. Make a poster warning people of the dangers of these common yard and house plants.

▲ Cabinet locks help prevent poisonings at home.

 What are two steps you can take to prevent poisonings?

Poison Proof Your Home

Here are some actions your parents or guardian can take to make your home poison proof.

- Keep the number of the local Poison Control Center near the phone.

- Store poisons in a locked cabinet. Get rid of old medicines.

- Keep medicines and cleaning products in their original labeled containers.

- Do not store medicines or cleaning products with food.

- Use products that have safety or tamper-resistant caps.

ACTIVITY

LIFE SKILLS

CRITICAL THINKING

Be a Health Advocate

More than half of the poisonings in the United States happen to children under the age of six.

1 **Choose a healthful action to communicate.** Suppose you want to help raise awareness about the number of children under six in your community who are poisoned.

2 **Collect information about the action.** Talk with a volunteer at a Poison Control Center. What actions does the center advise people to take to reduce poisonings?

3 **Decide how to communicate this information.** How will you tell classmates about what you have learned? You might make a brochure that states your message clearly.

4 **Communicate your message to others.** Give your brochure to everyone in your class to take home.

LESSON REVIEW

Review Concepts

1. **List** four rules to prevent falls at home and two rules to prevent falls at school.

2. **Describe** six safety rules for escaping fire in your home.

3. **List** three ways to be safe in an earthquake.

4. **Identify** five ways to prevent poisoning at home.

Critical Thinking

5. **Apply** Explain how you would develop an emergency fire escape plan for your home.

6. **LIFE SKILLS** **Be a Health Advocate** Suppose you learn that earthquakes can occur in your community. There is no information about how to stay safe if one occurs. How can you help prepare your community for an earthquake?

Being Safe Outdoors

You will learn . . .

- safety rules to follow for walking.

- safety rules to follow for swimming and ways to prevent drowning.

- ways to stay safe in different weather conditions.

Vocabulary

- **lightning**, *C54*
- **thunderstorm**, *C56*
- **hurricane**, *C56*
- **tornado**, *C56*
- **flood**, *C57*

During your lifetime you might walk more than 100,000 miles. That would be like walking around Earth five times! To prevent injury, walkers must be aware of cars, buses, trucks, and even bicycles. Knowing how to stay safe when walking is important to your health.

Walking Near Traffic

Wear walking shoes. Tie your shoelaces so that you will not trip on them. Keep your hands free. Carry books and other items in your backpack. Make sure your backpack is not too heavy. Your backpack should never weigh more than 10 to 20 percent of your total body weight.

Rules for Safe Walking

- Walk on the sidewalk, not on the street. If there are no sidewalks, walk facing traffic. That way you can see cars that are coming.

- Wear light-colored or reflective clothing at night so that others can see you.

- Learn what traffic signs mean and obey them.

- Do not step off the curb if the sign tells you not to walk.

- Cross the street only when the crossing guard or traffic signal tells you that it is safe.

- Walk inside the lines of a crosswalk when crossing the street.

- Do not cross the street without looking.

- Follow the left-right-left way to check for cars. This means look left, look right, and then look left again to make sure that no cars are coming.

What is the "left-right-left" way to check for cars?

▲ Don't run to beat a DON'T WALK signal. When the sign tells you it is safe to go, wait a moment before you step into the crosswalk. A car might be completing a turn.

Swim Safely

Many people enjoy the water and like to swim. At the same time, you have to be careful around water. Learn how to swim. If you have just learned to swim, practice but don't go into deep water, or you could drown or be seriously injured. These rules can help you stay safe while swimming.

Rules for Swimming Safely

- Follow pool or beach rules.

- Never swim alone. Make sure that a lifeguard or other responsible adult is nearby.

- Walk, don't run while at a pool.

  - Don't push others into a body of water.

  - Walk, don't run on a diving board.

  - Don't dive into water without checking the water depth with a responsible adult. Diving into shallow water can cause permanent injury.

  - Avoid getting tired and cold when you swim. It can put you in danger of drowning.

  - Do not swim when thunderstorms threaten. People can be killed if lightning strikes the water. **Lightning** is flashes of light caused by electricity in the air. The electricity may be moving between clouds or between clouds and the ground.

▼ **Never swim at a pool, or anywhere else, unless a lifeguard is on duty.**

Prevent Drowning

Always wear a personal flotation device (PFD) properly when you are on a boat. Some PFDs are also known as life jackets. PFDs can help you float. If you fall into the water, try to relax. If you struggle, the PFD may not be able to keep you facing up.

HELP and Huddle

These tips can help you if you fall from a boat into deep water.

- Keep your head *above* water.

- Most people lose body heat quickly. To save body heat, don't struggle or even try to swim toward shore.

- Pull your knees up and keep your arms close to your body. This is the HELP (Heat Escape Lessening Posture) position.

- If there are two or more of you in the water, huddle tightly together to save body heat until help arrives.

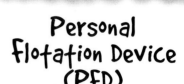

Con$umer Wi$e

ACTIVITY

Personal Flotation Device (PFD)

Research different kinds of PFDs or life jackets that are available. Select a model for children that is approved by the U.S. Coast Guard and that seems like a good buy.

What does HELP stand for?

▷ HELP can save you if you fall into cold water.

Weather Safety

▲ Avoid high ground or standing under trees when there is lightning.

Storms can also affect health. A **thunderstorm** is a storm that has thunder, rain, and lightning. During a thunderstorm, get inside. Stay away from windows. Do not use a telephone or a computer. Electricity from lightning can go through wires. You could get shocked. Some people unplug appliances during a storm. Don't shower or take a bath during a thunderstorm. Water conducts electricity.

A **hurricane** is a destructive storm that forms over the ocean. It produces high winds and heavy rain. **Tornadoes** are violent storms with funnel-shaped clouds and high winds that move over land. Tornadoes can occur during thunderstorms or hurricanes. Get inside if these types of storms threaten. In case of a tornado, get into the basement or a room without windows. Cover yourself with thick blankets or a mattress.

▲ Wear gloves or mittens. Frostbite happens when layers of skin freeze. Extreme frostbite can damage body tissues permanently.

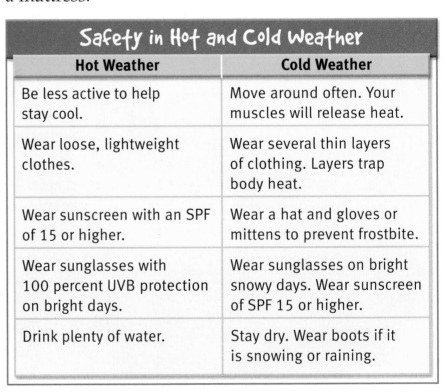

Safety in Hot and Cold Weather	
Hot Weather	**Cold Weather**
Be less active to help stay cool.	Move around often. Your muscles will release heat.
Wear loose, lightweight clothes.	Wear several thin layers of clothing. Layers trap body heat.
Wear sunscreen with an SPF of 15 or higher.	Wear a hat and gloves or mittens to prevent frostbite.
Wear sunglasses with 100 percent UVB protection on bright days.	Wear sunglasses on bright snowy days. Wear sunscreen of SPF 15 or higher.
Drink plenty of water.	Stay dry. Wear boots if it is snowing or raining.

Flood Safety

Heavy rains can cause a flood. A **flood** is a great flow of water onto normally dry land. To be safe in flood conditions, follow these rules.

- Do not swim or wade in flood water. Flood water moves very fast and you will not be able to control where it takes you, even if you are a strong swimmer.

- Do not ride in a car through a flooded area.

- Leave your home if told to do so.

HIGH WATER

 Why should you avoid flood waters?

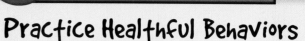

LIFE SKILLS · CRITICAL THINKING

Practice Healthful Behaviors

You are at the community pool. Your little sister is running around the pool deck. She just missed crashing into someone who was walking toward the diving board.

1. **Learn about a healthful behavior.** What are the risks of running at a pool? What is the healthful way to act at a pool?

2. **Practice the behavior.** Be a role model. Show your sister that it is safer not to run at the pool. How else can you get her to change her behavior?

3. **Ask for help if you need it.** If your sister won't listen to you, you may have to point out her behavior to the lifeguard.

4. **Make the behavior a habit.** Help your sister have fun without running. Make a list of things she can do.

LESSON REVIEW

Review Concepts

1. **Describe** three safety rules for walking.

2. **List** three safety rules for swimming and being around water.

3. **Identify** one danger each for cold weather, hot weather, thunderstorms, and floods. Make a table and write a way to keep safe from each danger.

Critical Thinking

4. **Apply** It is thundering and lightning outside and you are on the computer. You brother yells, "Log off now!" What safety rule is your brother following?

5. **LIFE SKILLS** **Practice Healthful Behaviors** You hear that the weather will be very hot today. What healthful behaviors can you practice to keep safe?

Ride Safely

Vocabulary

- **seat belt,** *C59*

Do you ride on a school bus? How do you and the other students behave on the bus? Loud, active riders can distract the driver. How can you be safe as you ride in a bus or in a car?

Car and Bus Safety

Cars and buses get you where you need to be quickly. Following safety rules for riding in cars and buses can save your life.

In a Car

- Always wear a seat belt. A **seat belt** is the lap belt and shoulder belt worn in a car.

- Ride in the back seat until you are 12 years of age. Riding in the back seat reduces the risk of injury if an airbag goes off.

- Lock the door when you are seated.

- Get out of the car on the curb side.

On a School Bus

- Stay seated while the bus is moving and wear a seat belt when available.

- Do not yell, throw things, get into fights, or trip people. Keep aisles clear.

- Gather your belongings before your stop.

- Get up only after the bus has stopped.

- Hold the handrail as you leave the bus.

- Watch for cars. People driving cars might not be paying attention.

- Never walk behind a bus. Walk well in front of the bus to cross a road. Look left, right, then left again. Cross only when it is safe.

▲ **Make sure that your seat belt fits snugly. Do not wear the shoulder belt under your arm. Always wear a seat belt even if the trip is short.**

 List three school bus safety rules.

C59

Bike and Scooter Safety

Riding a bicycle or a scooter can be a fun, pollution-free way to get around. There are steps you can take to reduce your risk of injury when you ride.

Safety Rules for Riding a Bike

- Wear an approved helmet that meets safety standards. Do not wear headphones.

- Check your brakes and tires often.

- Ride your bike on a bicycle path whenever possible, not on the street.

- Avoid swerving.

- Ride in the same direction that cars are moving.

- Obey traffic signs and lights. Use the hand signals shown below before you turn or stop.

- Walk your bike across busy streets.

- Don't carry a passenger on your bike.

- Slow down when the street or ground is wet. Allow more time to stop.

ACTIVITY

Consumer Wise

Wear It Right for Health!

Demonstrate how to wear a bicycle helmet correctly. The helmet should sit level on your head, two finger widths above the eyebrows. Buckle the straps tightly under your chin.

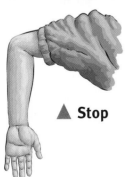

▼ **Signal with your left hand when you ride.**

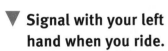

▲ **Stop**

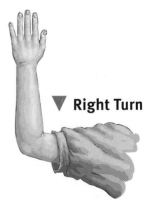

How should a bike helmet fit?

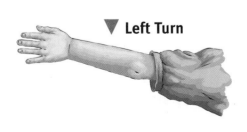

▼ **Left Turn**

▼ **Right Turn**

Ride a Scooter Safely

- Wear an approved helmet, elbow pads, and knee pads. Don't wear headphones.
- Ride on a smooth path. Avoid riding through water, or on gravel, sand, and slick surfaces.
- Stay out of traffic.
- Make sure that your brakes work.
- Wear sneakers.
- Do not ride at night.

Road Signs

These are some signs you might see when you are biking.

▲ **Follow local safety rules for where you can ride a scooter.**

Road Signs			
Sign	**What the Sign Means**	**Sign**	**What the Sign Means**
Bike lane sign	Bikes only can ride in the right lane.	Slippery when wet sign	The road is slippery when it rains or snows.
No walking sign	Do not walk in this area.	Stop sign	Come to a complete stop.
School crossing sign	School area ahead. Children cross the road here. Slow down and watch for walkers.	No bike zone sign	You are not allowed to ride a bike here.

Skate and Skateboard Safety

ACTIVITY

BUILD

Character

Following Rules

Citizenship Does your town have specific safety rules for skateboarding? When you follow safety rules for skateboarding, you are being a good citizen. List the safety rules for riding a skateboard where you live. Share these safety rules with your friends the next time you ride.

These rules can help you avoid injury when skating and skateboarding.

- Buy a skateboard that is the right size for your weight.

- Wear an approved helmet, elbow and knee pads, wrist guards, and non-slip shoes.

- Do not skate or skateboard in traffic.

- Never ride while holding on to a moving vehicle.

- Skate on smooth areas. Avoid puddles of water or places where oil has spilled. Don't try to ride on rough pavement.

- Do not skate at night. It is hard for you to see the path, and hard for people to see you.

- Use skateboard parks if available.

▶ **If you fall when skating, try to roll onto the softer, more muscular parts of your body. Try to roll like a ball, instead of landing on an outstretched arm or on an elbow. More than half of all skateboarding and skating injuries are to the hands, arms, and wrists.**

Think as You Ride

Ride and skate responsibly. Ask yourself these questions: How well do I ride or skate? Do I know how to fall? Is this a safe place to ride? Is anything blocking the path? How can I tell someone that I don't want to do something that I know is unsafe? For example, how do I tell someone that I don't want to ride double? Do I know what to do in case of an injury?

 Why is it not safe to skate at night?

 LIFE SKILLS **CRITICAL THINKING**

Set Health Goals

Luis fell and sprained an ankle while biking on a rough road two weeks ago.

1 **Write the health goal you want to set.** Luis might set the goal "I will follow safety rules for biking."

2 **Explain how your goal might affect your health.** Which safety rules will Luis follow to reach his goal? How can these rules help keep him safe?

3 **Describe a plan you will follow to reach your goal.** Keep track of your progress. Make a health behavior contract to help Luis plan and keep track of his progress for two weeks. Who can help him if he has trouble meeting his goal?

4 **Evaluate how your plan worked.** How did Luis do? If the plan didn't work, talk with a responsible adult to revise it.

LESSON REVIEW

Review Concepts

1. **List** two safety rules for riding in a car and two safety rules for riding a bus.

2. **Identify** three safety rules each for riding a bike and riding a scooter.

3. **Review** the safety rules for skating, riding a skateboard, and riding a bicycle. Tell how these rules are alike. Tell the ways in which they differ.

Critical Thinking

4. **LIFE SKILLS** **Make Responsible Decisions** Your parents say that you must wear a helmet when you ride your bicycle. As you hurry to bike with your friends, you forget your helmet. What responsible decision can you make to correct this situation?

5. **LIFE SKILLS** **Set Health Goals** Suppose that you are going on a ten mile bike trip. What health goal can you set for biking safely? Write a Health Behavior Contract to learn safety rules and road signs.

C63

Being Safe from Violence

You will learn . . .

- ways to stay safe from strangers, at home, at school, and in the community.

- about unsafe touch.

- ways to recover from violence.

- ways to prevent injuries from weapons.

Vocabulary

- **violence**, *C65*
- **safe touch**, *C67*
- **unsafe touch**, *C67*
- **victim**, *C67*
- **recovery**, *C67*
- **weapon**, *C68*

Suppose that you are at home in the family room on the ground floor. Your parent is upstairs. The doorbell rings. A stranger calls through the door and asks to use your phone. What should you do? There are many simple steps you can take to stay safe at home and away from home.

Staying Safe at Home

If a stranger asks to come into your home, there is a rule to follow. Never open the door to strangers. Ask a responsible adult for help. If a stranger harms you, that is a form of violence. **Violence** is harm done to yourself, others, or property.

Stay Safe from Strangers at Home

- Know how to lock windows and doors.

- Follow your family's rules. You might be told not to answer the door. You might have a password that the person has to give.

- Keep emergency numbers near the phone.

- Do not tell anyone at the door, on the phone, or on the Internet that your parents or a responsible adult is not with you. Say they cannot come to the phone. If the caller asks personal questions or calls a second time, tell a responsible adult.

- Never give your name or address to a caller on the phone or to anyone on the Internet.

- Tell your parents or guardian right away if anyone says disturbing things to you at the door, on the phone, or on the Internet.

 **What is violence?**

▲ A stranger might use the Internet to try to find out where you live or if you are home alone. Do not respond to e-mail from people you do not know.

Do you know that you do not need any money to call 9-1-1 from a pay phone?

School and Community Safety

Have you ever seen a student damage school property because he or she was angry? You might know of someone who brags that she can go to any store and steal candy without getting caught. Damaging or stealing property are examples of violence. You can protect yourself from violence.

Stay Safe from Strangers

Keep far away if someone in a car tries to talk to you. If you feel afraid, run in the direction opposite to the direction the car is moving.

Do not talk to strangers even if they act friendly. Back or run away. Keep looking for and moving toward a place where you could get help.

Don't walk alone at night. Never go to someone's house, a park, or a playground alone. Yell or scream for help and run away if you feel uncomfortable about someone. Run to a safe place, such as a fire station, if you think someone is following you.

Protect Yourself from Violence

- Choose friends carefully.
- Treat others with respect.
- Stay away from fights. Learn to resolve conflicts.
- Stay away from people who choose violence.
- Notice what goes on around you. Get away from dangerous situations.
- Report dangerous situations.

SafePlace℠

▶ Look for a police station, fire station, a store, or other place where you can be safe.

Unsafe Touch

It feels good when someone gives you a hug. This is a safe touch. A **safe touch** is a touch that is right and respectful. It is okay for your parents or guardian to hug you. It is all right for a doctor to examine you during a checkup. However, there is a kind of violence called unsafe touch. An **unsafe touch** is a touch that is wrong. An unsafe touch is a form of abuse. *Abuse* occurs when someone does harm to someone else. Study the tips on this page to protect yourself from an unsafe touch.

When a person is harmed by an unsafe touch, he or she might feel sad and ashamed. However, the person who has been harmed did not cause the violence to happen. That person is a victim of violence. A **victim** is a person who has been harmed by violence. A victim can recover. **Recovery** is a way to get well.

Recovering from Violence

To recover from violence, get medical treatment for any type of physical injury. Another important step is to talk to a responsible adult about your feelings as many times as you need to. You can talk to a parent, guardian, friend, religious adviser, or counselor.

 **What is a safe touch?**

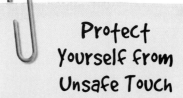

Protect Yourself from Unsafe Touch

If someone attempts to touch you in an unsafe way, do the following.

- Tell the person to stop touching you.
- Say "no" in a firm voice.
- Run away.
- Tell a responsible adult.
- Tell another adult, such as a teacher or counselor at school, if the first adult does not believe you.

▶ Talking with someone you trust is an important step in recovering from violence.

Staying Safe from Weapons

Almost every day on television, in movies, and in the news you hear about guns or knives being used to harm someone. A **weapon** is any object used to harm someone. You can stay safe from weapons.

Protect Yourself from Weapons

Do not touch or carry a weapon. Never pretend to have a weapon or pretend to shoot at someone. Don't bring real weapons or toy weapons to school or elsewhere. Do the right thing. Think of the consequences if the worst thing were to happen.

 List three ways to stay safe from weapons.

If You Find a Weapon, Think SAFE

S – Stop.

A – Avoid going near the weapon.

F – Find an adult.

E – Explain what you saw and where you saw it.

CAREERS

Police Officer

A police officer works to enforce community laws and tries to protect citizens from criminals and crimes. A police officer might help decide what is fair if citizens are having a dispute. He or she might visit schools and clubs to help educate people about drugs, safety, and weapons.

LOG ON www.mmhhealth.com
Find out more about health careers.

Make Responsible Decisions

For two days in a row, Sam has noticed a stranger in the neighborhood when he gets home from school. What should Sam do?

1 **Identify your choices. Check them out with a parent or trusted adult.** Sam lists his choices. He could ignore the stranger. He could tell his parents what he has observed.

2 **Evaluate each choice. Use the *Guidelines for Making Responsible Decisions™*.** Sam uses the six questions to evaluate each choice.

3 **Identify the responsible decision. Check this out with your parent or trusted adult.** Sam makes a decision. He decides to talk with his parents about the situation.

4 **Evaluate your decision.** Sam decided to tell his parents. How does his decision meet the *Guidelines for Making Responsible Decisions™*?

Guidelines for Making Responsible Decisions™

- **Is it healthful?**
- **Is it safe?**
- **Does it follow rules and laws?**
- **Does it show respect for myself and others?**
- **Does it follow family guidelines?**
- **Does it show good character?**

LESSON REVIEW

Review Concepts

1. **Explain** what you should never tell a stranger on the telephone.

2. **List** three safety rules for staying safe from strangers when you are not at home.

3. **Describe** how a victim can begin to feel better after being harmed by violence.

4. **Explain** why it is important to your health and the health of others not to touch a weapon.

Critical Thinking

5. **LIFE SKILLS** **Make Responsible Decisions** Your friend shows you a gun. He says it is not loaded. Your friend's parents are in another room. Use the *Guidelines for Making Responsible Decisions™* to write a plan for how you would handle this situation.

6. **LIFE SKILLS** **Make Responsible Decisions** You have just gotten home and locked the door. The doorbell rings and your parent is in the shower. Use the *Guidelines for Making Responsible Decisions™* to write a plan for how you would handle this situation.

Being Safe from Gangs

You will learn . . .

- reasons to stay away from gangs.
- ways to avoid gangs.
- safety rules to protect yourself from violence.

Vocabulary

- **gang**, *C71*

Friends are an important part of a healthy life. Spending time with responsible friends can protect you from people who might harm you. You can be safe and have fun.

What Is A Gang?

A **gang** is a group of people who may be involved in dangerous and illegal acts. The gang is known by a name and has a leader. Someone who joins a gang might think he or she is making new friends. The kinds of "friends" a person would have in a gang are those who could force you to steal, sell drugs, and harm other people.

Reasons to Stay Away from Gangs

Gang Members Might

- use weapons to hurt or even kill people.

- steal.

- use illegal drugs.

- make other members do harmful, illegal things.

- bully others to join or to obey.

- fight with members of their own gang or with members of other gangs.

If a person wants to join a gang, he or she may have to do what the gang members tell them to do. Gang members could force that person to attack and harm others.

If a person wants to leave a gang, he or she might be harmed. Gang members also might harm people in the family of the gang member who is trying to quit.

 **What is a gang?**

Health Online

Find a Positive Group of Friends

Members of gangs behave in a negative way. There are other groups people join that behave in positive ways. Research and report on a group that people join that acts positively in your community using the e-Journal writing tool. Visit **www.mmhhealth.com** and click on (e)-Journal.

ACTIVITY

On Your Own

FOR SCHOOL OR HOME

Make a "Nothing to Do" List

You've heard of a "To Do" list—usually a list of things that need to be done around the house. Ask your parents or guardian to spend time with you making a list of healthful activities that you can do when you think you have *nothing to do*. Refer to your list whenever you need something fun or useful to keep busy.

Nothing To Do List
Shoot Baskets
Read the Newspaper
Offer to set the table for dinner
Wash my own clothes
Fix a dessert
Clean out my closet
Take a walk
Learn a new game
Play with a younger brother or sister

▶ **If someone tries to bully you to do something you know you shouldn't do, the responsible decision is to say "no".**

Ways to Stay Out of Gangs

Gang members can be very persuasive. They may try hard to get people to join. You know that gangs are dangerous. Here are some ways to avoid gang members and stay out of gangs.

- Stay away from places where gang members hang out.

- Say "no" if you are asked to join a gang.

- Do not make friends with a gang member.

- Join an after-school program, or play a sport that you like instead of joining a gang.

- Find a hobby that you like. Join a hobby club to be with people who enjoy that hobby, too.

Why should you avoid gangs?

Resolve Conflicts

Beth has a friend who wants to join a gang and asks her to join too. Beth says "no." The friend becomes upset. What can Beth do? She knows that joining a gang is a harmful choice. Work with a partner. Role-play this situation.

1 **Stay calm.** Why does getting upset cause more problems?

2 **Talk about the conflict.** Beth needs to listen to her friend even though she disagrees with her choice. Then Beth should give her own opinion.

3 **List possible ways to settle the conflict.** If Beth can get her friend to stay calm, they can use the *Guidelines for Making Responsible Decisions™* to check out ways to settle the conflict.

4 **Agree on a way to settle the conflict.** You may need to ask a responsible adult for help. Beth may need to ask a responsible adult, someone they both trust, for help. This person may help them choose the best way to settle the conflict and help them commit to follow that choice.

DRUG FREE GUN FREE SCHOOL ZONE

VIOLATORS WILL FACE FEDERAL AND STATE PROSECUTION

LESSON REVIEW

Review Concepts

1. **List** three reasons for staying away from gangs.

2. **Name** two ways to stay away from a gang.

3. **Explain** why joining a gang can be unhealthful for mental health and physical health.

Critical Thinking

4. **Infer** Why can participating in an outside interest such as a hobby or a sport's team be a healthful way to avoid gang activities?

5. **LIFE SKILLS** **Resolve Conflicts** Write a skit about two sisters who have a conflict every night over who is to take the trash out. Use the life skills steps in your skit to help them resolve the conflict.

How to Handle an Emergency

You will learn . . .

- how to put together a first aid kit with a parent or guardian.
- what an emergency alert is.
- when and how to call for emergency help.

Vocabulary

- **emergency,** *C75*
- **first aid,** *C75*
- **first aid kit,** *C75*
- **Emergency Alert System,** *C76*
- **unconscious,** *C76*

Suppose someone on your sport team is injured during a game. Would you know how to help that person? Learn about actions you can take when you or someone else is hurt.

Be Ready for an Emergency

When someone is harmed, emergency help may be needed. An **emergency** is a serious and unexpected event in which help is needed right away. Bad cuts, breathing problems, and heart problems are examples of medical emergencies. Lightning, tornadoes, floods, hurricanes, and severe thunderstorms are weather emergencies.

People who are injured can be helped with first aid. **First aid** is the quick care given to a person who is injured or ill. If first aid is done correctly, a person's life may be saved. A **first aid kit** is information, equipment, and supplies that is used to care for a person who is injured or ill. Your family can decide where to put the kit. Make sure that it is properly prepared and in that place.

 What is a first aid kit?

 A first-aid kit should be checked every few months. Phone numbers may need to be updated and supplies replaced.

First Aid Kit Items

- telephone numbers to reach emergency help
- gauze pads
- bandages of several sizes
- wound cleaner
- scissors, tweezers, and safety pins
- blanket
- adhesive tape
- disposable gloves
- breathing mask
- elastic wraps
- splint

Getting Emergency Help

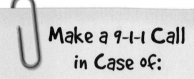

Make a 9-1-1 Call in Case of:

- fire.
- a crime taking place.
- a serious injury.
- a medical emergency.

Emergencies happen for many reasons. Some might be caused by severe weather conditions. Others may be caused by injuries or sudden changes in health.

Weather Emergencies

Some emergencies are due to weather. The **Emergency Alert System** (EAS) lets people know when a severe thunderstorm, snowstorm, tornado, or other health-threatening weather may be in the area. Often a weather emergency will be flashed on the television. It also can be heard on the radio. EAS also has been used to alert the public when a person has disappeared.

Medical Emergencies

▲ Learn how to make a 9-1-1 call.

Minor injuries often do not need treatment by a trained medical person. Sometimes, however, emergency medical help is needed. A *medical emergency* is one in which a person has a hard time breathing or stops breathing, has bad chest pains or pressure in the chest, has bleeding that will not stop, coughs or vomits blood, has a broken bone, or is in very bad pain.

Some people with major health problems such as diabetes or allergies, wear a medical ID bracelet. This is helpful, especially if the person wearing the bracelet cannot speak or is unconscious (un•KAHN•shuhs). To be **unconscious** means to be unaware of what is happening because you are not awake.

What is a medical emergency?

National Emergencies

A *national emergency* is one that could affect everyone in the country or a large section of the country. Your family can make an emergency supply kit. It should contain sleeping bags, batteries, duct tape, plastic bags, flashlights, a first aid kit, maps, and a radio. In addition, there needs to be enough food, water, and prescriptions for three days. Make a family communication plan with a list of all important family phone numbers.

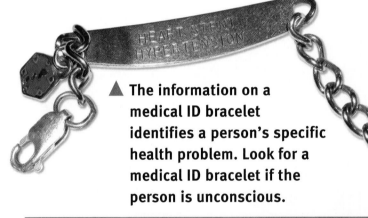

▲ The information on a medical ID bracelet identifies a person's specific health problem. Look for a medical ID bracelet if the person is unconscious.

ACTIVITY — LIFE SKILLS / CRITICAL THINKING

Use Communication Skills

One morning while fixing breakfast, your grandfather badly burns himself on the stove. How will you call for help? Work with a small group. Write a script that describes what you would do and say?

1. **Choose the best way to communicate.** Dial 9-1-1.

2. **Send a clear message. Be polite.** Explain the problem clearly. "My grandfather has burned his arm on the stove." Have your address and location ready.

3. **Listen to each other.** Answer the operator's questions. Listen carefully because the operator may ask you to repeat information.

4. **Make sure that you understand each other.** Do what is asked. Stay on the phone until help arrives. Make sure that you understand what the operator is asking you to do. Repeat what he or she has said to you.

LESSON REVIEW

Review Concepts

1. **List** five items that should be in a first aid kit.

2. **Explain** what an emergency alert system does.

3. **Identify** four possible situations for which you would make an emergency call.

Critical Thinking

4. **Apply** Suppose your aunt tells you that she is experiencing sharp pains in her chest. Do you need to call for emergency help? Explain.

5. **LIFE SKILLS** **Use Communication Skills** A friend is stung by a bee and becomes unconscious. Write a script for an emergency call about this situation.

Be a Health Advocate

Problem Every year, Brad's community is threatened with severe weather. What can he do to keep safe under these conditions?

"It's tornado season again, but you can plan ahead to be safe."

"Figure out a safe place for everyone in your family to go to."

"Keep a tornado emergency kit stocked with bottled water, flashlights, a radio, blankets, first aid kit, and batteries."

ON AIR

Solution Brad decides to be an advocate for safety in the event that severe weather threatens his community. He decides to write a Public Service Announcement (PSA). He uses the steps on the next page to help him.

Learn This Life Skill

Follow these steps to be a health advocate.

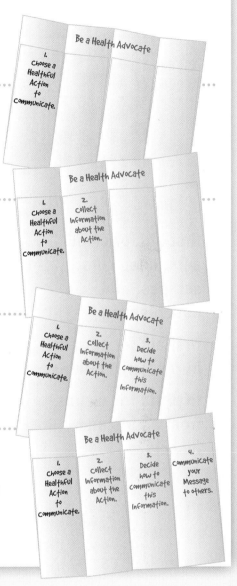

1 **Choose a healthful action to communicate.**
Brad wants to communicate how to stay safe during a tornado.

2 **Collect information about the action.**
Brad lists the safety steps a person should take when a tornado approaches.

3 **Decide how to communicate this information.**
Brad writes a script for his Public Service Announcement (PSA).

4 **Communicate your message to others.**
Brad gathers two friends. They record the PSA. They get permission to air the tape during morning announcements.

Practice This Life Skill

Choose a type of weather that sometimes threatens your community. Write a PSA telling others how to stay safe. Use the steps above as you develop your PSA.

C79

First Aid Skills

You will learn . . .

- first aid for small cuts, deep cuts, scrapes, and nosebleeds.
- first aid for sprains, burns, and choking.
- first aid for rashes from plants and insects.

Vocabulary

- **infection**, *C81*
- **universal precautions**, *C81*
- **sprain**, *C82*
- **choking**, *C83*

Bleeding, burns, and choking can be serious conditions that can require first aid. Using first aid correctly can help avoid further injury until medical help arrives.

First Aid for Bleeding

Do you know what the emergency treatment is for a cut? A cut is a break in the skin. The correct treatment can help prevent infection. An **infection** is growth of bacteria that harms the body.

Universal precautions must be used when helping someone who is bleeding. **Universal precautions** are steps taken to keep people from having contact with body fluids that may be infected. Goggles, gowns, gloves, and masks should be worn when another person's blood, vomit, or other body fluids are present.

 What is the importance of universal precautions?

First Aid Procedures	
Problem	**What to Do**
Small cuts	If you get a cut clean it with soap and water. Press it gently with a clean cloth for 10–15 minutes. Cover the cut with a bandage.
Deep cuts	If you get a deep cut tell an adult right away. Place a clean cloth over the cut, and press on it. Call for medical help. Keep pressing until medical help arrives.
Scrapes	If you get a scrape clean it with soap and water. Pat the area dry with a clean cloth. Cover with a bandage.
Nosebleeds	If you get a nosebleeed tell an adult right away. Sit upright. Pinch together the soft end of your nostrils for 10 minutes. Breathe through your mouth. Get medical help if your nose bleeds for more than 10 minutes or if it starts to bleed again.

Sprains, Strains, and Burns

▲ Taking care of minor injuries immediately can help them heal faster.

Your body is made up of tissues that can be injured. Sprains, strains, and burns are tissue injuries. A **sprain** is an injury to the tissue that connects bones to a joint. A *strain* is an injury to muscle tissue. A mild sprain or strain means that the tissue has been stretched. A severe sprain or strain means that tissue has been torn. If tissues are severely injured, the area swells and is painful. Always tell an adult about a sprain or a strain. First aid can be used to treat slight sprains and strains. Severe cases need medical treatment.

A *burn* is an injury to skin tissue caused by a heat source, such as fire or the Sun. There are also chemical and electrical burns. Always tell an adult about any kind of burn. Get medical treatment immediately for a severe injury.

 What is a sprain?

First Aid for Sprains, Strains, and Burns	
Sprains and Strains	**Burns**
Tell an adult.	Tell an adult.
Treat the injured area with **PRICE: P**rotection, **R**est (for 48 hours), **I**ce, **C**ompression (apply gentle pressure), and **E**levation.	Run cold water over the burn. Do not use ice.
Do not move the injured part.	Dry the area gently.
Place ice or a cold pack on the injured part.	Place a bandage loosely over the burn.
Raise the injured part above the level of the heart.	Don't break blisters. Don't use ointment.
Use heat on the area only after the swelling has gone down.	Get medical help if the burn is serious.

Choking

Imagine that while eating lunch your friend suddenly stops telling a story. He is trying to cough and grabs his throat. He is choking. **Choking** is being unable to breathe because of a blocked air passage.

First Aid for a Person Who Is Choking

Ask the person, "Are you choking?" The person might nod or grab his or her throat in the universal sign for choking. Get an adult right away. Here are the steps the adult should follow.

1. Stand behind the person.

2. Wrap arms around the person's waist.

3. Make a fist with one hand, and grasp it with the other. Press into the person's stomach just above the navel. Use quick, upward pushes. Don't press so hard that a rib is broken or injured.

4. Give pushes until the food comes out. Call 9-1-1 if the person does not stop choking.

First Aid If You Are Alone and Choking

1. Make a fist with one hand. Grab the fist with your other hand.

2. Lean forward over the back of a steady chair.

3. Push upward into your stomach with five quick, hard pushes.

4. Repeat until the food comes out.

 What is first aid for someone who is choking?

▲ The universal sign for choking is to grab the throat.

▲ Stand behind the person who is choking. Use quick, upward pushes into the stomach with your fist.

▲ If you are alone and choking, get behind a chair. Make quick, hard pushes upward with your fist.

C83

Poison ivy

Rashes from Plants

You can get a rash from touching certain plants, such as poison ivy, poison oak, and poison sumac. Some rashes may be painful. Others may be itchy. First aid can help treat these reactions. Learn to recognize poisonous plants in your area and stay away from them.

First Aid for Rashes from Plants

- Run cold water over the area within five minutes of coming into contact with the plant, if you can.

- Go to the doctor if the rash gets in your eyes.

- Do not scratch or rub the rash. Scratching could cause infection. Scratching can spread some rashes.

- Have an adult put on calamine lotion to help with the itching.

- Wash your clothes after you have been exposed to poison ivy or poison oak. Your clothes might have oils from the plant on them.

► The oil from some plants, such as poison ivy and poison oak, can cause an allergic reaction such as the blisters on the skin shown here. Study what these plants look like so that you can avoid them in the wild.

Poison oak

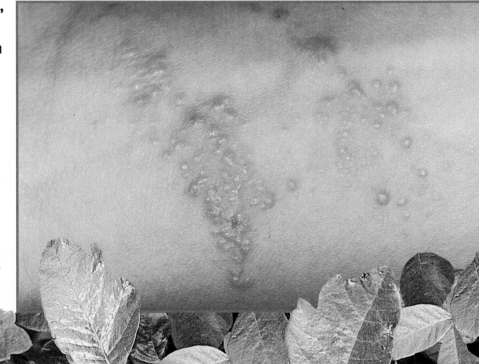

First Aid for Insect Bites and Stings

Some insect bites or stings require emergency medical help. Always tell an adult about an insect bite or sting.

For serious reactions A person who can't breathe well, passes out, vomits, or has chills, fever, or muscle aches, should be taken to the hospital immediately.

For more common reactions Have an adult scrape off the stinger with the edge of an index card. Scrape away from the direction of entry. Wash the area with soap and water. Apply ice for 15 minute periods over the next few hours. See a doctor if the bite or sting becomes infected.

 What is first aid for insect bites or stings?

Access Health Facts

You want to add directions to your family's first aid kit on treating bee stings. What should the instructions be? Work with a partner to find valid facts.

1. **Identify when you might need health facts.** Look for specific information about bee stings.

2. **Identify where you might find health facts.** Will you work with a parent or guardian to find it? Will you go to the library? A doctor's office?

3. **Find the health facts you need.** Access the different sources of information. Record the recommended treatment on an index card.

4. **Evaluate the health facts.** Is your information valid? How might you tell if health information is valid or not?

LESSON REVIEW

Review Concepts

1. **Describe** the first aid steps for bleeding if you have a small cut.

2. **List** the first aid steps for burns.

3. **Explain** what to do for a friend who is choking.

Critical Thinking

4. **Apply** Make a plan to explain to a young child how to stop a nosebleed.

5. **LIFE SKILLS** **Access Health Facts** Suppose that you want to make a poster that shows first aid for a burn. What information would you include?

CHAPTER 6 REVIEW

Use Vocabulary

choking, *C83*

emergency, *C75*

first aid, *C75*

poison, *C50*

seat belt, *C59*

unsafe touch, *C67*

Choose the correct term from the list to complete each sentence.

1. The quick care given to a person who is injured or ill is called ___?___.

2. A touch that is wrong is a(n) ___?___.

3. Someone falls in an accident and is badly injured. Medical help is needed quickly. This situation is a(n) ___?___.

4. You should always wear a ___?___ when you ride in a car.

5. A person is ___?___ if he or she is eating and suddenly becomes unable to breathe.

6. A substance that can harm you if it is swallowed or gets on the skin is a(n) ___?___.

Review Concepts

Answer each question in complete sentences.

7. What are three points you should have in a home fire escape plan?

8. List two safe behaviors you can take to poison-proof your home.

9. What should be your behavior toward a stranger who makes you feel uncomfortable?

10. Why does huddling help save lives in the water?

11. What can you do to be safe when riding a skateboard?

Reading Comprehension

Answer each question in complete sentences.

Use universal precautions when you help someone who is bleeding. Universal precautions are steps taken to keep people from having contact with body fluids that may be infected with bacteria or viruses. Goggles, gowns, gloves, and masks should be worn when blood, vomit, or other body fluids are present.

12. How do universal precautions protect health?

13. Why are universal precautions used?

14. How can a person who is giving care protect himself or herself?

Critical Thinking/Problem Solving

Answer each question in complete sentences.

Analyze Concepts

15. How does using hand signals protect your health when you are on a bike?

16. Why is it important to have phone numbers in a first aid kit?

17. Why do you need to get out of the water when a thunderstorm is coming?

18. How can you help a friend who is angry because of a low grade in school?

19. How does your behavior on a school bus affect the health of everyone else on the bus?

20. How might playing a sport or getting involved in an after-school program help you stay away from gangs?

Practice Life Skills

21. **Make Responsible Decisions** You are walking home from school when you notice that someone is following you. At this point, you are across the street from a grocery store. What should you do?

22. **Be A Health Advocate** Write a plan to help students in your school become aware of health emergency groups available in your community.

23. **Practice Healthful Behaviors** You are at home when you see lightning and hear thunder. These are signs that a thunderstorm is starting up. Make a checklist of dos and don'ts you should follow when this happens.

Read Graphics

The hand signals below are used by bicycle riders to tell drivers around them what they are about to do. You are looking at the back of each biker. Study the graphic and answer questions 24–26.

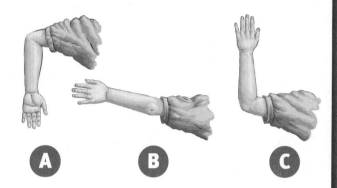

24. What action is Biker A signaling?

25. What action is Biker B about to take?

26. Describe the action that Biker C is signaling.

LOG ON www.mmhhealth.com
Find out how much you know about violence and injury prevention.

Effective Communication

Write a Speech

Write a speech to explain the importance of lifetime sports. Describe some lifetime sports that you can start doing now. Present your speech to your class.

Self-Directed Learning

Make a Chart

Work with a partner. Learn about your state's helmet laws for riding bikes, scooters, and skateboards. Organize your findings in a chart. Post the chart where your class can see it.

Critical Thinking and Problem Solving

Make a List

With a partner, make a list of sounds that you are familiar with. Order the list from softest to loudest. Which sounds are stressful to you? Tell how you deal with the stress.

Responsible Citizenship

Design a Display

Work with your class to gather items for a first aid kit. Make a display in your school for other students to see.

UNIT D

Drugs and Disease Prevention

CHAPTER 7

Alcohol, Tobacco, and Other Drugs, *D2*

CHAPTER 8

Communicable and Chronic Diseases, *D36*

SURGEON GENERAL'S WARNING: Smoking Causes Lung Cancer, Heart Disease, Emphysema, And May Complicate Pregnancy.

NOT TO BE TAKEN BY MOUTH

CHEW TABLETS BEFORE SWALLOWING

CHAPTER 7

Alcohol, Tobacco, and Other Drugs

Uc
N

PHARMACY

℞

IMPORTANT
FINISH ALL THIS MEDICATION UNLESS OTHERWISE DIRECTED BY PRESCRIBER.

What Do You Know?

How much do you know about drugs and their effects on a person's mental and physical health? Answer **yes** or **no** to each of the following statements.

_?_ Prescription drugs cannot be bought without a written order from a doctor.

_?_ Alcohol, tobacco, and other drugs can harm health.

_?_ Using resistance skills can help me say "no" to drug abuse.

_?_ People who abuse drugs can be helped.

Did you answer **yes** to all the statements? It is important for you to know that misuse and abuse of drugs can harm your health.

Read **Alcohol, Tobacco, and Other Drugs** to find out how you can avoid being harmed by drugs.

LOG ON www.mmhhealth.com
Find out more about staying drug free and healthy.

FOR EXTERNAL USE ONLY

Safe Drug Use

You will learn . . .

- what rules to follow in taking prescription drugs.
- what rules to follow in taking over-the-counter drugs.
- ways to prevent drug misuse.
- ways to prevent drug abuse.

When you have an earache, you go to your parents or guardian for help. They might decide that you need to have a check up from your doctor. The doctor will look into your ears and might give you medicine to treat the earache.

Vocabulary

- **drug**, *D5*
- **medicine**, *D5*
- **prescription drug**, *D5*
- **over-the-counter drug**, *D6*
- **drug misuse**, *D8*
- **drug abuse**, *D8*

Take Prescription Drugs Safely

Drugs are substances other than food that can change how the mind or body works. Drugs can change the way you feel, think, or behave. **Medicine** (MED•uh•sin) is a drug that you take to prevent or treat a health problem. Medicines are legal drugs. Some other drugs are illegal. It is against the law to use an illegal drug or to use medicine in an illegal way.

A **prescription** (pri•SKRIP•shuhn) **drug** is medicine that is obtained with a doctor's written order. The way to get a prescription drug is to take a written order from a doctor to a pharmacist (FAHR•muh•sist). A *pharmacist* is a person trained to prepare medicines. He or she may work at a drugstore, a hospital, or in a store that has a pharmacy.

 What is a prescription drug?

Robinson's Pharmacy

32 Orange Lane Bakersville, CA 90345 336-7851

RX 33458 **DR** PAUL HARPER
JEAN JOHNSON

TAKE ONE TEASPOONFUL
EVERY 4 HOURS

Cough Syrup **Refill** NONE

May cause drowsiness.

 Pharmacists fill prescriptions and prepare the prescription labels. Read the label carefully before you take any medicine.

> **Rules for Taking Prescription Drugs Safely**
>
> - Take only when given to you by your parents or guardian or a responsible adult who has their permission to give you that drug.
> - Take only if it was prescribed for you.
> - Never take another person's prescription medicine.

Take Over-the-Counter Drugs Safely

You might not need a prescription drug when you are ill. Suppose that you have a headache. Instead of a prescription drug, the doctor tells your parent or guardian to give you an over-the-counter (OTC) drug. An **over-the-counter drug** is medicine that can be bought without a doctor's prescription. OTC drugs might be used to relieve headaches, colds, or for minor aches and pains. An OTC drug should be taken only from your parents, guardian, or another responsible adult who has their permission. Always read the label on an OTC drug before taking it.

Parts of an OTC Label

- **Active Ingredient** The ingredient (ihn•GREE•dee•unt) that treats your symptom is the *active ingredient*.

- **Uses** Symptoms that the drug acts on

- **Warnings** Reasons to stop taking the drug; ways this drug might interact with other drugs; health conditions under which the drug should not be used.

- **Directions** When, how, and how much of the drug to take or use

- **Other information** How to store the drug

- **Inactive ingredients** These do not treat symptoms, but might flavor the medicine or keep it safe for use for a long time.

- **Questions or comments**

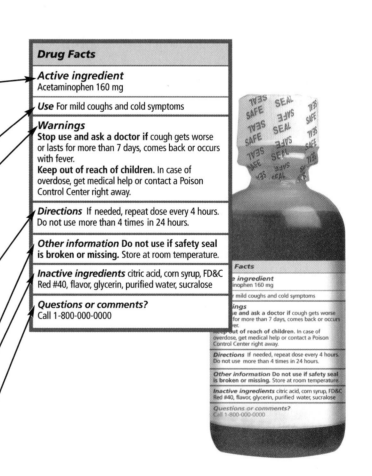

Drug Facts

Active ingredient
Acetaminophen 160 mg

Use For mild coughs and cold symptoms

Warnings
Stop use and ask a doctor if cough gets worse or lasts for more than 7 days, comes back or occurs with fever.
Keep out of reach of children. In case of overdose, get medical help or contact a Poison Control Center right away.

Directions If needed, repeat dose every 4 hours. Do not use more than 4 times in 24 hours.

Other information Do not use if safety seal is broken or missing. Store at room temperature.

Inactive ingredients citric acid, corn syrup, FD&C Red #40, flavor, glycerin, purified water, sucralose

Questions or comments?
Call 1-800-000-0000

Take Medicines Safely

Tamper-Resistant Seals A *tamper-resistant seal* or a safety seal is an unbroken seal that shows that a container has not been opened. An OTC drug that has a broken seal should never be bought.

Expiration Date A drug should not be used after its expiration (eks•puh•RAY•shuhn) date. An *expiration date* is the date on which the drug is no longer thought to work or be safe. Outdated medicines should be disposed of properly by an adult.

Side Effects A *side effect* is an unwanted feeling or illness after taking a drug. Examples of side effects are skin rashes and fever. Tell your parents or guardian right away if you have a side effect from a drug.

Taking Medicine Medicines come in many forms. Some are liquids. Others are creams or drops, pills or capsules. Pills or capsules should be taken with a full glass of water. Don't take them with hot drinks, milk, or fruit juice unless told to do so by a doctor or pharmacist.

On Your Own

ACTIVITY

FOR SCHOOL OR HOME

Make a Home Drug Survey

With your parents or guardian, make a list of all the drugs in your home. List each expiration date. Are any outdated? Should these be thrown away?

✔ **What is a side effect?**

▼ Pills or capsules should be taken with water.

Juice   Tea   Milk   Water

Ways to Prevent Drug Misuse and Abuse

ACTIVITY

Health Online

Finding Help

People who abuse drugs need help. Find out how people can get help with their drug abuse problems. Use the e-Journal writing tool to write a report on your findings. Visit **www.mmhhealth.com** and click on e-Journal.

Prescription drugs and OTC drugs can be harmful if they are not taken correctly. **Drug misuse** is the accidental, unsafe use of a medicine. For example, a person is supposed to take 2 tablets every 4 hours for an allergy. By mistake the person takes 4 tablets every 2 hours. This is an example of drug misuse. Drug misuse can be prevented by carefully reading the label on the package.

Drug abuse is the use of an illegal drug or the harmful use of a legal drug on purpose. Illegal drugs are drugs that are not allowed to be made, sold or used. Legal drugs also can be abused. For example, a man is supposed to take 1 teaspoonful of cough medicine every 6 hours. He decides to take 2 teaspoonfuls every 6 hours because it makes him feel relaxed. The man uses the medicine for a purpose other than for treating the cough. What he has done is a form of drug abuse. A person who abuses a drug might become *dependent* on the drug's emotional and physical effects. A person who depends on a drug is *addicted* (uh•DIK•tuhd) to it.

You can prevent drug abuse. Stay away from illegal drugs or the illegal use of drugs. Stay away from people who sell or use illegal drugs.

▲ **Take medicine only from a responsible adult. Report any side effects right away.**

 What is the difference between drug misuse and drug abuse?

D8

Make Responsible Decisions

You have a bad headache. Your friend offers you a pain pill her mom gives her. What will you do?

1 **Identify your choices. Check them out with your parent or trusted adult.** What are two choices that you have?

2 **Evaluate each choice. Use the *Guidelines for Making Responsible Decisions™*.** What answer will you give to each question in the guidelines for each possible choice?

3 **Identify the responsible decision. Check it out with your parent or a trusted adult.** How can you know if your decision is responsible?

4 **Evaluate your decision.** Do you feel right about your decision? Share with your friend how and why you made your decision.

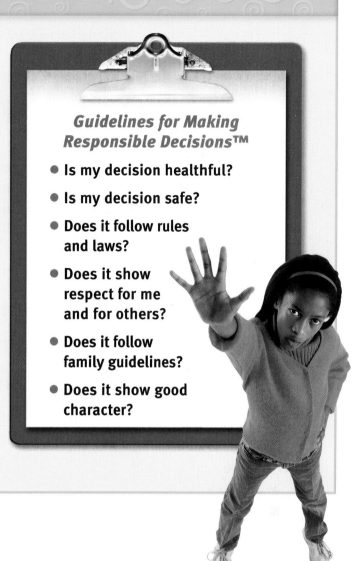

Guidelines for Making Responsible Decisions™

● **Is my decision healthful?**

● **Is my decision safe?**

● **Does it follow rules and laws?**

● **Does it show respect for me and for others?**

● **Does it follow family guidelines?**

● **Does it show good character?**

LESSON REVIEW

Review Concepts

1. **List** three safety rules about prescription drugs.

2. **Name** three ways that OTC drugs can be used safely.

3. **Identify** two ways to prevent drug misuse.

4. **Identify** three ways to prevent drug abuse.

Critical Thinking

5. **Analyze** Why is it important for parents to read the label before giving an over-the-counter drug?

6. **LIFE SKILLS** **Make Responsible Decisions** You have a painful ear infection. It is time for your prescription medicine. Your parents or guardian are busy talking to a neighbor. What should you do?

D9

Alcohol and Health

You will learn . . .

- ways that alcohol harms physical health, mental and emotional health, and family and social health.

- how to use resistance skills if pressured to drink alcohol.

- what types of help are available to someone with a drinking problem.

The boys pictured here know how to have fun and enjoy being with one another without drinking alcohol. Living healthfully without abusing drugs is a goal everyone can have.

Vocabulary

- **alcohol,** *D11*

- **depressant,** *D11*

- **alcoholism,** *D13*

Alcohol Harms Health

   Alcohol is a depressant drug found in some beverages and some medicines. A **depressant** is a drug that slows down body functions. It is illegal and harmful for people your age to drink alcohol. The abuse of alcohol harms all parts of your health.

Alcohol Harms Physical Health

   If a person your age drinks alcohol, it can slow growth and development. It takes less alcohol to harm a young person's body than that of an older person who weighs more. The diagram on this page shows body organs that can be harmed by alcohol. It also describes the harmful effects that alcohol has on parts of the body.

 **What is alcohol?**

How Alcohol Harms Physical Health

- **Nervous System** Alcohol can cause dizziness, loss of balance, unclear speech, and loss of muscle control. It can cause memory loss and destroy brain cells. Alcohol also can cause accidents and death if someone drinks and drives.
- **Mouth and Esophagus** Alcohol can cause cancer of the mouth and esophagus.
- **Heart** Alcohol can raise blood pressure, cause heart failure, and damage the heart muscle.
- **Liver** Long-term, heavy alcohol drinkers can damage the liver and cause liver cancer.
- **Stomach and Intestines** Alcohol can damage the cells lining the stomach and intestines.

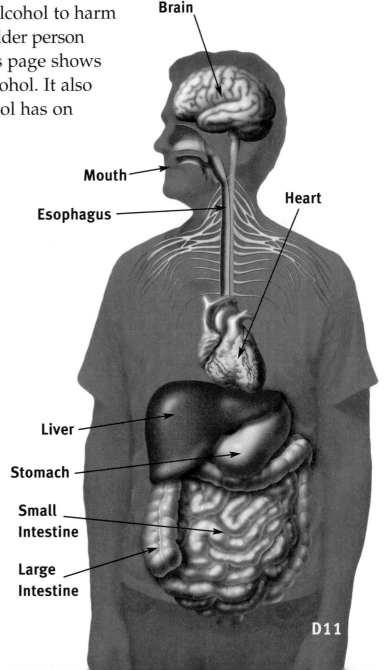

Brain

Mouth

Esophagus

Heart

Liver

Stomach

Small Intestine

Large Intestine

IS YOUR LIFE AFFECTED BY SOMEONE'S DRINKING?

My Father

My Friend

My Child

My Spouse

To help them, you have to help yourself first.
Call Al-Anon/Alateen.
1-888-4AL-ANON (1-888-425-2666)
www.al-anon.alateen.org

▲ **Alcoholism can bring unhappiness and stress to people, but there are ways to get help.**

Alcohol Harms Mental and Emotional Health

Drinking alcohol harms memory and a person's ability to make healthful decisions. Some people become mean when they drink alcohol. Others become depressed. Drinking alcohol does not show good character. It can harm self-esteem.

Alcohol Harms Family and Social Relationships

Drinking alcohol can change the way a person thinks and acts. A person who drinks alcohol might say things that he or she might not usually say. The person might also make wrong decisions. This can affect others. This kind of behavior could harm relationships with family and friends.

It is illegal for someone under the age of twenty-one to drink. When a person your age drinks, he or she is being dishonest and breaking the law. Parents and guardians may feel that they cannot trust their child. Family relationships are harmed when someone your age drinks alcohol.

Problem drinking is drinking that can cause wrong decisions and bad judgments to be made. Family and social relationships are harmed by problem drinking. Sometimes people with problem drinking do not think about the needs of other family members. They might cause family arguments. They might harm or disappoint themselves and cause other family members to be fearful. They might neglect their job.

If the problem drinker is a parent or guardian, all other family members are affected. They might not be able to count on that person for comfort, food, protection, an income, or safe shelter.

 How can problem drinking affect family health?

Alcoholism

Alcoholism (AL•kuh•HAW•LI•zuhm) is a disease in which a person is dependant on alcohol. A person who has alcoholism is an *alcoholic*. Alcoholism lasts through a person's lifetime. There is no cure for alcoholism.

Treatment for Alcoholism

Some people who have alcoholism are treated in a hospital. A doctor helps these people stop drinking and treats physical problems connected with the disease. People who have alcoholism often attend group meetings where help is available. *Alcoholics Anonymous* (AA) is a support group for people with alcoholism. The goal of AA is to support people who stop drinking alcohol. Family members and friends of people with alcoholism might go to other support groups. At *Al-Anon* meetings, family members and friends can get help. *Alateen* is a group for young people who are close to someone who has alcoholism.

CAREERS
Health Advocate

A health advocate is a person who teaches people about behaviors that will keep them well. This person may help families affected by alcoholism and other diseases find support resources. Other health advocates help people find health-care providers in their community. They also might help people understand their health insurance.

LOG ON www.mmhhealth.com Find out more about health careers.

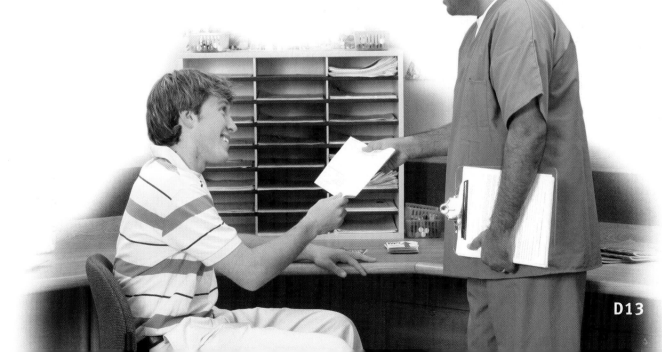

◄ Doctors can provide health resources.

Music
LINK

A Thousand Times, No!
Have your class set to music the 10 reasons to resist alcohol at right. Each reason can be sung or recited by a pair of students.

Ten Reasons to Resist Alcohol

Someone might try to pressure you into drinking alcohol. Here are ten reasons you can give in saying "no" to alcohol.

1. **I want to obey the law.** It is against the law for someone my age to drink alcohol.

2. **I want to act responsibly.** My mind would not be sharp. I might say or do something that I regret.

3. **I want to grow and develop properly.** Alcohol damages body organs.

4. **I want to avoid accidents.** My muscles would be affected if I drink.

5. **I want to have healthful relationships.** Drinking alcohol would keep me from learning right ways to talk and act around other people.

6. **I want to follow my family's guidelines.** I would have to hide my drinking and lie to my family. I would lose their trust.

7. **I want to keep from getting depressed.** Drinking alcohol will make me depressed and sad. Problems will seem worse.

8. **I want to avoid arguments and getting angry.** I might not be able to control anger if I drink.

9. **I want to keep from getting diseases.** Alcohol can damage my body organs.

10. **I want to keep from having alcoholism.** I do not want to become dependent on alcohol.

List five reasons for saying "no" to alcohol.

Use Resistance Skills

You can use the following resistance skills in saying "no" to alcohol.

- Look at the person. Be polite. Say "no" in a firm voice.

- Give one or more of the ten reasons for saying "no."

- Keep away from places where alcohol is used. Stay away from peers who drink alcohol.

- Tell a responsible adult if someone tries to talk you into drinking alcohol.

ACTIVITY

LIFE SKILLS

CRITICAL THINKING

Analyze What Influences Your Health

A role model is someone that you admire and want to be like.

1. **Identify people and things that can influence your health.** List people you admire who do not drink alcohol.

2. **Evaluate how these people and things can affect your health.** Ask a few people on your list to share how they resist drinking alcohol. List ways these people's choices make their lives more healthful.

3. **Choose healthful influences.** Choose a healthful action by a person on your list to imitate. What can you do to make yourself more like that person?

4. **Protect yourself against harmful influences.** Avoid people who make unhealthy choices.

◀ **A role model can influence how you take care of your health.**

LESSON REVIEW

Review Concepts

1. **Describe** three ways that alcohol harms physical health.

2. **Explain** ways that alcohol use could harm family and social relationships.

3. **List** ten reasons to say "no" to drinking alcohol.

4. **Describe** how Alateen and Al-Anon help people who are living with a person who abuses alcohol.

Critical Thinking

5. **Analyze** Why might a person recovering from alcoholism require treatment for physical problems?

6. **LIFE SKILLS** **Analyze What Influences Your Health** Think about television ads you have seen for alcoholic beverages. How do these advertisements try to influence people to use alcohol?

Tobacco and Health

You will learn . . .

- ways tobacco harms health.
- ways secondhand smoke harms health.
- ten reasons to say "no" to tobacco use.
- ways to quit tobacco use.

Vocabulary

- **nicotine**, *D17*
- **stimulant**, *D17*
- **tar**, *D17*
- **secondhand smoke**, *D18*
- **smokeless tobacco**, *D19*

When you go to a restaurant with your family, do you sit in the nonsmoking section? Some states have laws that do not allow people to smoke in restaurants at all. These actions help protect the health of both patrons and workers.

Tobacco Harms Health

Tobacco is a plant. Tobacco leaves are dried, shredded, and made into products such as cigarettes, cigars, smokeless tobacco, and pipe tobacco.

Smoking Harms Physical Health

Nicotine, tar, and carbon monoxide are three of the harmful chemicals found in tobacco smoke. Every tobacco product contains nicotine. **Nicotine** (NI•kuh•teen) is a stimulant drug found in tobacco. **Stimulants** are drugs that speed up the body's functions. Nicotine is addictive. It reaches the brain about ten seconds after it is inhaled into the lungs. **Tar** is a gummy substance found in tobacco smoke. Tar damages cells in lungs and air passages. Carbon monoxide enters the blood instead of oxygen in the lungs. This increases heart rate and blood pressure. Other effects of smoking are shown below.

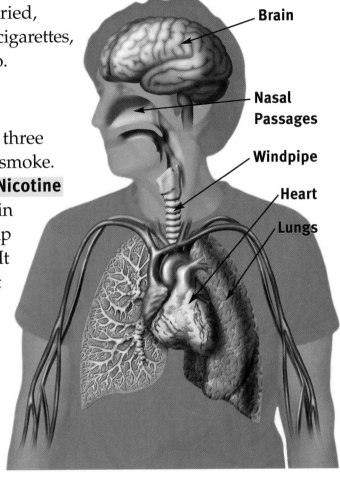

Brain

Nasal Passages

Windpipe

Heart

Lungs

 Name three harmful effects of smoking.

Harmful Effects of Smoking	
Short-Term Effects	**Long-Term Effects**
You risk becoming addicted to nicotine.	You become addicted to nicotine.
You get more colds and flu.	Cigarette smoking causes about 430,000 premature deaths every year in the United States.
Your risk of cancer increases.	Smoking is related to almost all cases of lung cancer. Smoking contributes to cancers in the mouth, esophagus, stomach, kidney, and bladder.
Your heart rate and blood pressure increase.	Smoking increases the risk of heart disease and of having a stroke.
You become short of breath, and you tire more easily.	Smoking increases your risk of emphysema in which lung tissue is gradually destroyed.
Your teeth get stained.	Smoking increases the risk of gum disease.

Secondhand Smoke

Explanatory Writing A new family restaurant in your town will have a nonsmoking policy. Suppose that you are the restaurant owner. Write a statement that tells the public why the restaurant doesn't allow smoking.

Secondhand smoke is smoke that a person breathes out. It could also come from a burning cigarette, cigar, or pipe. This smoke is harmful to people your age because your body is still growing and developing. When you sit in a room with people who are smoking, you are breathing in the smoke they exhale and smoke from their burning cigarette.

A *nonsmoker* is a person who does not smoke. A nonsmoker can get lung cancer by breathing in secondhand smoke over time. There are ways a nonsmoker can protect himself or herself from secondhand smoke.

- Ask others not to smoke around you.
- Ask to be seated in the nonsmoking section in restaurants or to go to restaurants where smoking is not allowed.

What is secondhand smoke?

SURGEON GENERAL'S WARNING: Smoking Causes Lung Cancer, Heart Disease, Emphysema, and May Complicate Pregnancy.

SURGEON GENERAL'S WARNING: Quitting Smoking Now Greatly Reduces Serious Risks to Your Health.

SURGEON GENERAL'S WARNING: Smoking by Pregnant Women May Result in Fetal Injury, Premature Birth, and Low Birth Weight.

◀ The harmful effects of smoking and smokeless tobacco products must be shown on all tobacco products.

Smokeless Tobacco

Smokeless tobacco is a tobacco product that can be chewed, placed between the cheek and gums, or inhaled through the nostrils. *Chewing tobacco* is leaf tobacco that is held in the mouth and chewed. A second kind of smokeless tobacco is snuff. *Snuff* is finely ground tobacco that is inhaled through the nose.

Smokeless tobacco contains nicotine. Nicotine in smokeless tobacco enters the body through the tissues in the mouth or nose. Smokeless tobacco can harm your body and is known to cause cancer.

▲ Snuff, or dip, is powdered tobacco. It is inhaled through the nose or held between the cheek and gum.

► Chewing tobacco, or chaw, is chewed in the mouth. Juices produced by chewing are spit out.

 List types of cancer that can be caused by smokeless tobacco.

Harmful Effects of Smokeless Tobacco

Short-Term Effects	Long-Term Effects
Your lips and gums may sting and bleed.	You may get cancer of cheeks, gums, and throat; white patches can appear in the mouth.
Your teeth will become stained.	You can get tooth decay. You can lose teeth.
Your blood pressure can increase.	You can become dependent on or addicted to nicotine.
You will have bad breath.	Your heart and lungs can be damaged.

Under 18 No Tobacco

We Card

STATE LAW PROHIBITS THE SALE OF TOBACCO TO MINORS

Please Have ID Ready

Reasons to Avoid Tobacco Use

What will you do when someone pressures you to smoke a cigarette? Here are some reasons you should refuse such an offer.

1 **Tobacco causes cancer.** Tell them you want to be cancer free.

2 **Tobacco causes heart disease.** It can make you tired because your heart and lungs have to work harder. Tell them that you want to keep your heart healthy. You want to be healthy and have plenty of energy. You want to reduce your risk of premature death.

3 **The nicotine in tobacco is addictive.** Tell them that you don't want to become addicted to nicotine.

4 **Nicotine and tar stain teeth, harm your mouth, gums, and teeth and give you bad breath.** Tell them that you want to have healthy teeth and gums. You want your teeth to last a lifetime. Tobacco smoke makes skin, hair and clothing smell bad. You want to have clean clothes and a clean body.

5 **Secondhand tobacco smoke can make others ill.** Tell them that you want to protect others from secondhand smoke.

State four reasons why you and others say "no" to tobacco use.

Ways to Quit Using Tobacco

Some people stop smoking without help. Most people, however, need help to recover from nicotine addiction. Family doctors and groups like the American Lung Association and the American Cancer Society have many plans that can help people quit smoking.

These plans might include using medicines, such as nicotine gums, patches, or nasal sprays. A person also might go to a clinic for counseling or attend smoking cessation (se•SAY•shuhn) classes.

TOBACCO USE
PROHIBITED

USO DE TABACO
ES PROHIBIDO

ACTIVITY LIFE SKILLS CRITICAL THINKING

Practice Healthful Behaviors

You have learned that secondhand smoke causes health risks. Suppose that you want to protect yourself against secondhand smoke.

1 **Learn about a healthful behavior.** What are some ways that you can avoid the risks of secondhand smoke? Work with a partner. Make a list of ideas.

2 **Practice the behavior.** Choose an idea from your list. Role-play this behavior. For example, you might practice asking to be seated in the nonsmoking section of a restaurant.

3 **Ask for help if you need it.** What will you do if seating is only available in the smoking section? Ask your parents or guardian for ideas.

4 **Make the behavior a habit.** Now that you have practiced what to do, make the behavior a habit. For instance, what would you do when you go to a fast-food restaurant with your family?

LESSON REVIEW

Review Concepts

1. **List** two long-term effects of smoking.

2. **Explain** ways secondhand smoke harms health.

3. **Name** two types of smokeless tobacco and list ways that each harms health.

4. **List** five reasons to say "no" to using tobacco products.

Critical Thinking

5. **Apply** A local clinic has a program to help people who smoke. The clinic would like a poster that helps people to quit. What should the poster show and say?

6. **LIFE SKILLS** **Be a Health Advocate** A friend wants to try chewing tobacco. Explain the harmful effects.

Learning LIFE SKILLS

Use Resistance Skills

Problem Two older girls offer Shawna a cigarette. They tell her that smoking one cigarette is no big deal. She'll look cool. She isn't being asked to smoke a whole pack. Is Shawna tempted to give it a try?

Try this cigarette. It's a new brand that won't hurt you.

No, thanks.

Tobacco won't hurt you unless you smoke all the time.

Solution Shawna can resist the pressure by using resistance skills. The steps for using resistance skills appear on the next page.

Foldables™ To Learn Life Skills

Learn This Life Skill

Follow these steps to help you use resistance skills.
The Foldables™ can help you.

1 **Look at the person. Say "no" in a firm voice.**

Practice saying "no" with your classmates.

2 **Give reasons for saying "no."**

Shawna can tell them that tobacco contains nicotine, which can harm the body. What other reasons can Shawna give?

3 **Match your behavior to your words.**

Shawna can walk away. She can try to keep away from these girls in the future.

4 **Ask an adult for help if you need it.**

What advice would you give Shawna about looking to a responsible adult for help?

Practice This Life Skill

How would you use resistance skills in a situation like Shawna's? Can *you* resist the pressure? Work with two classmates and role-play the situation. Include all four steps as you role-play the use of resistance skills.

Drug Abuse

You will learn . . .

- ways marijuana harms health.
- ways that the misuse or abuse of stimulants and depressants harms health.
- why it is harmful to abuse inhalants and steroids.

Vocabulary

- **marijuana**, *D25*
- **cocaine**, *D27*
- **ecstasy**, *D27*
- **inhalant**, *D28*
- **steroid**, *D29*

Illegal drug use is the use of a drug in a way that breaks the law. It can be the use of an illegal drug such as marijuana or heroin. It also can be the abuse of a legal drug. These students know that they can enjoy healthful relationships and stay drug free.

Marijuana

Marijuana (MEHR•uh•WAH•nuh) is an illegal drug that affects memory and concentration. Some names for marijuana are pot, grass, and weed. A stronger form of marijuana is *hashish*, which can be eaten or smoked.

Marijuana is smoked in cigarette or cigar form and in pipes. When smoked, THC, a chemical found in marijuana, moves quickly from the lungs to the bloodstream and to the brain. Marijuana affects memory, the ability to concentrate, and muscle coordination. It also affects mood.

Marijuana is sometimes added to food. Marijuana in food may be stronger and have more lasting effects than when smoked. In most places, it is against the law to possess, smoke, or sell marijuana in any form.

A few states allow medical use of marijuana for cancer patients. Such use requires a doctor's prescription. Medical marijuana may help relieve certain side effects of cancer treatment.

▲ Marijuana is made from the leaves and flowers of the cannabis plant. It affects physical health, mental and emotional health, and family and social health.

 Give three reasons not to use marijuana.

Effects of Marijuana Use

Short-Term Effects	Long-Term Effects
Red eyes	Frequent lung infections; asthma
Dry mouth and thirst	Hallucinations (seeing and hearing things that are not there)
Increased heart rate and blood pressure	Inability to think properly
Become forgetful	Stop caring about friends and family
Inability to do simple things	Stop caring about self
Hunger	Others lose trust in you
Risk of legal action for possession	Risk of legal action for possession
Panic or anxiety for no real reason	Feelings of guilt

Stimulants and Depressants

In the last lesson, you learned that *stimulants* speed up body functions. This means that under the influence of a stimulant, the heart beats faster. *Depressants* are drugs that slow down the functions of the body, especially the nervous system.

Stimulants

Some stimulants can be used legally. One of these stimulants is nicotine, found in tobacco. However, nicotine is a controlled drug. A *controlled drug* is one whose sale, use, and advertising are regulated by law. For example, in the United States, tobacco advertisements are controlled. Tobacco cannot be advertised on TV. It is illegal to sell tobacco products to persons under the age of 18. Tobacco products cannot be sold within a certain distance of schools. Other countries have similar laws about tobacco products.

Other legal stimulants are caffeine and amphetamines (am•FE•tuh•MEENZ). *Caffeine* is the stimulant found in some over-the-counter headache and cold medicines, coffee, tea, chocolate, cocoa, and some soft drinks. Caffeine causes some people to have trouble sleeping. It makes some people get headaches and feel jumpy. *Amphetamines* are stimulants prescribed by a doctor to treat certain health conditions, but some people abuse them.

▲ **When you have a choice, choose caffeine-free beverages. Why is this a healthful choice?**

D26

Cocaine, crack, and ecstasy are illegal stimulants. **Cocaine** is an illegal stimulant made from the leaves of the coca plant. Cocaine can be inhaled or injected. *Crack* is a form of cocaine that is smoked. Both cocaine and crack are illegal to use and are harmful. **Ecstasy** is an illegal stimulant drug that can increase or decrease the actions of the body. It can be either a tablet or capsule. Cocaine, crack, or ecstasy can cause death.

Depressants

Depressants affect the body by slowing down heart rate and nerve messages, making a person feel tired. They can prevent people from thinking clearly.

In Lesson 2 you learned that alcohol is a legal depressant. Laws control the sale of alcohol. For instance, people younger than 21 cannot legally buy alcohol. Some over-the-counter medicines, such as mouthwash and cough syrup, contain alcohol. While these products are helpful, some people abuse them because they contain alcohol.

Sleeping pills and tranquilizers are two other examples of depressants. These also are legal drugs. Doctors write prescriptions for sleeping pills to treat people who have trouble sleeping. Some sleeping pills are sold as OTC medicines. Tranquilizers help to relax the body. Prescriptions for tranquilizers are written for people who are depressed or have anxiety. Depressants like these are necessary to treat some health conditions, but they are sometimes misused and abused.

List two illegal stimulants.

▲ Sleeping pills, some cough syrups, and alcoholic beverages contain depressants.

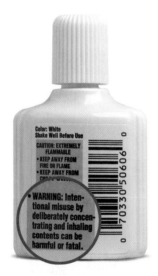
Inhalants and Steroids

Two other types of drugs that have medical uses, but also are abused by some people are inhalants and steroids. If abused, these drugs can harm health.

Medical Inhalants

You may have seen someone with asthma (AZ•muh) use an inhaler. An *inhaler* provides the user with medicine called an inhalant. An **inhalant** is a chemical that is breathed into the lungs. The inhalant is in the form of vapor or tiny droplets. It contains medicine that opens up the tubes leading to the lungs. The person then can breathe more easily.

Abusing Inhalants

Some everyday household products contain chemicals that vaporize easily. Paint thinner, spray paints, and certain glues release vapors of chemicals that are harmful. When inhaled the harmful chemicals enter the bloodstream and are carried to all the parts of the body, but especially to the brain. Follow safety directions on the label when using these products.

Some people breathe in the vapors or fumes of chemicals because it gives them a high. When inhaled, the chemicals in the vapor can cause irregular heartbeat, suffocation, choking, and brain damage in a healthy person within minutes of breathing the vapors just one time. There have been cases where users have died. This is called "sudden sniffing death."

 **What is an inhalant?**

Steroids

Steroids (STAYR•oydz) are chemicals that occur naturally in the body. Sometimes synthetic steroids are prescribed by doctors for medical reasons. Steroids help the body develop muscle tissue. Some people abuse steroids because they want to make their muscles larger and enhance their strength and appearance. This is an illegal use of steroids. Abuse of steroids happens most often among athletes. Steroid abuse can stop bone growth and can damage the liver, heart, and kidneys. It can cause severe mood swings and severe depression.

ACTIVITY

LIFE SKILLS

CRITICAL THINKING

Use Resistance Skills

You are on a community soccer team. A teammate's older brother thinks you should try steroids to improve performance. What can you do about this situation?

1 **Look at the person. Say "no" in a firm voice.** How will you respond to this person's suggestion?

2 **Give reasons for saying "no."** Write out how you will defend your position.

3 **Match your behavior to your words.** Think of two or three things that he could say that would make you doubt yourself. Plan an answer to each one. Avoid situations and people who influence you to make harmful decisions.

4 **Ask an adult for help if you need it.** Ask your parents or your guardian or your coach for help if you have problems with this person.

LESSON REVIEW

Review Concepts

1. **Describe** the short-term and long-term harmful effects of marijuana use.

2. **List** one legal stimulant and one illegal stimulant. How can each be harmful?

3. **Explain** why it is harmful to misuse and abuse depressants.

4. **Explain** why it is harmful to abuse inhalants.

Critical Thinking

5. **Analyze** You have trouble sleeping at night. Your mother suggests keeping track of how much caffeine you take in each day. Why would she make this suggestion?

6. **LIFE SKILLS** **Use Resistance Skills** A group of kids on the swim team is trying to get Ashley to use steroids. How should she use resistance skills to resist their peer pressure?

Stay Drug Free

You will learn . . .

- ten reasons to say "no" to drug abuse.

- what strategies help you say "no" to abusing drugs.

- ways people who abuse drugs might be helped.

Vocabulary

- **protective factor,** *D31*

When you refuse to abuse drugs, you show respect for yourself. You show that you care about your health. Staying drug free protects your health, safety, and your future.

Say "No" to Drug Abuse

You have made a decision to be drug-free. You want to be responsible. You want to be healthful and safe. You want to follow laws and family guidelines. You want to have self-respect and good character.

Surround yourself with protective factors. A **protective factor** is something that increases the chances of a positive outcome. Suppose you and your friends do not abuse drugs. You encourage each other to choose healthful activities instead of activities that will harm you. When you do so, you and your friends are protecting one another. The following protective factors can help you to say "no" to drugs.

- Having self-respect encourages you to stay healthy.

- Being active in school activities gives you goals to aim for.

- Being around adults and friends who do not abuse drugs gives you positive role models to imitate.

- Doing your best in school helps your self-respect and helps you value your abilities.

- Following rules, laws, and guidelines makes you aware of consequences for actions.

- Having goals and plans helps you think about planning a healthful future.

- Having a plan to manage stress lets you know that you don't have to give in to behaviors that harm health.

Tell five reasons for saying "no" to drugs.

Reasons to Stay Drug-Free

You know that drugs can be harmful. Repeat these reasons for choosing health, not drugs.

- **I want to follow laws.**
- **I want to respect my parents or guardian.**
- **I want a healthy body.**
- **I want a healthy mind.**
- **I want healthful friendships.**
- **I want to be able to learn.**
- **I want to be in school activities.**
- **I want to be safe.**
- **I want to have fun.**
- **I want to live.**

◄ **Staying drug-free helps you be your best.**

Help for People Who Abuse Drugs

There is help for people who abuse drugs. People who abuse drugs often need outside help to stop taking the drug. They may need to be in a hospital where they cannot get drugs. There a doctor can treat any medical health problems caused by their drug abuse. Patients also receive counseling. Some people who abuse drugs do not go to hospitals. They might receive counseling at a drug treatment facility.

Always tell a responsible adult right away if you suspect someone is abusing drugs. If possible, stay away from anyone who abuses drugs, because you cannot predict their actions. Develop friendships with people who choose healthful lifestyles.

 Name two ways people who abuse drugs can get help.

ACTIVITY

BUILD Character

A Helping Hand

Citizenship There are probably many organizations in your community that work to help people who abuse drugs. Make a poster illustrating how these organizations accomplish their work. Research local libraries, hospitals, and church and civic groups to find the names of some organizations. Gather materials and information about the organization of your choice. Illustrate your poster with photographs or drawings. Include information on how to contact the organization. Display your posters in your class.

Choose a Drug-Free Lifestyle

There are things you can do with friends that do not harm health. Check in your community to see what activities are available. At school or elsewhere you can join hobby groups, musical groups, or sport teams. There are places in every community where you can volunteer your time. Libraries, nursing homes, church groups, and many civic groups depend on volunteer help. By volunteering, you may find out what you want to do for life.

Be a Health Advocate

You have volunteered to make posters for an anti-drug rally.

1 **Choose a healthful action to communicate.** What do you want your poster to communicate about drugs? Record your ideas.

2 **Collect information about the action.** Where will you find information? You can start with your textbook. Record the information about being drug-free.

3 **Decide how to communicate this information.** You already know you are making a poster. Design it to be effective at the rally.

4 **Communicate your message to others.** Present your poster to the class. Hang it in the classroom, if possible.

LESSON REVIEW

Review Concepts

1. **Name** seven protective factors that help a person say "no" to drug abuse.

2. **List** the ten reasons to say "no" to drug abuse.

3. **Identify** adults you could talk with at school and outside of school who could get treatment for someone who abused drugs.

Critical Thinking

4. **Analyze** How is having a plan to manage stress a protective factor that can keep you from abusing drugs?

5. **LIFE SKILLS** **Be a Health Advocate** You and a friend are using markers to make a poster. Your friend says, "I love the smell of these markers. They make me feel so happy." What is going on? What will you do?

CHAPTER 7 REVIEW

Use Vocabulary

alcoholism, *D13*

drug, *D5*

drug abuse, *D8*

inhalant, *D28*

nicotine, *D17*

Choose the correct term from the list to complete each sentence.

Write the word on a separate sheet of paper.

1. A substance that changes how the mind or body works is a(n) __?__.

2. A stimulant found in tobacco is __?__.

3. The use of an illegal drug or the harmful use of a legal drug on purpose is __?__.

4. A disease in which a person is dependent on alcohol is __?__.

5. Any chemical that is breathed into the lungs is a(n) __?__.

Review Concepts

Answer each question in complete sentences.

6. What are safety rules for taking prescription drugs?

7. How can a person keep from misusing drugs?

8. How does alcohol harm family and social health?

9. What drug is in cigarettes, chewing tobacco, and snuff? How does it harm health?

10. What are three long-term effects of smoking?

Reading Comprehension

Answer each question in complete sentences.

Alcoholics Anonymous (AA) is a support group for people who have alcoholism. The goal of AA is to support people who stop drinking alcohol. Family members and friends of people who have alcoholism might go to other support groups. At *Al-Anon* meetings, family members and friends can get help. *Alateen* is a group for young people who are close to someone who abuses alcohol.

11. What is the goal of AA?

12. How do these support groups help family and social health?

13. How is Alateen different from Al-Anon?

Critical Thinking/Problem Solving

Answer each question in complete sentences.

Analyze Concepts

14. Explain how secondhand smoke can affect your lungs even though you don't smoke.

15. How can marijuana affect your ability to be a good student?

16. How do cocaine, crack, and amphetamines harm mental and emotional health?

17. How is treating alcoholism different from treating a sore throat?

18. Why is it just as important to take OTC drugs safely as it is to take prescription drugs safely?

Practice Life Skills

19. **Use Resistance Skills** You are at a classmate's house after school. The parents are at work. How would you use resistance skills to say "no" if you were pressured to drink alcohol?

20. **Make Responsible Decisions** A friend wants to stay up all night to finish a report due tomorrow. He asks his older brother to buy over-the-counter caffeine pills. He says, "I'm not doing anything wrong. Caffeine is legal." What is he doing that could be harmful to his health? Would his actions pass the *Guidelines for Making Responsible Decisions*™? Why? Why not?

Read Graphics

Use the illustration below to answer questions 21–24.

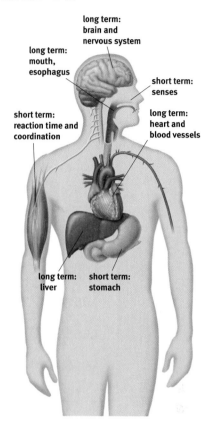

long term: brain and nervous system

long term: mouth, esophagus

short term: senses

short term: reaction time and coordination

long term: heart and blood vessels

long term: liver

short term: stomach

21. What type of effect does alcohol have on the heart and blood vessels?

22. What type of effect does alcohol have on the stomach?

23. List the areas of the body where alcohol has long-term effects.

24. List the areas of the body where alcohol has short-term effects.

 LOG ON www.mmhhealth.com Find out how much you know about health concepts related to drug use.

CHAPTER 8

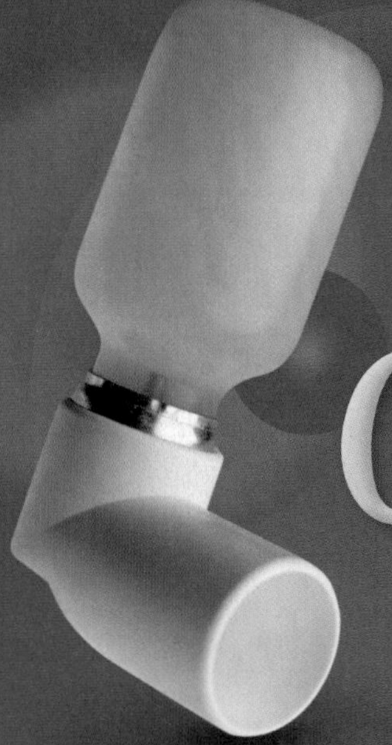

Communicable and Chronic Diseases

NDC 0501-3250-06

Calamine

antibiotic ointment
polymyxin B sulfate/bacitracin zinc/neomycin sulfate

What Do You Know?

Are you prepared to fight the battle against disease? Read the following statements and rate your disease-fighting habits.

__?__ I wash my hands before and after I eat.
__?__ I cough or sneeze into a tissue and then throw it away.
__?__ I never let anyone use my comb or brush.
__?__ I need to exercise every day.
__?__ I put sunscreen on before I go outside.

Do you practice each of these habits? If you do, then you know how to reduce the risk of many health problems. Everyone can form these habits and be healthy. Read **Communicable and Chronic Diseases** to find out.

LOG ON **www.mmhhealth.com**
Find out more about ways to keep healthy and disease free.

Diseases That Spread

You will learn ...

- kinds of pathogens that cause disease.
- ways pathogens enter the body.
- habits that keep germs from spreading.

Vocabulary

- **disease**, *D39*
- **communicable disease**, *D39*
- **pathogen**, *D39*

Many illnesses are spread by people, animals, or objects in the environment. Keeping your hands clean is one simple way to stop the spread of many illnesses.

Kinds of Pathogens

A **disease** is any condition that keeps the body from working as it should. A **communicable disease** is one that is spread from person to person, from animals to people, or from objects in the environment to people. Diseases that spread are caused by bacteria, viruses, fungi, or protists. Other diseases, such as heart disease and cancer, are not spread from person to person. Diseases that do not spread are called *noncommunicable diseases*.

Communicable diseases are caused by pathogens (PATH•uh•juhnz). A **pathogen** is a germ that causes disease. Some bacteria, fungi, viruses, and protists are pathogens. The chart below gives you some information about these types of pathogens.

 What is a pathogen?

Science LINK — ACTIVITY

Watch a Fungus at Work

Place a slice of fresh white bread in a sealable plastic bag in a warm place. Check the bread each day for seven days. Do not open the bag. Observe the bread each day. Describe how the bread changes.

Types of Pathogens				
Pathogen	**Bacteria**	**Fungi**	**Viruses**	**Protists**
What is it?	One-celled organism	Plantlike but cannot make their own food	Nonliving particles	One-celled or many-celled living things
Where does it live?	In air, soil, water, in and on plants and animals	In air, soil, water, in and on plants and animals	In plants and animals	In animals, soil, and in water
What are some diseases that it causes in humans?	Strep throat, some forms of pinkeye	Ringworm, athlete's foot	Common cold, flu, chicken pox, polio, West Nile virus, some forms of pinkeye	Malaria, sleeping sickness, dysentery
What does it look like?				

How Pathogens Get Into the Body

Pathogens can be in the air that you breathe, in soil, in water, and on food that you eat. There are pathogens on people and other animals, plants, and objects that you touch such as doorknobs and handlebars. Pathogens, such as bacteria and fungi, can get into the body through the eyes, the nose, the mouth, and through breaks in the skin.

Your body has many ways to protect you from pathogens. To cause illness, a pathogen has to break down these protections. Your body has ways to destroy the pathogen before it can make you ill. For example, tears and saliva contain chemicals that destroy many pathogens before they can cause harm.

 What are four places pathogens can get into the body?

 **Write About It!**

Write a Poem Write a poem or make up a saying that will remind you to wash your hands often and keep them away from your face. Read your poem or saying out loud to your class. Keeping your hands clean and away from your face can help you stay healthy.

▶ **Skin** Clean, unbroken skin helps keep pathogens from getting into the body.

▶ **Nose** A person with a cold releases droplets containing cold viruses into the air when he or she coughs or sneezes. You breathe in these droplets through your nose.

▼ **Eyes** When you touch an object that has pathogens on it, you may transfer them to your eyes if you rub your eyes.

◀ **Mouth** If you bite your nails or wipe your mouth with your hands, any pathogens on your hands can get into your mouth.

Your Skin

Cuts and Scrapes Your skin is like a waterproof covering. However, pathogens can get into scrapes and cuts in your skin. Washing small cuts and scrapes with soap and water removes many pathogens. Cover a larger cut or scrape with a bandage after it has been cleaned up. Tell your parents or guardian if a cut or scrape becomes red, swollen or sore.

Puncture Wounds Objects such as nails, staples, or other pointed objects can go deep into your skin and make a deep hole called a *puncture* (PUNK•chur) *wound*. Bacteria can grow in a puncture wound. See a doctor for a tetanus (TET•en•us) shot if you get a puncture wound.

Animal bites Some ticks and mosquitoes can carry diseases that affect humans. When you are outside, wear long pants, a long-sleeved shirt, and a hat. Tuck your pants into your socks if you are in wooded areas where ticks might be. Use insect repellent.

Rabies is a viral disease carried in the saliva of some warm-blooded animals. Rabies causes harm to the nervous system of a person who is bitten by an infected animal. You can't always tell if the animal is infected, so tell your parents or guardian immediately if you are bitten by a dog, cat, raccoon, skunk, or bat. Get care from a doctor immediately.

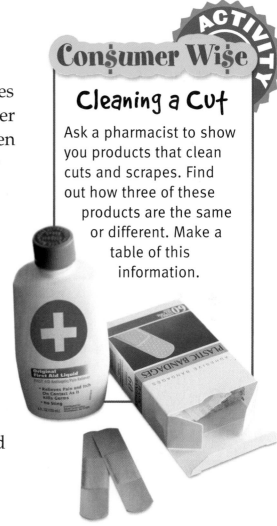

Con$umer Wi$e — ACTIVITY

Cleaning a Cut

Ask a pharmacist to show you products that clean cuts and scrapes. Find out how three of these products are the same or different. Make a table of this information.

► Raccoons can carry rabies. Dogs and cats that are not vaccinated against rabies also may carry the rabies virus. Be careful around unfamiliar animals.

Keep Pathogens From Spreading

What can you do to keep yourself healthy? You can develop simple habits to keep pathogens from getting into your body.

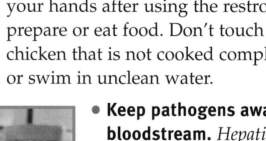
- **Keep pathogens away from your nose and eyes.** Keep your hands clean and away from your eyes and nose. Cover your mouth and nose with a tissue when you cough or sneeze. Throw the used tissue away. Then wash your hands.

- **Keep pathogens away from your mouth.** Do not put objects or your fingers in your mouth. Wash your hands after using the restroom and before you prepare or eat food. Don't touch or eat pork or chicken that is not cooked completely. Do not drink or swim in unclean water.

▲ Covering your nose and mouth when you sneeze helps stop the spread of pathogens.

- **Keep pathogens away from your bloodstream.** *Hepatitis B* is a viral disease of the liver. A person is exposed to this disease when he or she has a cut that comes in contact with blood that is infected with hepatitis B virus. People who abuse drugs and share needles expose themselves to this disease. If you must help a person who is ill or bleeding, use the universal precautions described in Chapter 6.

 List three healthful habits to practice when you cough or sneeze.

Make Responsible Decisions

You are at a playground. You step on a nail and get a puncture wound. How will you take care of this responsibly?

1 **Identify your choices.** Write two choices. Check them out with your parent or trusted adult.

2 **Evaluate each choice. Use the *Guidelines for Making Responsible Decisions™*.** Under each choice, write the answer to each of the six questions in the guidelines.

3 **Identify the responsible decision.** Circle the choice that will be the responsible decision. Check your decision with your parent or a trusted adult.

4 **Evaluate your decision.** How does the choice match the guidelines? What is the health consequence of each of your original choices?

Guidelines for Making Responsible Decisions™

- **Is my decision healthful?**
- **Is it safe?**
- **Does it follow rules and laws?**
- **Does it show respect for me and others?**
- **Does it follow family guidelines?**
- **Does it show good character?**

LESSON REVIEW

Review Concepts

1. **List** four kinds of pathogens that can cause disease.

2. **Name** four ways that pathogens can enter the body.

3. **Write** a paragraph describing habits you can practice to prevent the spread of pathogens at school.

Critical Thinking

4. **Apply** You and a friend go hiking in the woods. You insist on using insect repellent and wearing long sleeves and long pants tucked into your boots. What does this tell your friend about the seriousness of your goal to prevent illness?

5. **LIFE SKILLS** **Make Responsible Decisions** Your friend's dog bites you. Your friend asks you not to say anything. Explain what you should do and why.

The Body's Defenses

You will learn . . .

- how body defenses work.
- habits that help protect you from diseases spread by pathogens.

Vocabulary

- **mucus**, *D46*
- **white blood cell**, *D47*
- **antibody**, *D47*
- **immune**, *D47*
- **vaccine**, *D47*

"Ouch! That hurts!" When you get a cut or scrape, your first thought may be about how much it hurts. But your body is already at work fighting pathogens that are trying to invade your body.

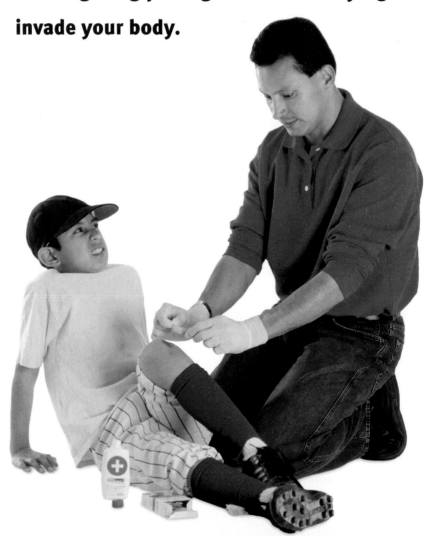

Body Defenses At Work

Pathogens are found everywhere—in shoes, on food, and even on your pets. Yet you are healthy most of the time. That's because your body is always at work fighting off these invaders. Your body has two main defenses that protect you from most diseases. *First-line defenses* work to keep pathogens out of your body. *Second-line defenses* go to work when pathogens have entered your body.

First-Line Defenses

First-line defenses are like a suit of armor. They are the first defenses that most pathogens meet as they try to attack your body. First-line defenses are

- unbroken skin
- hairs in your nose
- tears
- saliva
- mucus
- stomach acids.

 What are six first-line defenses against illness?

BUILD ACTIVITY

Character

Tag, You're It!

Responsibility Stand in a circle with your classmates. Name a way you can take responsibility for protecting yourself from disease. For example, you might say, "I take responsibility by taking a bath every day." Then tag a classmate. The classmate names another way to take responsibility. Keep going until everyone has stated a way to stay healthy.

◄ **Why could you compare the body's defenses to a suit of armor?**

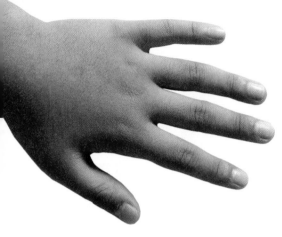

The Six First-Line Defenses

Unbroken Skin Unbroken skin keeps pathogens out of the body. Wash with soap and water right after scraping your skin. Cover the cut with a bandage.

Tears Tears wash away dust particles that might contain pathogens. Tears also contain substances that kill some pathogens.

Mucus (MYOO•kuss) **Mucus** is a moist coating that lines your nose and throat. It traps dust and pathogens and keeps them from reaching your lungs.

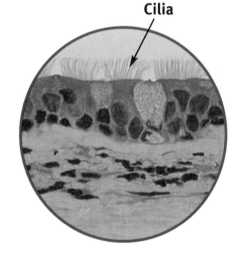

Cilia

Tiny Hairs Tiny hairs in your nose trap dust and some pathogens that you inhale. You get rid of them when you sneeze, cough, or blow your nose. Other fine, hairlike structures called *cilia* (SIL•ee•uh) in your windpipe trap particles as air moves into your lungs.

Saliva The liquid in your mouth is saliva. Saliva makes food easier to swallow. Saliva protects you from illness because it has a chemical that can kill some pathogens.

Stomach Acid Acid in your stomach breaks down food. The same acid is strong enough to kill many pathogens that might be on food you eat.

 How do first-line defenses fight disease?

◀ Inside the stomach as seen through a microscope.

Second-Line Defenses

If a pathogen gets past your first-line defenses, your body still has ways to fight off the invaders. Second-line defenses include white blood cells, antibodies, and vaccines.

White Blood Cells White blood cells are blood cells that fight illness if pathogens get into the body. Some types of white blood cells surround and destroy pathogens in your blood. They also can move out of the bloodstream into body tissues to attack pathogens.

Antibodies An antibody is a substance that your body makes to fight a pathogen as it is attacking you. Suppose that you get the measles virus. Your body starts to make antibodies that fight the measles virus right away. Measles antibodies stay in your body after you are well. If the measles virus attacks you again, the antibodies that you made the first time prevent you from getting the disease again. Once your body makes antibodies against a certain disease, you are immune (ih•MUNE) to that disease. To be immune to a disease is to be protected from that disease.

Vaccines A vaccine (vak•SEEN) is a substance that makes you immune to a disease. You have probably received vaccines for measles, mumps, chicken pox, and polio. Some vaccines provide immunity for life. Others need to be followed up by a booster to keep the person immune to a disease.

Science LINK ACTIVITY

Dr. Salk's Vaccine

Read about Dr. Jonas Salk, the scientist who won the race to make the first polio vaccine in the 1950s. Role-play Dr. Salk for your class. As Dr. Salk, explain how you discovered the vaccine and how it has helped people's health.

Bacteria

White blood cell

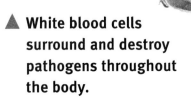

How do second-line defenses fight pathogens?

▲ White blood cells surround and destroy pathogens throughout the body.

Ways to Stay Well

You can form habits or behaviors that will protect you from many diseases that spread. Many of these behaviors also will speed your recovery if you are ill. These behaviors are to eat healthful foods, be physically active, and get plenty of rest and sleep.

Eat Healthful Foods The cells of your body need materials for growth, tissue repair, and other jobs. Eat whole grains for energy, fiber, and minerals. Fruits and vegetables give you many vitamins and minerals that help your body fight disease. Lean meats, poultry, and fish give you proteins for growth and cell repair. Dairy products provide vitamins, calcium, and other minerals. To stay healthy, use small amounts of fat, sugar, and salt in your diet.

▼ **A short nap can help you get the rest you need.**

Be Physically Active The American Heart Association says that people who are your age need at least 30 minutes of physical activity every day. Being active helps you stay at a healthful weight and makes your heart, lungs, bones, and muscles stronger.

Get Plenty of Rest and Sleep *Rest* is a period of relaxation. *Sleep* is deep relaxation. During sleep, you are not aware of what is happening around you. At your age, you need about nine to ten hours of sleep each night. Sleep gives body organs a chance to rest and repair themselves.

 List two habits that can protect you from communicable diseases.

Your Healthful Habits Kit

Practice these healthful habits to avoid pathogens and reduce your risk of disease.

- Wash your hands often.
- Keep hands away from your face.
- Do not share towels, combs, and brushes.
- Do not share cups, cans, bottles, straws, or eating utensils.
- Avoid touching or eating uncooked meats.
- Avoid people while they are ill.
- Use a tissue when you cough or sneeze. Then throw it away and wash your hands.
- Use universal precautions when you are near body fluids.

LIFE SKILLS · ACTIVITY

CRITICAL THINKING

Practice Healthful Behaviors

What behavior can your class practice this year to reduce the risk of spreading colds?

1. **Learn about a healthful behavior.** Have classmates brainstorm a list of healthful behaviors everyone could practice when they sneeze or cough. Choose one behavior from the list to practice.

2. **Practice the behavior.** Place creative reminders around the classroom to make sure that everyone practices this behavior.

3. **Ask for help if you need it.** Ask your teacher to help remind students about the risks of not practicing this behavior.

4. **Make the behavior a habit.** How can you tell if everyone in the class practices this healthful habit?

LESSON REVIEW

Review Concepts

1. **Explain** how two of the body's first-line defenses keep pathogens from getting into the body.

2. **Describe** how white blood cells fight pathogens that enter the body.

3. **Explain** the benefits of being physically active and getting plenty of sleep.

Critical Thinking

4. **Analyze** You have just recovered from the flu. Now a family member has it. Can you get the same flu again? Explain.

5. **LIFE SKILLS** **Practice Healthful Behaviors** What healthful behaviors can you practice to protect yourself from pathogens at home?

Treating Disease

You will learn . . .

- symptoms of communicable diseases.
- treatments for communicable diseases.
- the causes, symptoms, and treatments for some common childhood illnesses.

Vocabulary

- **symptom**, *D51*
- **treatment**, *D52*
- **antibiotic**, *D52*

Your body's defenses work hard to fight disease. Sometimes, however, pathogens do get into your body. When this happens, you may have symptoms of illness.

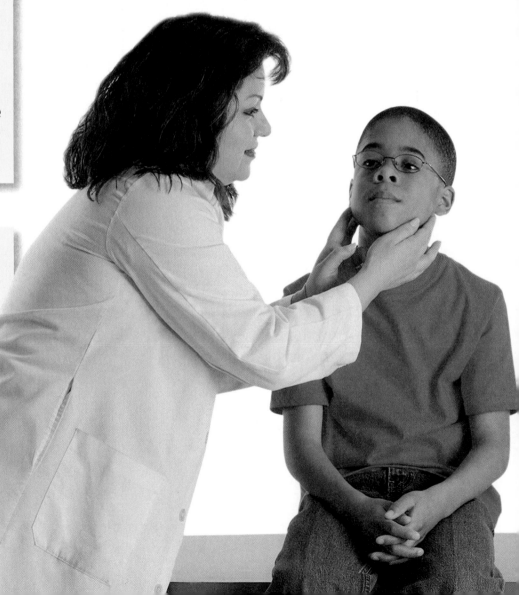

Signs and Symptoms of Disease

You've learned how diseases are spread and how the body fights them off. Often you know that you are ill because you have one or more symptoms (SIMP•tuhmz) and signs. A **symptom** is a change in the body's condition that signals disease. Examples of symptoms are having a headache, pain, or feeling tired. *Signs* are specific changes in health that the patient, doctor, and nurse notice. Examples of signs of illness are fever, rash, red eyes, vomiting, coughing, or sneezing.

Fever Normal body temperature is 98.6°F for most people. A *fever* is a higher than normal body temperature. You may get a fever when your body is defending itself against viruses that cause the common cold or if you have strep throat.

Swollen Lymph Nodes Lymph nodes are glands containing white blood cells. When a doctor feels your neck under your jaw, he or she is checking for swollen lymph nodes. Swollen lymph nodes are a sign that your white blood cells are fighting pathogens.

Coughing Coughing is one way the body gets rid of excess mucus and particles that irritate the throat or lungs. Mucus traps smoke particles, pathogens, dust, and pollen. Coughing also can be a sign of a lung infection.

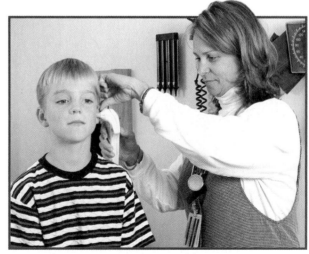

▲ **A thermometer is used to measure body temperature.**

 **What is a fever?**

Treating Diseases

ACTIVITY

Physical Education
LINK

Antibiotic Hopscotch

With a partner, write the names of illnesses on index cards. Write whether each illness is caused by bacteria, viruses, or fungi. Mark five boxes on the ground or floor. On your turn, take a card. If the disease can be treated with antibiotics, hop forward one box. If it can't, stay in the same box. Can you get to the last box?

Treatment is the care given to a person who is ill. The kind of medicine or care that is given depends on the cause of the illness.

Treating Bacterial Diseases An **antibiotic** is a drug that is used to kill or slow the growth of bacteria. *Strep throat* is an example of a disease caused by bacteria. Someone with strep throat usually has a sore throat and a fever. Antibiotics are used to treat strep throat and other bacterial diseases.

Treating Viral Diseases Antibiotics are not used to treat viral diseases. There are antiviral medicines that stop certain viruses from getting into cells or stop them from making copies of themselves.

The common cold, West Nile virus, and flu are caused by viruses, but there are no medicines to cure them. There are medicines, however, to treat the symptoms. They might reduce fever, soothe a sore throat, or stop you from coughing.

Vaccines protect you before you get certain viral diseases. A vaccine might keep you from getting a certain flu, chicken pox, polio, and other viral diseases.

Treating Fungal Diseases Fungi grow well in warm, moist places, such as between toes. Many fungal diseases can be avoided by keeping skin dry, by not sharing infected socks or other clothing, and by wearing your own shower slippers at a pool.

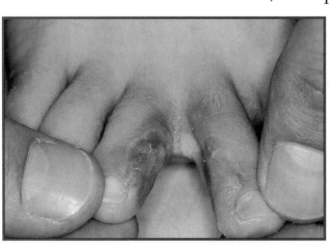

▲ Athlete's foot is a fungal disease that occurs between the toes and on the sole of the foot. It is treated with over-the-counter creams.

 What is an antibiotic?

Access Health Facts, Products, and Services

Why do you have to take an antibiotic for ten days when you have strep throat? How can you find the answer to this question?

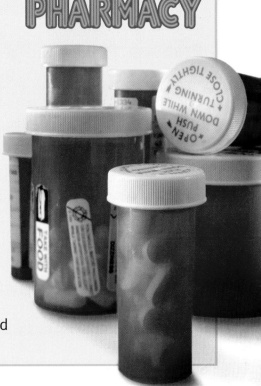

PHARMACY

1 **Identify when you might need health facts, products, and services.** You need valid health facts whenever you have a question about a medicine you are taking.

2 **Identify where you might find health facts, products, and services.** Answers to questions about medicines that you are using can be provided by health-care professionals such as your doctor or pharmacist.

3 **Find the health facts, products, and services you need.** If you or your parents or guardian have a question, write it down. Take the question with you when you talk to your doctor or pharmacist.

4 **Evaluate the health facts, products, and services.** Was your question answered completely? Is the information you received valid? Explain your answer.

LESSON REVIEW

Review Concepts

1. **List** three signs of disease.

2. **Describe** how the common cold, athlete's foot, and strep throat are each treated.

3. **Explain** why chicken pox vaccine would not be given to someone who has a case of chicken pox.

4. **Explain** why an antibiotic is not used to treat the common cold or the flu.

Critical Thinking

5. **Apply** Your uncle is bitten by a mosquito and gets West Nile virus. Why doesn't his doctor treat the illness with antibiotics?

6. **LIFE SKILLS** **Advocate for Health** Several people at the community pool have athlete's foot. How would you help stop the spread of this disease at the pool? Describe a plan to explain what this disease is and how it can be controlled. How will you check on the success of your "No More Athlete's Foot" campaign?

Set Health Goals

Problem Pinkeye is a common childhood infection of the clear covering of the eye and the inside of the eyelid. You have learned that pinkeye is going around your school. What steps can you take to keep from getting pinkeye?

Health Behavior Contract

Name _____   Date _____

Health Goal: I will choose habits that prevent the spread of pathogens.

Effect on My Health: Pathogens can enter my body through my eyes, nose, mouth, skin, and blood. I will practice habits to keep pathogens out of my body. I will choose habits that prevent the spread of pathogens.

My Plan: I will make a chart of habits I can practice to prevent the spread of pinkeye. I will track my progress for one week. Each day, I will make a check next to habits I have practiced.

	S	M	T	W	Th	F	S
Washed hands after using the restroom							
Washed hands before and after eating							
Stayed away from anyone who had pinkeye							
Kept from touching my face, especially my eyes							

How My Plan Worked: (Complete after one week) _____

_____

Solution Select a health goal about controlling the spread of disease. Write a Health Behavior Contract to outline what you will do to prevent pinkeye.

Learn This Life Skill

Follow these steps to help you set your health goal.
The Foldables™ can help you.

1 **Write the health goal you want to set.**

You might choose the health goal that says: I will
choose habits that prevent the spread of pathogens.

2 **Explain how your goal might affect your health.**

Write a statement that tells how practicing these habits
will keep you or your classmates from getting pinkeye.

3 **Describe a plan you will follow to reach your goal.
Keep track of your progress.**

Make a Health Behavior Contract like the one on the
previous page. Decide how long you will work at your
goal. Who can help you practice the health habits you
have listed?

4 **Evaluate how your plan worked.**

Did you have any problems? How would you change the
Health Behavior Contract to deal with the problems?

Practice This Life Skill

Write a plan to follow in order to prevent another
disease from spreading at school.

Chronic Diseases

If you get a cold, you usually have it for about seven days. People with allergies or asthma can be bothered off and on all of their lives. They can learn how to manage their health problems.

Causes of Chronic Disease

A **chronic disease** is a disease that lasts a long time or comes back from time to time, often over a lifetime. Chronic diseases have four main causes: pathogens, environmental factors, unhealthful habits, and inherited traits.

 What are four main causes of chronic diseases?

Chronic Diseases			
Cause	**Disease Agent**	**Disease/Reaction**	**Prevention/Treatment**
Pathogens	Bacteria, viruses, or other pathogens carried by ticks, mosquitos or other agents	Lyme disease Rocky Mountain spotted fever West Nile virus Encephalitis	Wear long sleeve shirts. Wear pants tucked into boots. Use sprays to keep ticks or mosquitos off.
Environmental factors	Secondhand smoke	Lung cancer	Stay away from secondhand smoke.
	Sun	Skin cancer	Don't get sunburned. Use sunscreen with SPF 15 or higher.
	Allergens	Allergy Skin rashes Difficulty breathing	Allergies may be treated with various medicines.
Harmful habits	Alcohol	Alcoholism Liver disease	Do not drink alcohol.
	Tobacco	Lung disease	Do not smoke cigarettes.
	Harmful eating habits/lack of exercise	Heart disease Obesity Type 2 diabetes	Eat healthful foods. Follow dietary guidelines. Get physical activity every day.
Inherited traits	Some diseases are traits that are passed from birth parents.	Cystic fibrosis Sickle-cell disease Hemophilia	These diseases require long-term treatment by a doctor.

Diabetes

The cells of your body use sugar from food for energy. **Diabetes** is a chronic disease in which there is too much sugar in the blood. There are two main forms of diabetes: *type 1 diabetes* and *type 2 diabetes*.

Type 1 Diabetes *Type 1 diabetes* is a chronic disease that begins in childhood and is a lifelong illness. In this form, the body makes little or no insulin. *Insulin* (IN•suh•luhn) is a substance that helps your cells obtain and use sugar. The exact cause of type 1 diabetes is not known.

A person with type 1 diabetes must control blood sugar level by testing his or her blood each day. He or she has to take shots of insulin each day. The person needs to exercise regularly and follow a healthful diet that is low in sugar.

Type 2 Diabetes *Type 2 diabetes* is the more common form of diabetes. In this form, the body makes some insulin, but does not use it well. Type 2 diabetes can be prevented or controlled with a healthful diet and exercise.

Type 2 diabetes usually occurs in adults, but it is becoming more common in children. Children who are overweight and physically inactive have increased risk for type 2 diabetes. You can reduce your risk for this disease by keeping a healthful weight and by being active every day.

ACTIVITY

Art LINK

Design a Poster

Design a poster to encourage people to walk more. Walking helps prevent people from developing type 2 diabetes. Display your poster in the classroom.

▲ Thirty to sixty minutes of physical activity each day reduces your risk of type 2 diabetes.

 What are ways you can reduce your risk of developing type 2 diabetes?

Allergies

An **allergy** (AL•uhr•jee) is the body's overreaction to a substance. *Allergens* are substances that cause allergies. Common allergens are dust mites, pollen, mold, oils from poison ivy or poison oak, and pet dander. Dust mites are tiny insects that live in carpets and soft furniture in everyone's home. They feed on dander. *Dander* is tiny flakes of skin often attached to hair or feathers. Wheat products, nuts, seafood, eggs, and milk are common food allergens.

Reactions to Allergens

Eating a food you are allergic to may cause stomach cramps or breathing difficulty. You might get a rash and itch if you have an allergy to some medicines, poison ivy or poison oak. Breathing in pollen can cause your eyes to water, your nose to become stuffy, or you might have difficulty breathing. Some people have trouble breathing, pass out, or have other reactions to the venom in insect stings. You can reduce your risk of an allergy attack by keeping away from substances to which you know you are allergic.

- Stay away from pets if you are allergic to them.

- Don't smoke. Avoid secondhand smoke.

- Wear a mask if you or someone near you uses cleaners or other products that give off fumes. And open a window to allow ventilation.

What is an allergy?

CAREERS

Allergist

An allergist is a doctor who diagnoses and treats allergies. Allergists perform skin tests to find out what a person is allergic to. If the cause of an allergy is found, the allergist may give the person shots or other medicines to treat the allergy.

LOG ON www.mmhhealth.com
Find out more about other health careers.

Asthma

Asthma (AZ•muh) is a condition in which the small airways of the respiratory system become narrow. During an asthma attack, it is hard to breathe. A person with asthma may wheeze, sigh, cough, and gasp for air.

Anything that causes an asthma attack is called a *trigger*. Some common asthma triggers are colds, cold air, exercise, tobacco smoke, and some foods. Other triggers are allergens. Many people with asthma receive shots so that they will not react to allergens.

The best way to prevent reactions to triggers is to keep away from them. Here are some ways to reduce triggers that are breathed in.

- **Vacuum often.** Vacuum rugs and soft furniture often to remove particles that can trigger an attack.

- **Wash bedding weekly.** Soak sheets in warm water with laundry detergent and bleach for four hours every week. Then wash them in warm water. This will get rid of most dust mites and the flecks of skin that they feed on.

- **Don't put carpet in bedrooms.** Carpet collects dust, dust mites, and pet dander.

- **Stay away from wood burning stoves and fireplaces.** Many people with asthma choose not to have stoves or fireplaces because the particles in the smoke that are produced by burning wood can bring on an asthma attack.

▼ Vacuuming every week helps reduce pet dander and other particles in carpets. Special filters in some vacuum cleaners can remove a large number of particles that can make breathing difficult for people with allergies and asthma.

 **What is a trigger?**

Analyze What Influences Your Health

How can you choose a behavior that reduces your risk for a chronic disease?

1 **Identify people and things that can influence your health.** Suppose you have two friends with different habits. One likes to spend time in front of the TV after school. The other likes to play outside after school. Both friends want you to spend time with them today.

2 **Evaluate how these people and things can affect your health.** Think about each friend's actions. How might each affect your health? Record your ideas in a two-column chart.

3 **Choose healthful influences.** Which friend's influence is more healthful?

4 **Protect yourself against harmful influences.** Work with a partner. Role-play a conversation you might have to encourage the friend who watches TV to be more active.

LESSON REVIEW

Review Concepts

1. **List** the four main causes of chronic diseases.

2. **Describe** ways to prevent type 2 diabetes.

3. **Describe** three ways you can prevent allergy attacks.

4. **List** four ways to reduce triggers that can cause an asthma attack.

Critical Thinking

5. **Contrast** Describe the differences between type 1 and type 2 diabetes.

6. **LIFE SKILLS** **Analyze What Influences Your Health** Sandra has asthma and is allergic to pet dander. A friend who has a dog invites Sandra to a party. What should Sandra do?

Heart Disease

You will learn . . .

- what causes a heart attack.
- ways that you can reduce the risk of heart disease and having a premature heart attack.

Vocabulary

- **heart disease**, *D63*
- **heart attack**, *D63*
- **premature heart attack**, *D64*

Do you enjoy running and getting lots of exercise each day? Practicing healthful habits now can help reduce your risk of heart disease as an adult.

Causes of Heart Attack

Your heart is a muscle. It pumps blood to your body through blood vessels called arteries and veins. Blood carries oxygen to your body's cells. All body cells, including those that make up the heart, need a continuous supply of oxygen.

Heart disease is a chronic disease of the heart and blood vessels. The most common cause of heart disease is blocked blood vessels. *Coronary arteries* are blood vessels that carry blood to the heart muscle itself. Sometimes fat builds up inside the walls of the vessels. The opening becomes narrow. Blood flow slows down or stops. A **heart attack** is a sudden lack of blood to the heart muscle. When blood flow to the heart stops, oxygen does not reach the heart muscle. The cells of the heart muscle begin to die.

A heart attack is very serious. Many people who have a heart attack die. This can happen if a major artery to the heart is blocked. Many other people who have heart attacks live. They get help in time. They may have surgery or be given medicine to open the blocked artery.

 **What are warning signs of a heart attack?**

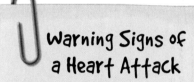

Warning Signs of a Heart Attack

If you see someone having any of these signs, get help immediately.

- pain in the jaw, chest, or upper body
- shortness of breath
- dizziness
- breaking out in a cold sweat

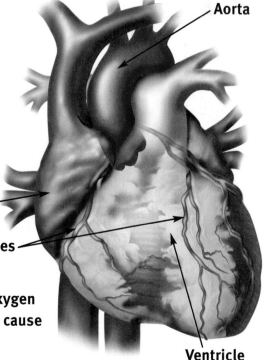

Aorta

Atrium

Coronary arteries

Ventricle

▶ Coronary arteries carry blood containing oxygen to the heart. A blocked coronary artery can cause a heart attack.

Reduce Risks for Heart Disease

Healthful habits that you form now can help reduce your risk of developing heart disease. If you make it a habit to practice heart healthy behaviors as you get older, you will reduce your risk of heart disease and premature heart attack. A **premature heart attack** is one that occurs before age 60. There are five actions you can take to reduce your risk.

1. **Eat a healthful diet.** Limit the amount of fatty foods you eat. Choose lean meats and poultry products. Choose low-fat dairy foods. Eat 3–5 servings of vegetables and 2–4 servings of fruits every day starting today. Eat whole-grain foods that are rich in fiber.

2. **Keep a healthful weight.** A person who is obese has too much body fat. If someone is obese as a young person, the chance of being obese as an adult is increased. Your heart must pump more often to move enough blood to your body cells if you are obese. This stresses the blood vessels and can lead to heart disease.

3. **Keep blood pressure in a healthful range.** *Blood pressure* is the force that blood puts on artery walls. The walls of arteries can be damaged if the force is too strong. You can help keep your blood pressure in a healthful range by staying at a healthful weight. Follow a diet that is low in salt. Be physically active every day.

ACTIVITY

On Your Own

FOR SCHOOL OR HOME

Make a Health Job Jar

Find ways to keep physically active. Take a jar and twelve index cards or pieces of paper about the same size. Label the jar **My Health Job Jar.** On each piece of paper, write a physical activity that you can do easily when you get home from school. One might be "Walk 1000 paces." Another might be "Walk up and down the stairs four times." Each afternoon when you get home, pick out one "job" to do that day. Record the date on the paper and return it to the jar.

4. Get regular physical activity.
Physical activity makes your heart muscle strong. A strong heart does not have to pump as often as a weak heart. Physical activity helps you stay at a healthful weight.

5. Keep away from tobacco.
Cigarettes contain nicotine and carbon monoxide. Nicotine makes the heart beat faster. It also raises blood pressure. Carbon monoxide replaces oxygen in the blood. The younger a person is when he or she starts to smoke, the greater the risk of a heart attack when the person is older.

 How does physical activity help your heart?

CRITICAL THINKING

Be a Health Advocate

Create a "Seven Days to Better Heart Health" booklet for someone you care about. On each page, make a suggestion for better heart health.

1 **Choose a healthful action to communicate.** List healthful habits that are important for heart health.

2 **Collect information about the action.** Decide which information to include.

3 **Decide how to communicate this information.** You want to make a booklet. Will it have a statement about a good health habit for each day? Will it have a place to write a journal each day?

4 **Communicate your message to others.** Share your booklet with your class.

LESSON REVIEW

Review Concepts

1. **Define** heart disease.

2. **Explain** what causes a heart attack.

3. **List** five ways to reduce risk of heart disease and premature heart attack.

Critical Thinking

4. **Infer** Your best friend's father is 35 and smokes regularly. How might this habit affect his father's heart and blood vessels? How might it affect your friend's heart later in life?

5. **Be a Health Advocate** Design a colorful poster that encourages your family to choose habits that prevent heart attacks. What important facts will you include?

Cancer

You will learn . . .

- ways to reduce the risk of skin cancer.
- ways to reduce the risk of lung cancer.
- ways to reduce the risk of colon cancer.

Vocabulary

- **cancer**, *D67*
- **radon**, *D67*

Many parts of the body can be affected by cancer. Habits that you choose now, including the types of snacks you eat, can reduce your risk of the most common forms of cancer.

Types of Cancer

Cancer is a disease in which cells grow in ways that are not normal. There are many types of cancer, including skin cancer, lung cancer, and colon cancer.

Skin Cancer According to the Centers for Disease Control, skin cancer is the most common kind of cancer in the United States. Skin cancer can be caused by harmful rays from the sun and by sun lamps and tanning beds. You are at risk for skin cancer if you spend time unprotected in the sun. Factors that increase your risk for skin cancer later in life are having serious sunburns as a child and having fair skin. You can reduce your risk. Use sunscreen with an SPF (Sun Protection Factor) of 15 or higher and stay covered when you are out in the sun.

Lung Cancer More people die from lung cancer each year than from any other form of cancer. The leading cause of lung cancer is cigarette smoking. Cigar and pipe smokers also are at risk. People who do not smoke are at risk if exposed to secondhand smoke.

Another substance that can lead to lung cancer is radon. **Radon** is a colorless, odorless gas that comes from rocks and clay soils. It leaks into buildings through cracks in basement floors.

Colon Cancer The colon is the large intestine. Undigested food moves through the colon as waste. A bowel movement removes the waste from the colon. Eating foods with fiber and drinking plenty of water helps you have a daily bowel movement. Colon cancer is more common among people over 50 years of age. It is the second most common cause of cancer-related death.

What is cancer?

Con\$umer Wi\$e

Analyze Food Labels

Collect food labels from 10 different food products. Make a poster that compares the foods according to the amount of fiber per serving. You can find out if a food contains fiber by reading the label. A food is low in fiber if its Percent Daily Value of fiber is less than 5 percent. A food with a Percent Daily Value of 20 percent or more is high in fiber.

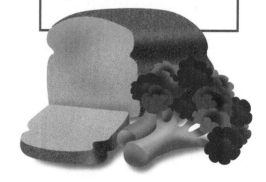

Reduce the Risk of Cancer

You have read about skin, lung, and colon cancers. You can learn about and practice behaviors that reduce your risk of getting these cancers.

Reduce the risk of skin cancer.

- Do not sunbathe to try to get a tan.
- Limit the time in the sun between 10:00 A.M. and 4:00 P.M. The sun's harmful rays are strongest during these hours.
- Wear a sunscreen with a SPF of 15 or higher when you go outside. Wear sunscreen all year long, not just in summer.
- Wear long-sleeved shirts, long pants, wide-brimmed hats, and sunglasses when outdoors.
- Do not use a sunlamp or a tanning bed. These devices have the same harmful rays as the sun.

Reduce the risk of colon cancer.

- Eat plenty of fiber. You can get fiber in fruits, vegetables, and whole-grain products.
- Eat few fatty foods. Choose low-fat foods and snacks. Eat lean meats and poultry.

Reduce the risk of lung cancer.

- Do not smoke. This rule includes cigarettes, pipes, and cigars.
- Avoid breathing secondhand smoke.

TOBACCO USE PROHIBITED

USO DE TABACO ES PROHIBIDO

Set Health Goals

Marisa knows that she needs to eat more vegetables, but she says that she just doesn't like them. How can you help Marisa to plan to eat more healthfully?

1 **Write the health goal you want to set.** Help Marisa start a journal. In it she can write I will eat the correct number of servings from the Food Guide Pyramid.

2 **Explain how your goal might affect your health.** Explain that she can reduce her risk of certain forms of cancer later in life by eating healthfully now.

3 **Describe a plan you will follow to reach your goal. Keep track of your progress.** Tell Marisa that she can begin by eating small amounts. In her journal, Marisa can write a Health Behavior Contract for what vegetables she will try each day.

4 **Evaluate how your plan worked.** Did Marisa's plan work? What obstacles, if any, prevented her from completing her plan? What new ways might she try?

LESSON REVIEW

Review Concepts

1. **Explain** what kinds of foods you should eat to help prevent colon cancer.

2. **Discuss** how you can find out if there is radon where you live.

3. **List** three habits that decrease your risk of getting skin cancer.

Critical Thinking

4. **Synthesize** What healthful habits protect you from lung and colon cancer and also from heart disease?

5. **LIFE SKILLS** **Set Health Goals** Set a health goal to choose habits that prevent skin cancer. Make a Health Behavior Contract to show your plan. Evaluate your plan.

CHAPTER 8 REVIEW

Use Vocabulary

antibody, *D47*

cancer, *D67*

diabetes, *D58*

heart attack, *D63*

pathogen, *D39*

symptom, *D51*

Choose the correct term from the list to complete each sentence.

1. A substance that your body makes to fight a pathogen while it is attacking you is a(n) __?__ .

2. Having a headache may be a __?__ of disease.

3. Cells that grow in ways that are not normal may be a sign of __?__ .

4. A(n) __?__ occurs when blood flow stops to the heart muscle.

5. A germ that causes a communicable disease is a(n) __?__ .

6. A chronic disease in which there is too much sugar in the blood is called __?__ .

Review Concepts

Answer each question in complete sentences.

7. Name four pathogens and a disease that each one causes.

8. What habits help protect you against diseases spread by pathogens?

9. What are the symptoms of strep throat? How is strep throat treated?

10. List three common triggers of asthma. Tell how you can reduce asthma triggers.

11. What is a premature heart attack? How can it be avoided?

Reading Comprehension

Answer each question in complete sentences.

Right away, your body starts to make antibodies that fight the measles virus. Measles antibodies stay in your body after you are well. If the measles virus attacks you again, the antibodies that you made the first time keep you from getting the disease again.

12. What does your body do when it is attacked by the measles virus?

13. Why don't you get measles again if the virus attacks you again?

14. What happens to measles antibodies after you are well?

D70

Critical Thinking/Problem Solving

Answer each question in complete sentences.

Analyze Concepts

15. What are the first-line defenses to keep pathogens from entering the body?

16. What are the differences between type 1 and type 2 diabetes?

17. What is the most common cause of heart disease?

18. How does keeping a healthful weight reduce the risk of heart disease?

19. Why should a person with asthma avoid putting a carpet in his or her bedroom?

Practice Life Skills

20. **Practice Healthful Behaviors** Heart disease is a chronic disease of the heart or blood vessels. What healthful behaviors can you practice to keep your heart healthy?

21. **Make Responsible Decisions** It's picture day at school. Your turn is next. You want to comb your hair, but you didn't bring a comb with you. A classmate offers you his. Should you use the comb? Explain.

Read Graphics

Use the chart below to answer questions 22–25.

Signs and Symptoms of Some Diseases	
Illness	**Signs and Symptoms**
Cold	Tiredness, cough, sore throat, stuffy or runny nose, sneezing, watery eyes
Flu	Fever, tiredness, cough, headache, decreased appetite, body aches, chills
Strep throat	Sore throat, gray and white patches on throat, body aches, fever, loss of appetite, often swelling in the throat
Chicken pox	Fever, itchy skin rash that looks like small blisters or spots
Lyme disease	"Bull's-eye" rash, tiredness, headache, stiff neck, fever, chills, muscle and joint pain
West Nile virus	Fever, headaches, body aches, upset stomach. Serious cases can sometimes lead to shaking, numbness, and vision problems.

22. Describe the differences between the symptoms of a cold and the flu.

23. Which illnesses usually cause a fever?

24. In serious cases, which illness could cause vision problems?

25. Describe the differences between the skin rashes caused by chicken pox and Lyme disease.

 LOG ON **www.mmhhealth.com** Find out how much you know about health concepts.

Effective Communication

Make a Comic Book

Draw a series of pictures in comic book format in which a friendly character describes how to wash your hands and how it reduces the risk of becoming ill.

Self-Directed Learning

Learn About a Disease

Research the history of a disease such as smallpox, malaria, yellow fever, or cholera. Find out where the disease has occurred in different parts of the world and how it is treated.

Critical Thinking and Problem Solving

Use a Diagram

The ways in which your body fights disease is called "defense." Make a diagram to explain how the body fights disease and what happens when the pathogens break through.

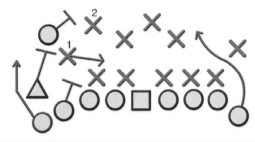

Responsible Citizenship

Interview an EMT

Ask your teacher to invite an Emergency Medical Technician (EMT) to your class to explain the training that he or she undergoes. What types of work do EMTs perform in your community?

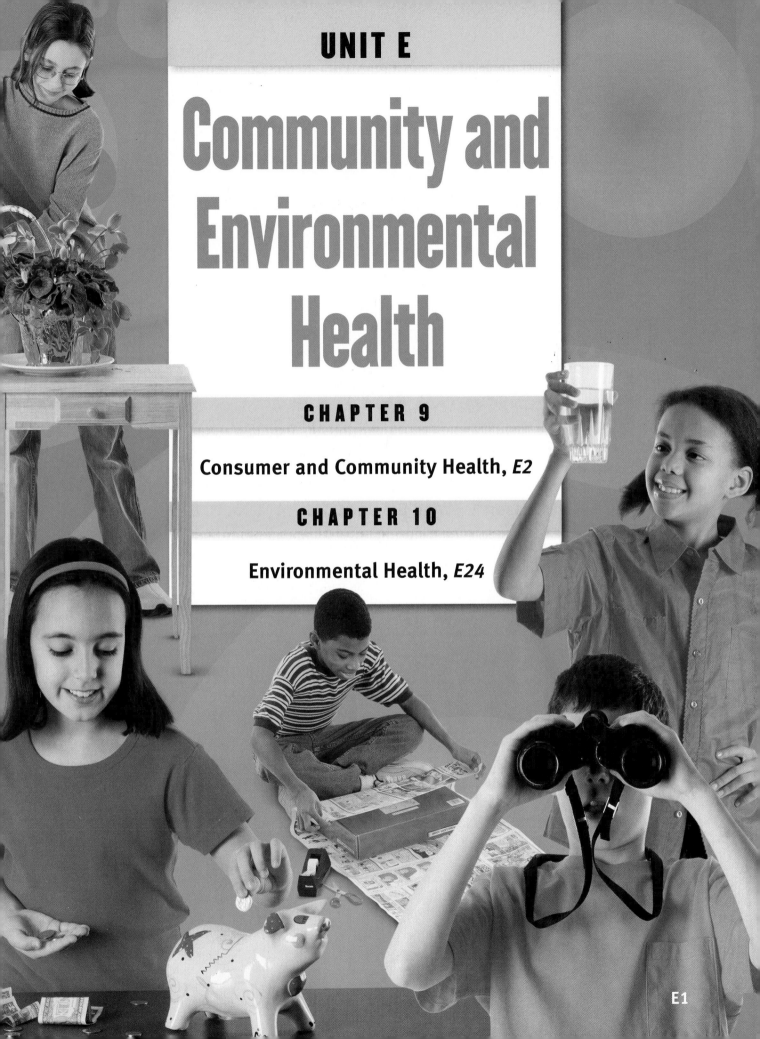

UNIT E

Community and Environmental Health

CHAPTER 9

Consumer and Community Health, *E2*

CHAPTER 10

Environmental Health, *E24*

CHAPTER 9

Consumer and Community Health

PERFECTVIEW

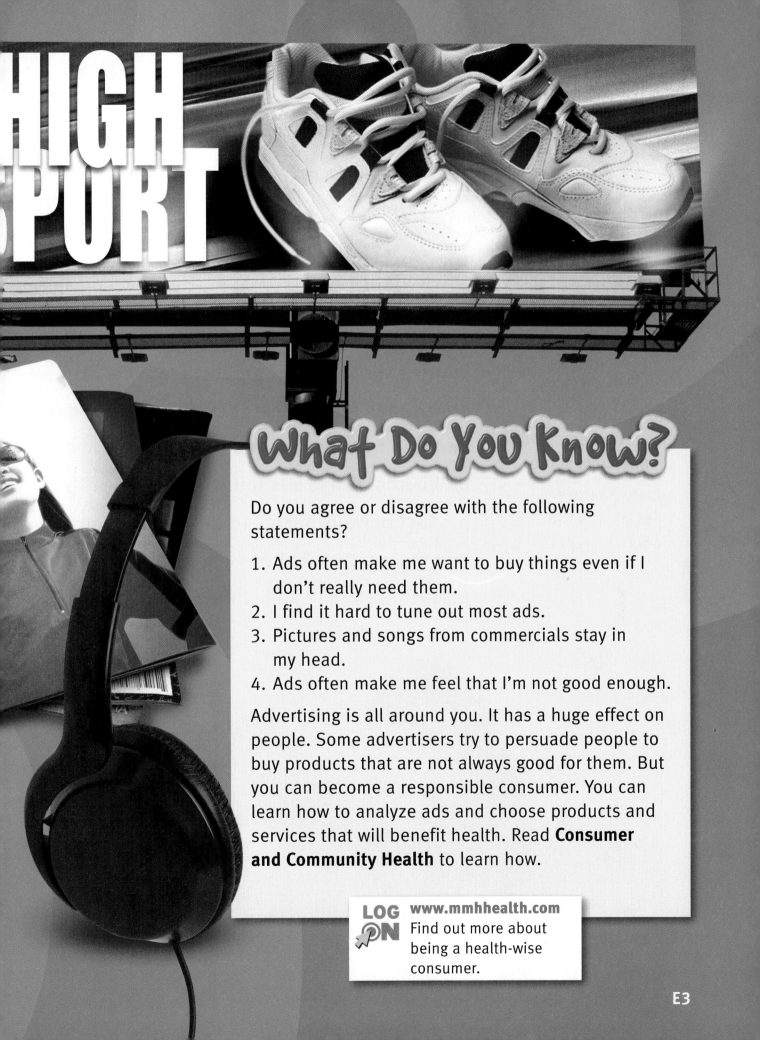

HIGH
SPORT

What Do You Know?

Do you agree or disagree with the following statements?

1. Ads often make me want to buy things even if I don't really need them.
2. I find it hard to tune out most ads.
3. Pictures and songs from commercials stay in my head.
4. Ads often make me feel that I'm not good enough.

Advertising is all around you. It has a huge effect on people. Some advertisers try to persuade people to buy products that are not always good for them. But you can become a responsible consumer. You can learn how to analyze ads and choose products and services that will benefit health. Read **Consumer and Community Health** to learn how.

LOG ON www.mmhhealth.com
Find out more about being a health-wise consumer.

E3

Consumers and Advertising

You will learn . . .

- what purpose advertisements and commercials serve.
- how to analyze messages in the media.

Vocabulary

- **commercial,** *E5*
- **media,** *E5*

You see thousands of products for sale in stores. Ads for many of these products appear on TV, in newspapers and magazines, and on billboards. These ads tell you about the product in ways designed to convince you to buy the product. But do they always tell you everything you need to know to make wise consumer choices?

Advertising and the Media

You may see ads in the media. **Media** are ways of sending information to people. TV, radio, movies, newspapers, and magazines are media. An ad, or *advertisement*, that uses words and pictures can be found in printed materials and on billboards. A **commercial** is an ad on the radio or television.

Companies place commercials in TV shows that young people like to watch. They put ads in magazines that young people like to read. Do you ever wear clothing with the name of the clothing company on it? You advertise that company's name every time you wear that pair of jeans, shoes, shirt, or hat.

Suppose you see ads for a particular sports drink on TV, in magazines, and in newspapers. You are more likely to remember a product that is advertised often. Advertisers hope that you are more likely to want to buy it, too. Some ads are for health-care products. A *health-care product* is an item that is used for health. Toothpaste, bandages, and aspirin are examples of health-care products.

ACTIVITY

Art LINK

Design a Label

Choose a health-care product such as shampoo. Design a new label for it. Make sure it shows a person who has benefited from the product. You can exaggerate the benefits to add comic effect. Describe the product. After reading your description, everybody should want to buy the product.

What are three kinds of media?

▶ **TV, radio, magazines, and newspapers are all media.**

Analyzing Ads

Ask Five Questions

Choose an ad. Then ask yourself these questions:

- Who made the ad?

- What is the ad trying to make me do?

- How does the ad appeal to me?

- Is the ad trying to make me do something responsible?

- Did the person who wrote the ad leave out any facts? Why?

Write your answers on a sheet of paper. Present the ad and your answers to your class.

You may see dozens of ads each day. Companies spend millions of dollars to make ads. They use many tricks to make you want to buy their brands.

Ads may show famous entertainers or sports stars. Famous people are paid to be in ads. Companies think that using famous people will make you notice the ad. They know that this method of advertising will make you more likely to buy the product.

Ads also may use humor. They may use catchy tunes. If you think an ad is funny or you like the music in an ad, you might be more likely to remember it. You also might be more likely to buy the product.

Read ads carefully. Use the five questions listed here to analyze the ads. This will help you to make responsible decisions about products.

- **Who made the ad?** You watch an ad for sneakers on TV. The sneakers seem great. Who made the ad? The company that makes the sneakers designed the ad.

- **What is the ad trying to make me do?** The ad is trying to make me buy the sneakers. It might try to make you think that the sneakers will help you jump higher. Is this true?

- **How does the ad appeal to me?** Why do I like the ad? Does liking an ad make the sneakers better?

▲ Think about what makes an ad appealing to you.

- **Is the ad encouraging me to do something responsible?** You see a sports star on TV. The sports star wears expensive sneakers. You like the sports star. Is this a good reason to buy the sneakers?

- **Did the ad leave out any facts? Why?** Are the sneakers very expensive? The ad isn't going to tell you this. A few facts might make you less likely to buy the product. Ads might leave these facts out.

  Reading an ad carefully can help you make responsible decisions about health care products.

Why might you see famous people in ads?

ACTIVITY — LIFE SKILLS · CRITICAL THINKING

Make Responsible Decisions

You see an ad for a video game that offers free Internet time if you purchase the game by a certain date. Would buying the game based on the ad offer be a responsible decision?

1. **Identify your choices. Check them out with your parent or trusted adult.** Make a list of your choices.

2. **Evaluate each choice. Use the _Guidelines for Making Responsible Decisions™_.** Ask the six questions for each choice. Make a checkmark next to the choice each time you answer "yes."

3. **Identify the responsible decision. Check this out with your parent or trusted adult.** Underline the choice with the most checkmarks.

4. **Evaluate your decision.** Explain why you think your decision was responsible.

LESSON REVIEW

Review Concepts

1. **Explain** why an ad might use humor.

2. **List** five questions to use to analyze an ad carefully.

3. **Define** the term _media_.

4. **Explain** how a TV commercial is different from a newspaper ad.

Critical Thinking

5. **Analyze** Why do companies spend millions of dollars to make ads?

6. **LIFE SKILLS** **Make Responsible Decisions** Your younger brother's favorite singing group appears in a TV ad, all wearing a new kind of sunglasses. Your brother tells you he wants the glasses. How can you help him decide?

Wise Buys

You will learn . . .

- to identify responsible ways to spend money.
- to identify responsible ways to spend time.
- how to choose healthful entertainment.

Vocabulary

- **entertainment**, *E12*

How do you spend your time? How do you spend your money? You have many choices. Plan to use both your time and your money wisely.

Be Money Wise

Do you have money to spend each week? Maybe you receive an allowance from your parents or guardian. Maybe you earn money for doing chores. It's important to manage your money.

Managing Your Money

Money that you receive or earn is called *income*. An *expense* is money that you spend for something you need or want. When you manage money wisely, your expenses are never more than your income.

- **Basic Expenses** Do you buy your lunch every day? Maybe you need a new notebook. Make sure that you have enough income to cover these expenses.

- **Other Purchases** For some purchases, you need to save a small amount of money each week.

- **Saving** In addition to basic expenses, it is wise to set aside a small part of your income for future purchases. You can save this money in a bank account.

 Why is it a good idea to save money?

In the first column write down the money you receive each week. This is your *income* for the week.

In a second column, list items that you need and want to buy. Include the price of each item. These are *expenses*.

Make a column for the amount you want to save for the future.

Add up each column. What is the amount in the expense column? It should be equal to or less than the amount in the income column.

▲ To save money, open a bank account with your parents or guardian.

▼ A *budget* is a plan for your money. Write your weekly budget in columns on a sheet of paper.

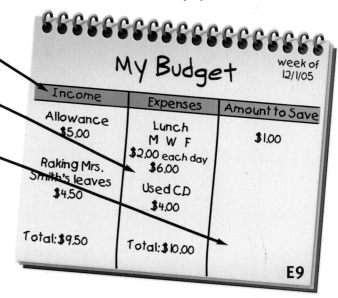

My Budget week of 12/1/05

Income	Expenses	Amount to Save
Allowance $5.00	Lunch M W F $2.00 each day $6.00	$1.00
Raking Mrs. Smith's leaves $4.50	Used CD $4.00	
Total: $9.50	Total: $10.00	

E9

Spend Time Wisely

Managing your time can be like managing money. There are twenty-four hours in a day. How do you spend that time?

Write down how much time you spend attending school, doing homework, being physically active, being with friends and family, or being alone. Include time spent eating and sleeping. Do you have any free time at the end of the day? Make a plan to spend your time wisely. Watching television or playing video games should not be a priority.

- **Homework** Try to do your homework at the same time each day. Maybe you can do it after sports practice or before dinner. Work in a quiet place to avoid distractions caused by TV, music, and other sounds. First make sure that you have what you need to do your homework. Then complete your homework in the time you planned.

- **Physical Activity** Where can you fit in time to ride your bike? Go skating? Take a walk? Play baseball? Being active improves mental and physical health. It helps lower stress. It is time well spent.

- **Interests** There are many fun, healthful things that you can do during free time. If you manage your time, you benefit because you have time to participate in sports, play music, or develop a hobby. You'll feel good about yourself and increase your self-respect.

- **Family and Friends** It's fun to be with family and friends. It can lower stress. Talk about your day. Talk about things that are important to you. Ask your family and friends about things that are important to them.

- **Time Alone** Spend time by yourself each day to relax. Relaxing after a busy day can give your body the rest it needs to repair and regain energy. Think about your day. Plan what you want to do. Some people daydream. Many musicians, poets, writers, and inventors spend a lot of time alone.

Think about this week. How will you spend your time? Make a plan to manage your time wisely.

On Your Own

ACTIVITY

FOR SCHOOL OR HOME

Time for Family

Brainstorm with your family, activities you can do together. You might take a walk together, visit a museum, or go to the park. You could attend a band concert or stay home and play a board game together. Choose an activity to do together.

► Spend time each week doing something you enjoy.

 List three ways to spend your time wisely.

Choose Healthful Entertainment

Reading stickers on computer games can help you avoid those with violence.

Entertainment is something that interests or amuses you. For entertainment, you might read a book, watch TV, or go to the movies. You might play a team sport, ice skate, or shoot baskets. Healthful entertainment helps you learn and have fun.

Some entertainment can be harmful. Some video games, movies, and TV programs show people practicing dangerous behaviors. They might show people hurting each other or using illegal drugs. Here are some suggestions to help you and your family choose healthful entertainment.

- **Choose entertainment that helps you learn.** You can learn about science, history, or other countries from TV shows. You can read a good book or play games that help you learn. You can have fun while you learn.

- **Choose video games, movies, and TV programs that show people with good character.** Think about the kinds of people you admire. Do they respect others? Do they care about others? Do they solve problems peacefully? Think about the actors you see in TV shows and movies. Do they show character traits that you should imitate?

- **Choose computer games carefully.** Using the computer can be fun. But some computer games show violence. Read the stickers on computer games. This helps you and your family avoid buying those that are violent.

What is healthful entertainment?

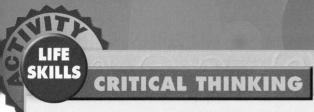
Set Health Goals

Many young people your age enjoy going to the movies. Some movies are healthful entertainment, but some are not. Following these steps can help a person choose healthful entertainment.

1 **Write the health goal you want to set.** I will choose healthful entertainment. Make a Health Behavior Contract. Describe what you should look for in movies for healthful entertainment.

2 **Explain how your goal might affect your health.** How will being responsible in choosing movies help you? Write this in your Health Behavior Contract.

3 **Describe a plan you will follow to reach your goal. Keep track of your progress.** Write your rules for choosing healthful entertainment. Choose movies that contain healthful entertainment. Make a check mark each time you do. Tell who can help you reach your goal.

4 **Evaluate how your plan worked.** Look at your chart after one month. Did you choose healthful entertainment? What other choices could you have made?

LESSON REVIEW

Review Concepts

1. **Explain** how a budget can help you spend money wisely.

2. **List** some healthful ways to spend your free time.

3. **Explain** what the term *healthful entertainment* means.

Critical Thinking

4. **Evaluate** Explain why video games that show characters harming others are not healthful entertainment.

5. **LIFE SKILLS** **Set Health Goals** You want a new skateboard. It costs more money than you have. You could ask your parents or guardian to buy it for you. What is a responsible way to obtain it?

Make Responsible Decisions

Problem Kevin and Gina are channel surfing. Kevin clicks to a program that has a lot of violence. What should Kevin do?

> "What's this? I've never seen it before . . . Who talks like THAT?"

> "I don't know, it might be fun to watch. Watching it once won't harm us."

Solution Sometimes it's difficult to decide if a TV show is healthful entertainment. Using the steps on the next page can help you make a responsible decision.

Learn This Life Skill

Follow these steps to help you make responsible decisions about TV programs and movies. The Foldables™ can help.

1 **Identify your choices. Check them out with your parent or trusted adult.**

Kevin can watch the program or change the channel. Write your choices for selecting TV shows and movies.

2 **Evaluate each choice. Use the *Guidelines for Making Responsible Decisions™*.**

For each choice, ask yourself the following questions.

- Is it healthful?
- Is it safe?
- Does it follow rules and laws?
- Does it show respect for myself and others?
- Does it show family guidelines?
- Does it show good character?

3 **Identify the responsible decision. Check this out with your parent or trusted adult.**

Talk with someone who can help you identify healthful programs and movies.

4 **Evaluate your decision.**

What should you do if a TV program shows behavior that is not healthful?

Practice This Life Skill

Your friend wants to see a film that is very violent. Draw a four-panel cartoon showing how you will use the four steps to make a responsible decision.

Community Health Care

You will learn . . .

- what health careers benefit your community.
- where health helpers work in your community.

Vocabulary

- **community**, *E17*
- **career**, *E17*
- **psychiatrist**, *E18*
- **clinic**, *E19*
- **inpatient**, *E20*
- **outpatient**, *E20*

Who are your community's health helpers? Where can you find them? It's good to know where you can get help. It's also good to know what health helpers do. You might want to be a health helper one day.

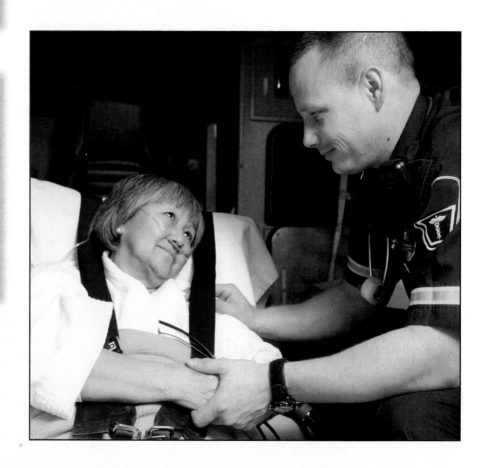

Community Health

A **community** is a place where a group of people live. Your community has many people who help you stay healthy. These people are *health helpers*. Doctors, nurses, and dentists are health helpers. Safety workers and sanitation workers are also health helpers.

Groups or associations such as the American Heart Association (AHA) help to improve community health. The AHA works to prevent and control diseases of the heart and blood vessels. The American Lung Association works to prevent and control diseases of the lungs. Health helpers with these groups learn about diseases and teach the public how to be healthy. They also may help raise funds for heart or lung research.

You might like to have a career as a health helper. A **career** is the work that a person prepares for and does throughout life. You can talk to health helpers in your community. You can learn about what they do.

BUILD ACTIVITY Character
Recycling at Your School

Citizenship Recycling helps the environment. It helps keep your community clean. Does your school have a recycling program? If it does, find out if you can volunteer to help. If not, why not start one? Set up a program to recycle paper, bottles, and cans. Ask your teacher for permission and for help.

◀ Safety workers include firefighters and police officers. They help protect you in an emergency.

 What groups in your community work to improve health?

▶ Sanitation workers keep the community clean. They pick up trash, collect materials to be recycled, and clean the streets. A clean community is a more healthful place to live.

Getting Health Care

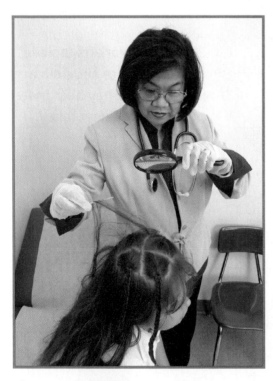
Who do you go to when you are ill? Who will help if you are injured? Who do you see when you need a health exam? There are many places in your community where you benefit from health care.

At Home You get health care at home. When you're ill, you tell your parents or guardians. They care for you at home if you have a cold. They might give you medicine.

At School Some schools have a nurse who cares for injured or ill students. The school nurse might also teach students about health. Many large schools also work with a doctor who specializes in sports-related health. This doctor goes to games and often travels with sports teams. He or she can help if there are injuries during a game.

Doctor's Offices Many doctors work at offices where they treat ill patients and provide checkups. Some doctors are general family practice doctors. Others are specialists. They treat specific illnesses or body systems such as bones or the heart.

Mental Health Centers Some people get care at mental health centers. People go to these centers to talk with a psychiatrist (sy•KY•uh•trist). A **psychiatrist** is a doctor who specializes in mental and emotional health. *Psychologists* (sy•KAWL•uh•jists) and *social workers* are also trained in mental and emotional health. *Counselors* help people with stress and changes in their lives. If you are worried or feel stress, you should talk with your parents or guardian.

▲ **Some schools have nurses to care for students.**

Community Health Departments A community health department is an agency that oversees the health of a town or city. Health department workers may give people vaccinations. They keep track of diseases that appear in the community to help stop dangerous diseases from spreading.

Some health department workers are health inspectors. They make sure that businesses such as grocery stores, hair salons, and restaurants are clean. They check that the people who work in these businesses are healthy. They also might check health conditions at nursing homes and day care centers.

Health Clinics A clinic provides many kinds of health care. A **clinic** is a place where health care is given to people who do not need to stay in a hospital. Workers at a health clinic might provide care for many kinds of health problems. Some clinics specialize. That means that workers in the clinic might treat just one type of health problem. There are eye clinics, mental health clinics, clinics for bone diseases, and clinics that specialize in children's health. Some communities have clinics that give low-cost health care.

Health Online

Locate Your Community Hospital

Research a hospital in your community. Find out what types of health care are provided there. Use the e-Journal writing tool to write a report on your findings. Visit **www.mmhhealth.com** and click on ℮-Journal.

Hospitals Doctors and nurses often work in hospitals. They are there to care for people all day and night. Some of the people who go to hospitals are inpatients. An **inpatient** is a person who must stay in a hospital at least overnight for treatment. Many people who have surgery stay in the hospital. A woman might stay in a hospital to have a baby.

Other people who go to hospitals are outpatients. An **outpatient** is a person who receives treatment in a hospital but does not stay overnight. Outpatients may visit the hospital for a health test. They may visit for an exam. As outpatients, they may stay in the hospital for a few hours and then go home.

You can get emergency health care at the hospital. Suppose you are riding a bike. You fall and hurt yourself. Your parents or guardian might take you to the emergency room. People hurt in car crashes are taken by emergency workers to an emergency room.

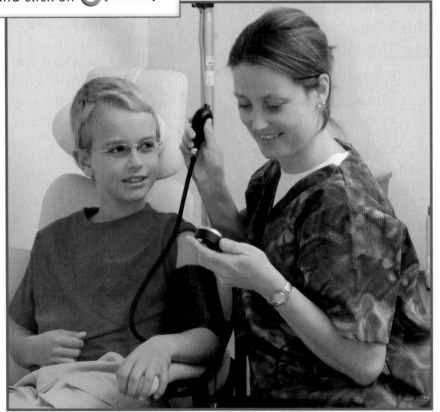

◀ A nurse is a health helper who works in many different types of facilities in the community.

 List three places where you can get health care in your community.

Access Health Facts, Products, and Services

Do you know where your community's health department is located? Where are the different kinds of clinics located in your community? Team up with a classmate to find out.

1 **Identify when you might need health services.** List the health care you might need. Where would you go if you needed emergency care?

2 **Identify where you might find health services.** How can you find health services? Where could you get a flu shot in your community? Look in a phone book. Where else might you find what you want to know?

3 **Find the health services you need.** Find the addresses of nearby hospitals and clinics. List them on a sheet of paper. Make a map of the area around your school. Hang the map on a cork board. Use push pins of one color to show where hospitals are. Use push pins of other colors to show other places where you can get health care.

4 **Evaluate the health services.** Where would people go for emergency health care? Where would they go if a tooth hurts? Write the information next to the map.

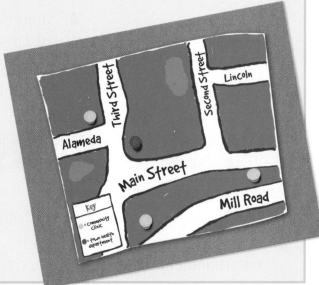

LESSON REVIEW

Review Concepts

1. **List** the workers who help keep your community healthy.

2. **Describe** what health inspectors do to keep your life healthy.

3. **Name** two health helpers who work in a mental health center.

4. **Explain** the difference between a hospital and a clinic.

Critical Thinking

5. **Contrast** Describe the difference between inpatient and outpatient hospital services.

6. **LIFE SKILLS** **Access Health Facts** A doctor says you must have an MRI on your knee. You want to know more about the test. Where can you learn what an MRI is and what this test will show?

CHAPTER 9 REVIEW

Use Vocabulary

career, *E17*

clinic, *E19*

commercial, *E5*

community, *E17*

entertainment, *E12*

media, *E5*

psychiatrist, *E18*

Choose the correct term from the list to complete each sentence. Write the word on a separate sheet of paper.

1. Sources of news and information are the __?__.

2. A place where medical care is given to outpatients is a(n) __?__.

3. The work that a person prepares for and performs throughout life is a(n) __?__.

4. An ad on the radio or TV is a(n) __?__.

5. A place where a group of people lives is their __?__.

6. Something that interests and amuses you is called __?__.

7. A doctor who specializes in mental and emotional health is a(n) __?__.

Review Concepts

Answer each question in complete sentences.

8. Describe an example of healthful entertainment that helps you learn.

9. List three kinds of health care that you can get at a hospital.

10. Identify the information that you list in a budget.

11. List two private groups that work to promote health knowledge.

12. List three kinds of health-care products.

13. Identify ways to spend free time wisely.

Reading Comprehension

Answer each question in complete sentences.

Ads may show famous entertainers or sports stars. Famous people are paid to be in ads. Companies think that using famous people will make you notice the ad. They know that this method of advertising will make you more likely to buy the product.

Ads also may use humor or catchy tunes. If you think an ad is funny or you like the music in an ad, you might be more likely to remember it. You also may be more likely to buy the product.

14. Why do companies use famous people in ads?

15. Why might ads use humor or catchy tunes?

Critical Thinking/Problem Solving

Answer each question in complete sentences.

Analyze Concepts

16. You made a time plan for your day. Every hour is filled with school, homework, chores, and activities you must do such as eating, bathing, and sleeping. How can you improve your plan?

17. Why do the media contain ads?

18. An ad tells you about a new drink. The ad makes it look like the drink will make you stronger. What can you do to find out if this is reliable health information?

19. A person is hurt in a car accident. Which community health helpers might aid the person?

20. You make a budget. The amount in the income column adds up to $4.50. The amount in the expense column totals $5.25. What does this mean?

Practice Life Skills

21. **Make Responsible Decisions** You have saved money to buy a notebook that you need. You go to the store and notice something that you want. You don't have enough money to buy both. Use the *Guidelines for Making Responsible Decisions*™ to help you decide what to do.

22. **Analyze Influences on Your Health** How do health helpers in your community influence you to stay healthy?

Read Graphics

Use the chart below to answer questions 23–25.

Community Health Care		
Community Services	**Hospitals**	**Clinics**
Food inspection	General hospital	Eye, ears, nose clinic
Senior care	Children's hospital	Sports clinic
Water department	Emergency care unit	Cancer clinic
Sanitation		Cardiac-care clinic

23. **a.** What group would you contact if you have a complaint about sanitation in a restaurant?

b. Where might a person go to have cancer treatment?

c. Where would you go to have a football injury treated?

d. Where would a person with a heart attack be taken?

24. Where might you go for emergency health treatment?

25. What group might be called on to clear the roads in a snowstorm?

LOG ON www.mmhhealth.com Find out how much you know about consumer and community health.

CHAPTER 10
Environmental Health

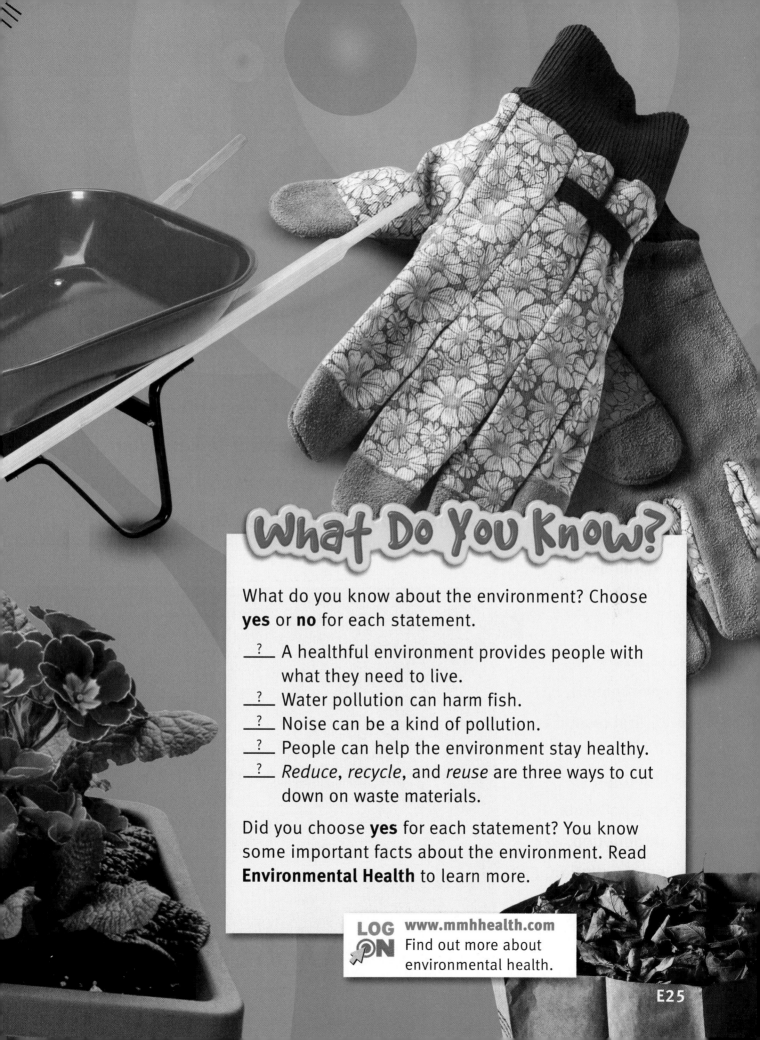

What Do You Know?

What do you know about the environment? Choose **yes** or **no** for each statement.

_?_ A healthful environment provides people with what they need to live.

_?_ Water pollution can harm fish.

_?_ Noise can be a kind of pollution.

_?_ People can help the environment stay healthy.

_?_ *Reduce*, *recycle*, and *reuse* are three ways to cut down on waste materials.

Did you choose **yes** for each statement? You know some important facts about the environment. Read **Environmental Health** to learn more.

LOG ON www.mmhhealth.com
Find out more about environmental health.

E25

A Healthful Environment

You will learn . . .

- what the term environment means.
- to identify kinds of land, air, and water pollution.
- ways to keep your environment friendly.

A healthful environment gives you clean air, land, and water. It offers outdoor places you can enjoy. It is important to keep your environment clean, healthful, and friendly. This helps you live a healthy life.

Vocabulary

- **environment,** *E27*
- **natural resources,** *E27*
- **pollution,** *E27*
- **land pollution,** *E28*
- **air pollution,** *E28*
- **water pollution,** *E29*
- **friendly environment,** *E30*
- **noise,** *E30*

Your Environment

The **environment** is everything around you. Air, water, soil, plants, and animals are all part of the environment.

Natural resources are materials found in nature, which are useful or necessary for life. Air and water are natural resources. You could not live without them. Soil is a natural resource needed for growing food. Mineral resources include coal, oil, iron, and copper. Coal is used for fuel. Oil is used for fuel and to make plastics. Iron and copper are used to make cars, buildings, tools, and many other products.

The environment is also used for recreation. *Recreation* is what you do for enjoyment or relaxation. Perhaps you have a hobby. Perhaps you play sports. You might enjoy swimming at a lake. You might enjoy hiking in the woods. These are all forms of recreation.

The environment can be harmed by pollution. **Pollution** occurs when land, water, or air contain harmful substances making them unhealthful to the environment. Pollution can make water harmful to drink. It can make air harmful to breathe. It can harm crops.

 **What makes up your environment?**

CAREERS
Park Ranger

Park rangers take care of our national parks. These parks are located in the country, the wilderness, and in cities. The wilderness is a place where no people live. A park ranger may teach visitors about plants and animals or about the history of a site. Part of a park ranger's job is to preserve the area and keep it safe for people to enjoy.

LOG ON www.mmhhealth.com
Find out more about health careers.

E27

Types of Pollution

Land, air, and water can all be harmed by pollution.

Land Pollution

Land pollution occurs when land contains harmful substances that make it unhealthful to the environment and people. These substances might come from factories, home owners, farms, and garbage dumps and landfills. Factories may give off wastes in the form of particles that settle on soil in the area. Chemicals used by homeowners and farmers to kill weeds and insects can soak into the ground. Garbage dumps and landfills sometimes leak chemicals into the ground. If people dispose of harmful chemicals incorrectly, these substances get into the ground as well. These actions can harm the soil and water. As a result, people can be harmed.

▲ **What can you do to help prevent littering?**

Air Pollution

Air pollution is air that contains harmful substances, often in the form of very small particles.

Some air pollution occurs when fuel is burned. Cars, trucks, and planes burn fuel. So do power plants and factories. The waste products from burning fuel go into the air as exhaust. Even the furnace that heats your home causes some air pollution. Burning leaves or trash causes air pollution, too. Some air pollution comes from natural causes. Forest fires add to air pollution.

Air pollution can cause your eyes to sting. It might make you cough or sneeze. Air pollution can make breathing difficult for people with allergies or asthma. People with heart conditions also can suffer if the air they breathe has a large number of pollutants.

▲ **Air pollution can make it hard for some people to breathe easily.**

Water Pollution

Water pollution occurs when water contains harmful substances, making it unhealthful to the environment and people. Water pollution can make water unsafe to drink. It can make fish unsafe to eat. It is not healthful to swim in polluted water.

There are many sources of water pollution. Sometimes people are careless about disposing of poisonous products, such as strong cleaners, motor oil, and paints. They may pour them down the drain or on the ground. The poisons then seep into ground water. *Ground water* is water in the pores of rock and soil. Farmers may use certain chemicals on farms to make crops grow better. Water containing these chemicals washes off the land, and is called runoff. *Runoff* is water that flows along surfaces and into streams, lakes, or oceans. Chemicals from factories also can leak into ground water and into wells. Harmful particles in the air may settle on rivers and lakes.

 List three ways that water pollution can occur.

◀ **Runoff from land can cause water pollution if it contains fertilizers, motor oil, or gasoline.**

A Friendly Environment

BUILD Character

Lose the Litter!

Citizenship As a class, find a way to reduce litter. Litter is a kind of pollution. Make a list of five ways to persuade people to stop littering in your community. Choose the best idea. Work with your teacher to develop the idea.

Your environment includes your home, school, and community. A **friendly environment** is one in which people respect one another. A friendly environment supports your family and social health.

Your environment is friendly when you are friendly to others. It is friendly when you help others. It is friendly when you respect the property of others. *Graffiti* are words or pictures scratched or painted on structures without the permission of the owner. Graffiti makes an environment less friendly. Some people think that graffiti is a form of pollution. It makes buildings look neglected and dirty. Graffiti is against the law in many places.

Noise in the environment can harm health. **Noise** is loud or constant sound. It can cause stress and harm hearing. Loud music and machines—such as jackhammers, a lawn mower, and airplanes—cause noise pollution. If you are near a loud machine for more than a few minutes, your hearing can be harmed. Wear ear plugs or other hearing protection when near loud machinery. Do you listen to loud music? Do you wear headphones? Keep the volume low. A high volume can harm your hearing.

▲ Your home, school, and community are all part of your environment.

What is a friendly environment?

E30

Resolve Conflict

You are reading a book at the kitchen table. Your brother comes into the kitchen and turns on the radio. The music is loud. The noise bothers you. You ask your brother to turn off the radio. He says he won't. How will you resolve the conflict? Pair up with a classmate to role-play this situation. Take turns playing the two roles.

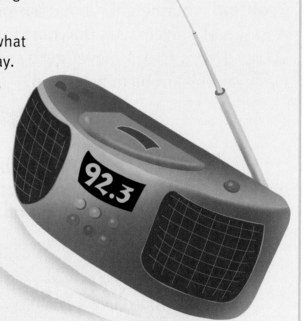

1 **Stay calm.** If you feel that you are getting angry, what can you do? Show a calm behavior as you role-play.

2 **Talk about the conflict.** What is your point of view about the problem? What is your brother's point of view? Do the people with the conflict really understand why they have different opinions? Discuss this with your classmate.

3 **List possible ways to settle the conflict.** Can you think of a solution that you could both accept? Describe it.

4 **Agree on a way to settle the conflict.** You may need to ask an adult for help. Share with your class how you solved the conflict.

LESSON REVIEW

Review Concepts

1. **Explain** what the environment is.

2. **Name** the three kinds of pollution in our environment?

3. **List** three ways that land pollution can occur.

4. **Explain** what makes an environment friendly.

Critical Thinking

5. **Synthesize** How does making the environment friendly show respect for other people?

6. **LIFE SKILLS** **Resolve Conflicts** You are doing your homework. It is quiet. Your sister starts practicing her tuba. It is distracting you. How might you settle this conflict?

Use Communication Skills

Problem Your neighborhood has one basketball court.
A group of players uses the court for hours every day.
You and your friends never get a chance to use it.
How can this problem be solved?

Solution People may do things that bother you.
You can use communication skills to explain how
you feel.

Learn This Life Skill

Follow these steps to learn how to communicate.
The Foldables™ can help you.

1 **Choose the best way to communicate.**

Decide how you will communicate with the people who won't share the court.

> Use Communication Skills
> 1. Choose the best way to communicate.

2 **Send a clear message. Be polite.**

Decide what you will say to the other group. Be ready with ideas for solving the problem. Use I-messages.

> Use Communication Skills
> 1. Choose the best way to communicate.
> 2. Send a clear message. Be polite.

3 **Listen to each other.**

Present your message. Then listen to what they have to say.

> Use Communication Skills
> 1. Choose the best way to communicate.
> 2. Send a clear message. Be polite.
> 3. Listen to each other.

4 **Make sure that you understand each other.**

Repeat what you think you heard the other group say. Ask them to repeat what they think you said. What can you do if the other group does not understand your point of view?

> Use Communication Skills
> 1. Choose the best way to communicate.
> 2. Send a clear message. Be polite.
> 3. Listen to each other.
> 4. Make sure you understand each other.

Practice This Life Skill

People litter at a local playground. Work with a small group. Describe how you could discuss this problem with a person you see littering. Use the four steps. Share your ideas with your class.

Reducing Pollution

You will learn . . .

- ways to keep land clean and safe.
- ways to keep the air clean and safe.
- ways to keep water clean and safe.

Vocabulary

- **sanitary landfill,** *E35*
- **smog,** *E36*
- **acid rain,** *E36*

Trees add beauty and shade to any environment. Did you know that they also help remove pollution from the air? Planting trees helps a community to stay clean and healthful.

Reducing Land Pollution

What can communities do to reduce land pollution? Communities can write a community environmental health plan. A *community environmental health plan* is a plan to reduce environmental health risks. The plan lists the community's environmental health problems. It then lists ways to solve the problems.

Suppose that a community needs to find a new way to get rid of trash. The community could build an incinerator (in•SIN•uh•ray•tuhr) or a sanitary landfill. A **sanitary landfill** is a large pit that holds trash as it decays. The pit is lined with clay or plastic. The liner keeps material from leaking out of the pit into the ground water. Layers of trash are put into the pit. Each layer of trash is covered with a layer of soil. The soil contains bacteria and fungi that will break down the trash. An *incinerator* is a building in which trash is burned and turned into ash. The ash is then buried in landfills.

What You Can Do

Litter is scraps of paper and other trash. You see litter on the sidewalk or along the road. Litter is a kind of land pollution. Everyone can help prevent litter. Don't throw trash on the ground. Put it in a trash can instead. Make a plan at school to take action against litter.

 What is the purpose of a community environmental health plan?

MAKE a Difference
Make It Green

Students in Portland, Oregon, wanted to help improve their community's environment. They looked into problems that they could help solve. They learned about a vacant lot near their school. The students made plans to make a small park and put in a garden with native plants. What could you do to improve your community's environment?

▲ **Some communities put their trash in a sanitary landfill. How does your community get rid of its trash?**

Reducing Air Pollution

Air pollution affects the health of many people. This type of pollution affects the air they breathe. Three substances that cause air pollution are ozone (OH•zohn), smog, and acid rain. Ozone normally forms high above Earth. There, it protects Earth from the sun's harmful rays. But ozone also can form close to Earth when automobile exhaust is acted on by sunlight. Ground level ozone can make your eyes feel scratchy. It can make it hard to breathe. Ozone that forms near the ground is part of smog. **Smog** is a haze that forms when sunlight strikes air pollution.

Acid rain forms when air pollution mixes with fog, rain, or snow. It can damage buildings. It can harm trees. Acid rain has been linked with the death of fish in lakes. When inhaled, it can harm people's lungs.

ACTIVITY

Art LINK

Converter Diagrams

Research a catalytic converter. Find out where it is located in an automobile, and how it makes the exhaust cleaner. Draw a diagram of the device and explain to your class how it works.

ACTIVITY

Science LINK

Checking the Air

What's in the air where you live? Here is a way to find out. Use two-sided sticky tape. Cut off a three-inch strip and stick the strip on a paper plate or plastic lid. Put it outside and wait 24 hours. Then use a hand lens to check the tape. Write a sentence describing what you see. Share your results with your classmates.

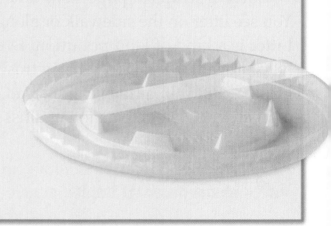

Air Quality

Air quality is the healthfulness of the air you breathe. The *Clean Air Act* is a law that helps keep the air healthy. It sets limits on the amount of harmful gases and particles that can be in the air. The quality of the air over the United States is checked every day. Sometimes the air might contain too much pollution. If so a plan is made to reduce the pollution. Sometimes those who cause the pollution have to pay a fine.

Reducing Air Pollution

Exhaust from cars, trucks, planes, boats, and lawn mowers causes air pollution. *Exhaust* is the waste gases from fuel that is burned in an engine.

Companies that build cars and trucks have made the exhaust cleaner. Some engines run on fuels that release less pollution. Some new cars run on a combination of electricity and gasoline. Factories and power plants have been required to reduce pollution from their smokestacks.

 What are three ways that air pollution has been reduced?

Health Online

Providing Clean Air

The Clean Air Act sets limits on air pollution so that people can breathe air that is healthful. Research whether or not the Clean Air Act has been successful. Use the e-Journal writing tool in reporting your findings. Visit **www.mmhhealth.com** and click on e-Journal.

▼ **Air quality improves as pollution is reduced.**

Reducing Water Pollution

Write About It!

Poem for the Planet
Write a short poem about water pollution. Tell what causes water pollution and how to prevent it. You can put your poem to music and make a song. Read your poem or perform your song for your classmates.

Water pollution harms the health of the environment. Chemicals from some factories can cause diseases. Fertilizers run off lawns and farm fields. They can seep into the ground and into streams. This can cause water pollution. Sometimes sewage enters lakes or rivers. *Sewage* is waste that you flush down the toilet or pour down your drain. Water that contains sewage is harmful to your health. It must be cleaned before it is let into lakes or rivers. The *Clean Water Act* sets limits on the amount of pollution that can enter the water.

Water Treatment

Water in most towns and cities is treated so that it is safe to use. Drinking water may come from rivers or lakes. Before the water goes to people's homes, it is sent through a *water treatment plant*. The water treatment plant removes waste materials that might cause health problems from the water. Then the water is safe to drink.

Sewage is waste water. Sewage moves from your home through pipes to a *wastewater treatment plant*. There the water is cleaned. Then it is let back into the environment.

◀ Since 1969, The Clearwater, a boat that sails on the Hudson River in New York, has presented environmental programs for teachers and students. Students learn about the importance of keeping the river clean.

What You Can Do to Reduce Water Pollution

The following tips will help to keep water clean and healthful.

- **Use community resources.** Dispose of waste materials, such as paint, paint remover, and hazardous household chemicals, at a hazardous waste collection center.

- **Avoid using products that can harm the environment.** Use cleaners that do not contain harsh chemicals. Don't pour paint or paint remover down a drain.

- **Limit the use of lawn and garden chemicals.** Using environmentally friendly garden materials reduces the amount of pesticides that will enter ground water.

 How does the Clean Water Act help control water pollution?

ACTIVITY — LIFE SKILLS — CRITICAL THINKING

Access Health Facts

Where does your town or city get its drinking water? How is the water made safe to drink?

1. **Identify when you might need health facts.** Write a list of questions. Where does the town's water come from?

2. **Identify where you might find health facts about water services.** Does your community have a water department?

3. **Find the health facts you need.** Talk to someone at the community water department.

4. **Evaluate the health facts.** Make a poster showing the way water is treated in your community.

LESSON REVIEW

Review Concepts

1. **Explain** how sanitary landfills help prevent land pollution.

2. **Identify** a law that helps keep the air clean and safe.

3. **Describe** two times when water is treated.

Critical Thinking

4. **Analyze** Black smoke is coming from a car's exhaust pipe. The owner can get it fixed right away or can save money by not fixing it. Which choice helps the environment? Explain.

5. **LIFE SKILLS** **Access Health Facts** Where can you find information about your community's environmental plan?

Conserving Resources

You will learn . . .

- ways to save water.
- ways to reduce, recycle, and reuse.
- ways to save energy.

Vocabulary

- **conserve**, *E41*
- **recycle**, *E42*
- **reduce**, *E43*
- **reuse**, *E43*
- **energy**, *E44*
- **insulation**, *E44*

Do you let the water run as you brush your teeth? This habit wastes as many as nine gallons of water each time you brush. To help conserve this vital resource, turn off the water as you brush.

Conserving Water

Earth seems to have plenty of water. Huge saltwater oceans cover much of the planet. But people need fresh water for drinking, cooking, and growing food. Fresh water comes from lakes, rivers, and wells.

To **conserve** something is to protect it from being lost or to use it carefully. Why should you conserve fresh water? You need to conserve fresh water because you can't live without it. Much of your body is made of water. You cook with water. You wash yourself with it. It flushes waste out of your house. Farmers can't grow food without fresh water. Here are some steps you can take to conserve fresh water.

- **Run a dishwasher** only when it is full.

- **Take a five-minute shower** instead of a bath.

- **Don't fill the tub to the top** when you take a bath.

- **Don't run water** as you brush your teeth.

- **Keep cold water** in the refrigerator. This way you won't waste water running the faucet until the water gets cold.

- **Tell your parents or guardian** if you see a leaky faucet at home. Leaks waste water.

- **Set the clothes washer** for a small load when you have only a few clothes to wash.

- **Don't let rinse water run** when you do dishes.

- **Use buckets of water** to wash the car. Don't let the hose run.

 Why is it important to conserve water?

ACTIVITY

Math LINK

Showers Add Up

Find enough containers to hold four gallons. Many showers use this much water in one minute! Suppose you take a ten-minute shower every day. How many minutes do you spend in the shower each week? If your shower uses 4 gallons of water per minute, how much water do you use in one week?

▲ **You can save water by running the dishwasher only when it is full.**

Recycle

ACTIVITY

Con$umer Wi$e

Look Before You Buy

Research paper products with your parent or guardian. Look for the words "post consumer" on the label. This tells you that the paper is made from paper that was used before. The package may say "20 percent post consumer" or "50 percent post consumer." A higher number means more of the product is made of recycled paper.

How much paper do you use each day? How many bottles and bags do you throw out? How can you save resources? You can put cans, bottles, and paper into recycling bins.

Everything you use comes from natural resources. Paper comes from trees. Trees take time to grow. Many things we use are made from oil or metals. These are pumped or mined from the ground. There is only a certain amount of each of these natural resources. Conserving resources helps make them last longer.

Many things can be used again or changed into something new. To **recycle** is to change waste products so that they can be used again in a new way. Many materials can be recycled. These include paper, glass, plastic, and metal. *Aluminum* (ah•LOO•mih•nuhm) is a metal that is easily recycled.

▶ Many cans are made from recycled aluminum.

1 You put an aluminum can in the recycle bin.

2 Workers clean and crush the cans.

3 Machines shred and melt the cans.

4 Melted aluminum is formed into bars, pressed, and rolled.

5 New cans are formed.

6 People buy the products and recycle the cans again.

Reduce and Reuse

To **reduce** means to use less of the things that become trash. Think about all the paper that you use each day. Reducing the amount you use conserves trees, water, and energy resources. You can reduce and conserve in other ways, too. Take a moment before you buy something. Ask yourself the questions listed on the clipboard.

Reuse as many things as you can. To **reuse** something is to use it again instead of throwing it away. Suppose that you buy a new pair of shoes. You also need a box to hold hobby supplies. You can reuse the shoebox to hold your supplies. Reusing something you already have for a new purpose saves energy.

Here are some ways to reduce and reuse.

- **Write on both sides** of a sheet of paper.

- **Save wrapping paper** to use again.

- **Carry a cloth bag** with you when you shop. Put what you buy in that bag. You won't need paper bags from the store.

- **Take your lunch** in a reusable container.

- **Use cloth napkins** instead of paper napkins.

- **Buy products** with as little packaging as possible. There will be less to throw away.

- **Give a magazine you have read** to someone else instead of throwing it away.

 Why should you choose the product with the least packaging?

▶ **Use cloth shopping bags instead of paper bags.**

Before You Buy

- Do I really need this item?

- Will I use it more than once?

- Could I borrow one from someone else?

- Is there too much packaging?

- Will most of the packaging just be thrown away?

- Can I use the parts of the packaging for something else?

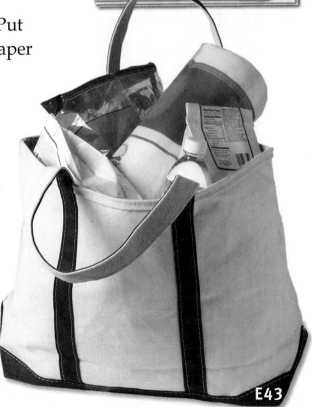

Save Energy

Energy is the ability to do work. Energy used to heat homes and run cars comes from fossil fuels, such as coal, oil, and natural gas. These forms of energy also are used in power plants to make electricity. However, these energy sources pollute the air when they are burned. There are sources of energy that do not pollute air or water. *Solar* (SOH•luhr) *panels* turn sunlight into electricity. Wind *turbines* (TUHR•bynz) make electricity from wind. Sunlight and wind do not form air pollutants. Nuclear power is also used in some areas.

Save Energy at Home

A *thermostat* (THER•muh•stat) controls your furnace, electric heater, and air conditioner. Set the thermostat on a lower temperature when you need heat. Set it on a higher temperature when you run the air conditioner. Less energy will be used.

Using insulation can save energy. **Insulation** (in•suh•LAY•shuhn) is material that stops or slows the passage of heat. In winter, insulation helps keep heat in. In summer, it helps keep heat out. Other ways to conserve energy include the following.

- Turn off lights and computers when not in use. Do not hold a refrigerator or freezer door open longer than you need to.

- Dry clothes on a clothesline instead of using an electric or gas dryer.

- Walk or ride a bike instead of riding in a car.

- Reduce how often you use air conditioning.

 Why is it important to conserve energy?

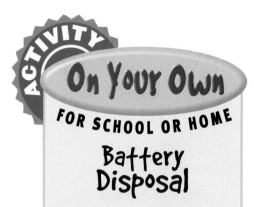

On Your Own

FOR SCHOOL OR HOME

Battery Disposal

Don't throw used batteries away with the rest of the trash. They contain harmful materials. Find out where your family can dispose of batteries safely in your community.

▲ **Wind turbines are clean sources of energy.**

CRITICAL THINKING

Set Health Goals

You can cut back on the amount of energy you use in your home. Write a Health Behavior Contract to set a goal to use less energy.

1 **Write the health goal you want to set.** Write your goal on your Health Behavior Contract: I will cut back on energy use.

2 **Explain how your goal might affect health.** List reasons you should save energy at home. Write the list on your Health Behavior Contract.

3 **Describe a plan you will follow to reach your goal. Keep track of your progress.** List the steps you will take to conserve water and energy. Keep a record on your Health Behavior Contract telling what you do each day for a month.

4 **Evaluate how your plan worked.** Were you able to reduce the amount of energy your family used? If not, tell how you will change the plan to make it work better.

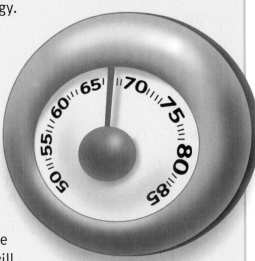

▶ **Drying clothes in the air saves fossil fuels and cuts down on air pollution.**

LESSON REVIEW

Review Concepts

1. **Describe** a plan to save water as you get ready for school in the morning.

2. **List** three ways to save paper.

3. **Analyze** How can saving electricity be good for the health of the community?

Critical Thinking

4. **Analyze** Identify an object you already own and tell how it might be reused for another purpose. Identify the purpose.

5. **LIFE SKILLS** **Set Health Goals** How does setting a goal to recycle help conserve natural resources?

E45

Use Vocabulary

Choose the correct term to complete each sentence.

natural resources, *E27*

pollution, *E27*

noise, *E30*

environment, *E27*

smog, *E36*

conserve, *E41*

recycle, *E42*

1. Everything that is around you makes up your __?__.

2. Materials found in nature that are useful or necessary for life are __?__.

3. To save natural resources is to __?__.

4. To process certain materials so that they can be used again is to __?__.

5. When the environment contains harmful substances it is called __?__.

6. A loud or constant sound is __?__.

7. A haze that forms when sunlight strikes air pollution is __?__.

Review Concepts

Answer each question in complete sentences.

8. What makes up your environment?

9. What are natural resources?

10. Describe three ways that you can help make your environment friendly.

11. Name four things that can be recycled.

12. Describe two ways that air pollution can be cleaned up.

13. Name three actions that you can take to conserve fresh water.

Reading Comprehension

Answer each question in complete sentences.

Air quality is the healthfulness of the air you breathe. The *Clean Air Act* is a law that helps keep the air healthy. It sets limits on the amount of harmful gases and particles that can be in the air. The quality of the air over the United States is checked every day. Sometimes the air might contain too much pollution. If so a plan is made to reduce the pollution. Sometimes those who cause the pollution have to pay a fine.

14. What does the Clean Air Act limit?

15. How does the United States keep track of air quality?

16. What may happen to those people who cause pollution?

Critical Thinking/Problem Solving

Answer each question in complete sentences.

Analyze Concepts

17. How does using less paper help conserve natural resources?

18. Suppose a community makes an environmental health plan to build a new landfill. How could this help everyone in a town or city stay healthy?

19. How does it help the environment when you buy items packaged in materials that you can reuse?

20. Describe three ways to save energy at school.

21. What are three causes of air pollution?

22. Explain why it is important to conserve water.

Practice Life Skills

23. **Use Communication Skills** Your family members often leave the lights on when they leave a room. How can you use communication skills to explain how you feel about their actions?

24. **Make Responsible Decisions** Why is it important to recycle the cans and bottles you use?

Read Graphics

Use the table to answer questions 25–27.

Keeping Land, Air, and Water Safe

Land	Air	Water
Reduce, reuse, and recycle waste	Drive cars with cleaner fuels, such as hybrid cars	Build sewage treatment plants in our communities
Don't dump trash or drop litter along the road	Pass laws such as the Clean Air Act	Build community water treatment plants
Don't put graffiti on buildings	Conserve energy and natural resources	Pass laws such as the Clean Water Act
Reduce the use of lawn chemicals at home		Don't throw chemicals into water

25. What is the law that sets limits on pollution to keep water safe?

26. How might people who drive cars cause less air pollution?

27. How do communities clean water?

 LOG ON **www.mmhhealth.com** Find out how much you know about environmental health.

Effective Communication

Make a Booklet

Describe in a booklet how to save energy at home. Fold a stack of several sheets of unlined paper in half to make a booklet. Include drawings to illustrate how to do this.

Self-Directed Learning

Write a Report

Learn about a kind of health helper. Report to your class explaining what the health helper does. Include information about the training needed to become that health helper.

Critical Thinking and Problem Solving

Make a How-to Book

As a class, brainstorm as many uses as you can for an empty plastic milk jug. Make a list of your ideas. Then make drawings of your ideas and describe how to make the object.

Responsible Citizenship

Design a Poster

Research types of recreation you can enjoy in your community. Make a poster describing these choices. Use words and drawings in your poster.

Glossary

A

abuse rough or harsh treatment (p. A76)

accident an unexpected event (p. C47)

acid rain forms when air pollution mixes with fog, rain, or snow (p. E36)

additive (AD•uh•tiv) anything added to a food to help it look or taste better or be more healthful (p. B51)

adolescence (AD•uhl•ES•uhns) the stage of growth from 12 to 18 years (p. B27)

adoption legally taking a child of other parents into the family (p. A66)

adulthood the stage of growth from 18 to 70 years and beyond (p. B28)

advertisement an announcement that tells people about a product or an event (p. B52)

aerobic (uhr•OH•bik) **exercise** exercise that uses a lot of oxygen at a steady pace over a long period of time (p. C31)

air pollution (puh•LOO•shuhn) air that contains harmful substances often in the form of very small particles (p. E28)

alcohol a depressant drug found in some beverages and some medicines (p. D11)

alcoholism a disease in which a person is dependent on alcohol (p. D13)

allergy (AL•ur•gee) the body's over-reaction to a substance (p. D59)

anaerobic (a•nuh•ROH•bik) **exercise** exercise that uses a lot of oxygen in a short period of time and faster than your body can supply it (p. C31)

antibiotic a drug that is used to kill or slow the growth of bacteria (p. D52)

antibody (AN•ti•bod•ee) a substance that your body makes to fight a pathogen as it is attacking you (p. D47)

asthma (AZ•muh) a condition in which the small airways of the respiratory system become narrow (p. D60)

attitude your way of thinking, acting, and feeling (p. A36)

B

balanced diet a daily eating plan that includes the correct number of servings from the five food groups (p. B55)

body image the way you feel about how your body looks (p. B68)

body system a group of organs that work together to do a certain job (p. B5)

bone marrow soft tissue in the center of long bones, such as those in your arms and legs (p. B9)

bored feeling restless and not knowing what to do (p. A30)

bully a person who threatens and frightens you (p. A76)

C

calorie a unit used to measure the energy produced by food in the body (p. B51)

cancer a disease in which cells grow in ways that are not normal (p. D67)

carbohydrate (kar•boh•HY•drayt) a nutrient that supplies the main source of energy for your body (p. B40)

career the work that a person prepares for and does throughout life (p. E17)

caring being kind to someone (p. A27)

cavity a hole in the enamel of a tooth (p. C12)

cell the smallest working part of a living thing (p. B5)

character the qualities that make a person different from others (p. A12)

childhood the stage of growth from 1 to 12 years (p. B24)

choking being unable to breathe because of a blocked air passage (p. C83)

chronic (KRAHN•ik) **disease** a disease that lasts a long time or comes back from time to time, often over a lifetime (p. D57)

circulation (sur•kyuh•LAY•shun) the movement of blood throughout the body (p. B16)

clinic a place where health care is given to people who do not need to stay in a hospital (p. E19)

clique (KLEEK) a group of people who keep others out of their group (p. A75)

cocaine (koh•KAYN) an illegal stimulant drug made from the leaves of the coca plant (p. D27)

commercial an ad on television or radio (p. B52); (p. E5)

communicable (kuh•MYEW•ni•kuh•buhl) **disease** disease that is spread from person-to-person, from animals to people, or from objects in the environment to people (p. D39)

communication the sharing of feelings, thoughts, or information (p. A46)

community a place where a group of people live (p. E17)

compete to play to win (p. C37)

conflict a strong disagreement or fight (p. A53)

conserve to protect something from being lost or to use it carefully (p. E41)

cool-down five to ten minutes of easy physical activity, done after exercising, that cools your muscles and gradually lets your heart rate return to normal (p. C38)

D

death the end of the life cycle (p. B30)

dental plaque (PLAK) a sticky film that coats teeth (p. C12)

depressant a drug that slows down body functions (p. D11)

dermis thick layer of cells below the epidermis (p. B12)

diabetes (digh•uh•BEE•tis) a chronic disease in which there is too much sugar in the blood (p. D58)

Dietary Guidelines suggested goals to help you stay healthy (p. B46)

digested changed into a form your body can use (p. B15)

disease a condition that keeps your body from working as it should (p. D39)

divorce a legal end to marriage (p. A65)

drug substances other than food that can change how the mind or body works (p. D5)

drug abuse the use of an illegal drug or the harmful use of a legal drug on purpose (p. D6)

drug misuse the accidental, unsafe use of a medicine (p. D6)

E

earthquake the movement of a part of Earth's crust caused by sudden shifting of rock along a fault (p. C49)

ecstasy (EK•stuh•see) an illegal stimulant drug that can increase or decrease the actions of the body (p. D27)

emergency a serious and unexpected situation in which help is needed right away (p. C75)

Emergency Alert System lets people know when health-threatening weather may be in their area and when a person has disappeared (p. C76)

emotion a feeling inside you (p. A27)

empty-calorie food a food that is low in vitamins and minerals but high in calories (p. B56)

energy the ability to do work (p. E44)

entertainment something that interests or amuses you (p. E12)

environment everything around you (p. A60); (p. E27)

epidermis the outer layer of skin cells (p. B12)

family a group of people who are related in some way (p. A59)

family guidelines rules set by parents or guardians that tell children how to act (p. A59)

farsighted able to see far objects clearly but close objects look blurry (p. C6)

fast-food restaurant a place that serves food quickly (p. B53)

fats nutrients that provide energy (p. B41)

fear a feeling of danger (p. A27)

first aid the quick care given to a person who is injured or ill (p. C75)

first aid kit a collection of information, equipment, and supplies that is used to care for a person who is injured or ill (p. C75)

flexibility the ability to bend and move your body (p. C23)

flood a great flow of water onto dry land (p. C57)

fluoride (FLOOR•ide) a mineral that hardens tooth enamel (p. C12)

food allergy (AL•ur•gee) a reaction to a food that is caused by the immune system (p. B63)

foodborne illness a sickness caused by eating food or drinking beverages that contain harmful germs (p. B64)

food group foods that contain many of the same types of nutrients (p. B45)

Food Guide Pyramid a guide that shows the number of servings from each food group your body needs each day (p. B45)

food intolerance a reaction of the body to a food or something within the food (p. B63)

food label nutrition information printed on a food container (p. B51)

foster child a child who lives with a family without being related by birth or adoption (p. A66)

friend a person who likes and supports you (p. A69)

friendly environment one in which people respect one another (p. E30)

gang a group of people who may be involved in dangerous and illegal acts (p. C71)

grief (GREEF) the discomfort a person feels after a loss (p. A27)

grooming taking care of your body and appearance (p. C17)

health the condition of your body, mind, and relationships (p. A5)

health advocate (AD•vuh•kut) a person who helps another person choose healthful behaviors (p. A48)

healthful behavior an action that increases the level of health for you and for others (p. A6)

healthful body composition having a lean body without too much fat (p. C23)

health goal something that you work toward to promote health (p. A5)

healthful weight the weight that is suggested for your age and size (p. B67)

hearing loss a problem in one or both ears that prevents a person from hearing properly (p. C8)

heart and lung endurance the ability to stay active without getting tired (p. C23)

heart attack a sudden lack of blood to the heart muscle (p. D63)

heart disease a chronic disease of the heart or blood vessels (p. D63)

heredity (huh•RED•uh•tee) the traits passed to you from your birth parents (p. A60); (p. B21)

hormone (HOR•mohn) a chemical produced by the body that controls certain body processes (p. B21)

hurricane a destructive storm that forms over the ocean (p. C56)

I-message a healthful way to communicate about a problem and how it affects you (p. A46)

immune to be protected from a disease (p. D47)

infancy the period of growth from birth to one year (p. B22)

infection growth of bacteria that harms the body (p. C81)

inhalant (in•HAY•luhnt) a chemical that is breathed into the lungs (p. D28)

injury damage or harm done to a person (p. C47)

inpatient a person who must stay in a hospital at least overnight for treatment (p. E20)

insulation (in•suh•LAY•shuhn) material that stops or slows the passage of heat (p. E44)

joint the place where two or more bones meet (p. B9)

joy the feeling of great happiness (p. A27)

lactose the sugar in milk (p. B63)

land pollution when land contains harmful substances that make it unhealthful to the environment and people (p. E28)

learning disability a difference that causes a person to have trouble learning (p. B25)

life cycle the order of change that each living organism passes through during its life (p. B22)

life skill a healthful action to learn and practice to improve and maintain your health (p. A7)

lifetime sport a sport that you can enjoy throughout your life (p. C32)

lightning flashes of light caused by electricity in the air moving between clouds or between clouds and the ground (p. C54)

long-term goal a goal that takes a long time to reach (p. A24)

marijuana (mayr•uh•WAH•nuh) an illegal drug that affects memory and concentration (p. D25)

media ways of getting information to people (p. E5)

mediation a process in which a responsible person helps settle a conflict (p. A54)

medicine a drug that you take to prevent or treat a health problem (p. D5)

mineral nutrient that helps your body's chemical processes (p. B42)

MSG a substance used to flavor meats, seafood, and soups (p. B63)

mucus a moist coating that lines your nose and throat (p. D46)

muscular endurance the ability to use your muscles for a long time without stopping (p. C22)

muscular strength the ability to use your muscles to push, pull, lift, throw, or kick (p. C22)

natural resources things found in nature that are necessary or useful for life (p. E27)

nearsighted able to see close objects clearly but far away objects look blurry (p. C6)

neuron (NOO•rahn) nerve cell (p. B18)

nicotine (NI•kuh•TEEN) a stimulant drug found in tobacco (p. D17)

noise loud or constant sound (p. E30)

nutrient (NEW•tree•uhnt) substance in food that your body uses to keep you healthy (p. B39)

one-mile run/walk measures your heart and lung endurance (p. C29)

organ a body part made of different kinds of tissues (p. B5)

outpatient a person who receives treatment in a hospital but does not stay overnight (p. E20)

overweight having a weight above your healthful weight (p. B68)

over-the-counter (OTC) drug medicine that can be bought without a doctor's prescription (p. D6)

pathogen (PA•thuh•juhn) a germ that causes disease (p. D39)

peer someone who is about the same age as you, but may or may not be your friend (p. A71)

peer pressure the influence people your own age have on you (p. A71)

percent body fat pinch measures the amount of body fat you have (p. C29)

permanent teeth teeth that, with care, should last a lifetime (p. C11)

personality how you look, think, act, and feel (p. A11)

physical fitness having your heart, lungs, muscles, and joints in good condition (p. C22)

poison a substance that can harm you if it is swallowed or gets on your skin (p. C50)

pollution when land, water, or air contain harmful substances making them unhealthful to the environment and people (p. E27)

posture how a person sits, stands, or moves (p. B9)

premature heart attack one that occurs before age 60 (p. D64)

prescription (pri•SKRIP•shun) **drug** a medicine that is obtained with a doctor's written order (p. D5)

preservative a substance added to food to keep it from spoiling (p. B51)

primary teeth teeth that grow in first (p. C11)

protective factor something that increases the chance of a positive outcome (p. D31)

protein nutrient needed to build, grow, and repair body cells (p. B39)

psychiatrist (sy•KY•uh•trist) a doctor who specializes in mental and emotional health (p. E18)

puberty the time when a person's body changes and becomes able to reproduce (p. B27)

pull-ups a test for upper body strength and endurance (p. C28)

radon a colorless, odorless gas that comes from rocks and clay soils (p. D67)

recovery a way to get well (p. C67)

recycle to change waste products so that they can be used again in a new way (p. E42)

reduce to use less of the things that become trash (p. E43)

relationship a connection you have with another person (p. A45)

resistance skills ways to say "no" to risk behaviors (p. A19)

respect treating others as you want to be treated (p. A45)

respiration the process by which cells release energy from food (p. B17)

responsible able to be trusted with a job, duty, or a concern (p. A13)

responsible decision a decision that is healthful and safe (p. A17)

reuse to use items again instead of throwing them away (p. E43)

ringworm a skin disease caused by a fungus (p. C18)

risk behavior an action that can be harmful to you and others (p. A6)

role model someone who shows behavior that other people copy (p. A48)

sadness the feeling of sorrow or unhappiness (p. A27)

safe touch a touch that is right and respectful (p. C67)

safety equipment the approved helmets, padding, and mouth guards that you wear to keep from getting injured during sports or other physical activity (p. C38)

sanitary landfill a large pit that holds trash as it decays (p. E35)

sealant a thin layer of plastic-like material painted on healthy molar teeth (p. C14)

seat belt the lap belt and shoulder belt worn in a car (p. C59)

secondhand smoke smoke that a person breathes out as well as smoke that comes from a burning cigarette, cigar, or pipe (p. D18)

self-concept what you think about yourself (p. A23)

self-control deciding not to say or do something that you know you shouldn't (p. A51)

self-respect thinking highly of yourself (p. A11)

self-statement a reminder to yourself as to what you should do (p. A14)

separation when a couple is still married but living apart (p. A65)

short-term goal a goal reached in a short time (p. A24)

shuttle run measures total body coordination (p. C28)

sit-ups or curl-ups a measure of the strength and endurance of your abdominal muscles (p. C28)

smog a haze that forms when sunlight strikes air pollution (p. E36)

smokeless tobacco a tobacco product that can be chewed, placed between the cheek and gums, or inhaled through the nostrils (p. D19)

snack food you eat between meals (p. B55)

sprain an injury to the tissue that connects bones to a joint (p. C82)

steroid chemicals that occur naturally in the body or are prescribed by doctors for medical reasons (p. D29)

stimulant (STIM•yuh•luhnt) a drug that speeds up the body's functions (p. D17)

stress the response to any demand on your mind or body (p. A33)

stressor something that causes stress (p. A33)

symptom a change in the body's condition that signals disease (p. D51)

tar a gummy substance found in tobacco smoke (p. D17)

thunderstorm a storm that has thunder and lightning (p. C56)

tissue a group of the same kind of cells (p. B5)

tornado violent funnel-shaped storm with high winds that moves over land (p. C56)

treatment care given to a person who is ill (p. D52)

trunk lift measures the strength and flexibility of your back muscles (p. C28)

unconscious (uhn•KAHN•shuhs) to be unaware of what is happening because you are not awake (p. C76)

underweight having a weight below your healthful weight (p. B68)

universal precautions steps taken to keep people from having contact with body fluids that may be infected (p. C81)

unsafe touch a touch that is not right (p. C67)

vaccine (vak•SEEN) a substance that makes you immune to a disease without having to get the disease (p. D47)

values beliefs that guide a person's behavior (p. A11)

victim a person who has been harmed by violence (p. C67)

violence harm done to yourself, others, or property (p. C65)

vitamins nutrients that help your body use proteins, carbohydrates, and fats (p. B42)

V-sit and reach or sit and reach measure the flexibility of the muscles in your back and legs (p. C28)

warm-up five minutes or more of easy physical activity done before you exercise (p. C38)

water pollution when water contains harmful substances, making it unhealthful to the environment and people (p. E29)

weapon any object used to harm someone (p. C68)

wellness the highest level of health you can reach (p. A6)

white blood cell blood cell that fights illness if pathogens get into the body (p. D47)

wrong decision a decision that is harmful and unsafe (p. A17)

Glosario

 Visita **www.mmhhealth.com** para escuchar el glosario en inglés y en español.

A

abuse/abuso Trato rudo o cruel. (pág. A76)

accident/accidente Evento inesperado que puede causar daño. (pág. C47)

acid rain/lluvia ácida Lluvia, nieve o niebla en la que se ha mezclado contaminación atmosférica. (pág. E36)

additive/aditivo Sustancia que se agrega a un alimento para que luzca o sepa mejor o para que sea más saludable. (pág. B51)

adolescence/adolescencia Etapa del crecimiento de los 12 a los 18 años de edad. (pág. B27)

adoption/adopción Acogimiento legal de un hijo de otros padres para formar parte de una familia. (pág. A66)

adulthood/adultez Etapa del crecimiento de los 18 a los 70 años de edad o más. (pág. B28)

advertisement/anuncio Mensaje que avisa sobre un producto o evento. (pág. B52)

aerobic exercise/ejercicio aeróbico Ejercicio que requiere un uso sostenido y continuo de oxígeno durante un periodo prolongado. (pág. C31)

air pollution/contaminación atmosférica Partículas o gases peligrosos en el aire. (pág. E28)

alcohol/alcohol Droga depresiva que se encuentra en algunas bebidas. (pág. D11)

alcoholism/alcoholismo Enfermedad en que una persona es adicta al alcohol. (pág. D13)

allergy/alergia Reacción negativa del cuerpo ante una sustancia. (pág. D59)

anaerobic exercise/ejercicio anaeróbico Ejercicio intenso que requiere mucho oxígeno durante un periodo corto y que sobrepasa la capacidad del cuerpo de proporcionar oxígeno. (pág. C31)

antibiotic/antibiótico Medicamento que ayuda al cuerpo a combatir infecciones causadas por bacterias u otros agentes patógenos. (pág. D52)

antibody/anticuerpo Sustancia en la sangre que ayuda a combatir agentes patógenos. (pág. D47)

asthma/asma Enfermedad crónica en la cual las vías respiratorias más pequeñas se estrechan. (pág. D60)

attitude/actitud Manera de pensar, actuar y sentir de una persona. (pág. A36)

balanced diet/dieta balanceada Plan de alimentación diaria que incluye la cantidad correcta de porciones de los cinco grupos alimenticios. (pág. B55)

body image/imagen corporal Sentimiento de una persona respecto a la manera como luce su cuerpo. (pág. B68)

body system/sistema corporal Grupo de órganos que funcionan en conjunto para realizar un trabajo determinado. (pág. B5)

bone marrow/médula ósea Tejido suave localizado en el centro de huesos largos, como los de los brazos y piernas. (pág. B9)

bored/aburrido Se dice de la persona que está inquieta y no sabe qué hacer. (pág. A30)

bully/intimidador Persona que amenaza y atemoriza a otras. (pág. A76)

calorie/caloría Unidad que se usa para medir la energía producida por los alimentos en el cuerpo. (pág. B51)

cancer/cáncer Enfermedad en la cual las células dañinas crecen en forma anormal. (pág. D67)

carbohydrate/carbohidrato Nutriente que suministra la principal fuente de energía que el cuerpo necesita. (pág. B40)

career/profesión Trabajo para el que una persona se prepara y que desempeña durante su vida. (pág. E17)

caring/afectuosidad Sentimiento bondadoso hacia alguien. (pág. A27)

cavity/caries Cavidad en los dientes que comienza en el esmalte. (pág. C12)

cell/célula Parte viva más pequeña del cuerpo de una persona. (pág. B5)

character/carácter Características de la forma de ser de una persona que la distinguen de las demás. (pág. A12)

childhood/niñez Etapa del crecimiento de 1 a 12 años de edad. (pág. B24)

choking/atragantamiento Dificultad para respirar por tener un conducto respiratorio bloqueado. (pág. C83)

chronic disease/enfermedad crónica Enfermedad que dura bastante tiempo o que se repite. (pág. D57)

circulation/circulación Transporte de la sangre a través del cuerpo. (pág. B16)

clinic/clínica Lugar donde una persona puede recibir atención médica sin tener que permanecer allí. (pág. E19)

clique/pandilla Grupo de personas que mantienen a otras apartadas de su grupo. (pág. A75)

cocaine/cocaína Droga estimulante ilegal que se extrae de las hojas de coca. (pág. D27)

commercial/anuncio comercial Anuncio en la televisión o en la radio. (págs. B52, E5)

communicable disease/enfermedad contagiosa Enfermedad que puede transmitirse a una persona desde otra, animales u objetos en el ambiente. (pág. D39)

communication/comunicación Intercambio de sentimientos, pensamientos o información entre personas. (pág. A46)

community/comunidad Lugar donde vive un grupo de personas. (pág. E17)

compete/competir Participar para ganar. (pág. C37)

conflict/conflicto Gran desacuerdo o pelea. (pág. A53)

conserve/conservar Impedir que algo se pierda o usarlo con cuidado. (pág. E41)

cool-down/enfriamiento De 5 a 10 minutos de actividad física ligera al terminar el ejercicio para enfriar los músculos y dejar que el ritmo cardiaco vuelva gradualmente a la normalidad. (pág. C38)

death/muerte Fin del ciclo de vida. (pág. B30)

dental plaque/placa dental Película invisible y pegajosa producida por bacterias que se forma sobre los dientes. (pág. C12)

depressant/sustancia depresiva Droga o medicamento que desacelera las funciones del cuerpo. (pág. D11)

dermis/dermis Capa interna y gruesa bajo la epidermis. (pág. B12)

diabetes/diabetes Enfermedad crónica que se presenta cuando hay mucha azúcar en la sangre. (pág. D58)

Dietary Guidelines/Pautas Dietéticas Metas sugeridas para alimentarse de manera saludable. (pág. B46)

digested/digerido Se dice del alimento transformado de forma que el cuerpo pueda utilizarlo. (pág. B15)

disease/enfermedad Afección que impide que el cuerpo funcione como debiera. (pág. D39)

divorce/divorcio Terminación legal de un matrimonio. (pág. A65)

drug/droga Sustancia no alimenticia que cambia la manera de funcionar del cuerpo o la mente. (pág. D5)

drug abuse/abuso de sustancias Uso de una droga ilegal o uso perjudicial e intencional de un medicamento legal. (pág. D6)

drug misuse/uso indebido de medicamentos Uso peligroso y accidental de un medicamento. (pág. D6)

earthquake/terremoto Movimiento de parte de la corteza de la Tierra debido al desplazamiento súbito de rocas sobre una falla. (pág. C49)

ectasy/éxtasis Droga ilegal que aumenta o disminuye la rapidez de las funciones del cuerpo. (pág. D27)

emergency/emergencia Situación seria e inesperada en la que se necesita ayuda inmediatamente. (pág. C75)

Emergency Alert System/Sistema de Alerta de Emergencia Sistema que permite a las personas saber cuándo una condición climática que amenaza la salud puede presentarse en su área, y cuándo una persona ha desaparecido. (pág. C76)

emotion/emoción Sentimiento fuerte de una persona. (pág. A27)

empty-calorie food/alimento con calorías vacías Alimento bajo en vitaminas y minerales pero alto en calorías. (pág. B56)

energy/energía Capacidad para hacer un trabajo. (pág. E44)

entertainment/entretenimiento Algo que interesa o divierte. (pág. E12)

environment/ambiente Todo lo que rodea a una persona. (págs. A60, E27)

epidermis/epidermis Capa externa de la piel. (pág. B12)

family/familia Grupo de personas emparentadas por vínculos de sangre, matrimonio o adopción. (pág. A59)

family guideline/norma familiar Norma establecida por los padres o tutores que ayuda a los niños a saber cómo actuar. (pág. A59)

farsighted/hipermetropía Afección en la que se tiene una visión clara de objetos lejanos y borrosa de los cercanos. (pág. C6)

fast-food restaurant/restaurante de comidas rápidas Sitio donde se preparan y se sirven alimentos rápidamente. (pág. B53)

fats/grasa Nutrientes que son una fuente de energía. (pág. B41)

fear/temor Sentimiento de peligro. (pág. A27)

first aid/primeros auxilios Atención rápida que se da a una persona herida o enferma. (pág. C75)

first aid kit/kit de primeros auxilios Información, equipo y elementos que se usan para atender a una persona herida o enferma. (pág. C75)

flexibility/flexibilidad Capacidad para doblar y mover el cuerpo con facilidad. (pág. C23)

flood/inundación Desbordamiento de una masa de agua sobre terreno normalmente seco. (pág. C57)

fluoride/fluoruro Sustancia química que endurece el esmalte dental. (pág. C12)

food allergy/alergia a un alimento Reacción desagradable al consumir un alimento, causada por el sistema inmunológico. (pág. B63)

food group/grupo alimenticio Alimentos que proporcionan los mismos tipos de nutrientes. (pág. B45)

Food Guide Pyramid/Pirámide Alimenticia Guía que indica cuántas porciones de cada grupo alimenticio necesita el cuerpo de una persona diariamente. (pág. B45)

food intolerance/intolerancia a un alimento Reacción negativa del cuerpo a un alimento o a una sustancia en del mismo. (pág. B63)

food label/rótulo nutricional Lista de ingredientes e información de nutrición impresa en un recipiente de alimentos. (pág. B51)

foodborne illness/intoxicación alimentaria Enfermedad causada por consumir alimentos o bebidas que contienen gérmenes nocivos. (pág. B64)

foster child/hijo de acogida Niño que acoge una familia sin estar relacionado por nacimiento ni adopción. (pág. A66)

friend/amigo Persona que tiene afecto y apoya a otra. (pág. A69)

friendly environment/ambiente acogedor Ambiente en que las personas se respetan entre sí. (pág. E30)

gang/ganga Grupo de personas usualmente involucradas en actos peligrosos e ilegales. (pág. C71)

grief/duelo Sentimiento de aflicción de una persona debido a una pérdida. (pág. A27)

grooming/aseo Mantenerse limpio y bien presentado. (pág. C17)

health/salud Estado del cuerpo y la mente de una persona, y la manera de relacionarse con los demás. (pág. A5)

health advocate/defensor de la salud Persona que ayuda a otra a tener comportamientos saludables. (pág. A48)

health goal/meta de salud Objetivo que una persona busca alcanzar para estar más sana. (pág. A5)

healthful behavior/comportamiento saludable Acción que aumenta el nivel de salud de las personas. (pág. A6)

healthful body composition/composición corporal saludable Cuerpo delgado sin demasiada grasa. (pág. C23)

healthful weight/peso saludable Peso recomendado según la edad, la estatura, el género y la contextura física de una persona. (pág. B67)

hearing loss/pérdida auditiva Incapacidad para escuchar bien con uno o ambos oídos. (pág. C8)

heart and lung endurance/resistencia cardiopulmonar Capacidad de permanecer activo sin sentirse cansado. (pág. C23)

heart attack/ataque cardiaco Falta repentina de sangre hacia el corazón. (pág. D63)

heart disease/enfermedad cardiovascular Enfermedad del corazón o los vasos sanguíneos de una persona. (pág. D63)

heredity/herencia Rasgos que se heredan de los padres biológicos. (págs. A60, B21)

hormone/hormona Sustancia química producida por el cuerpo que controla ciertos procesos. (pág. B21)

hurricane/huracán Tormenta destructiva que se forma sobre el océano. (pág. C56)

I

I-message/mensaje inteligente Manera saludable de comunicar un problema y sus efectos en una persona. (pág. A46)

immune/inmune Se dice de la persona que está protegida contra una determinada enfermedad. (pág. D47)

infancy/infancia Etapa de crecimiento desde el nacimiento hasta el primer año de vida. (pág. B22)

infection/infección Crecimiento de bacterias que causan daño al cuerpo. (pág. C81)

inhalant/inhalante Sustancia química que se aspira. (pág. D28)

injury/lesión Daño o detrimento corporal causado a una persona. (pág. C47)

inpatient/paciente interno Persona que debe permanecer en un hospital al menos una noche para recibir tratamiento. (pág. E20)

insulation/aislamiento Material que evita o retarda el paso del calor. (pág. E44)

J

joint/articulación Punto del cuerpo donde se unen dos o más huesos. (pág. B9)

joy/alegría Sentimiento de gran felicidad. (pág. A27)

L

lactose/lactosa Azúcar que se encuentra en la leche. (pág. B63)

land pollution/contaminación del suelo Presencia de sustancias nocivas en la tierra que hace que no sea saludable para el ambiente ni para la gente. (pág. E28)

learning disability/discapacidad de aprendizaje Desigualdad que hace que una persona tenga dificultad para aprender. (pág. B25)

life cycle/ciclo de vida Orden de los cambios por los que pasa un ser vivo durante su vida. (pág. B22)

life skill/destreza para la vida Acción saludable que se aprende y se practica para mejorar y mantener la salud. (pág. A7)

lifetime sport/deporte para toda la vida Deporte que una persona puede practicar durante toda su vida. (pág. C32)

lightning/rayo Destello de luz causado por la electricidad presente en la atmósfera. (pág. C54)

long-term goal/meta a largo plazo
Objetivo para el que se necesitará
mucho tiempo para alcanzarlo.
(pág. A24)

marijuana/marihuana Droga ilegal que
afecta la memoria y la concentración.
(pág. D25)

media/medios de comunicación Fuentes
de noticias e información. (pág. E5)

mediation/mediación Proceso en el que
una persona responsable ayuda a
resolver un conflicto. (pág. A54)

medicine/medicamento Droga legal
que se usa para prevenir, tratar o
curar una enfermedad o lesión.
(pág. D5)

mineral/mineral Nutriente que ayuda a
los procesos químicos del cuerpo.
(pág. B42)

MSG/glutamato monosódico Sustancia
usada para dar sabor a carnes,
comidas de mar y sopas. (pág. B63)

mucus/moco Capa húmeda que
recubre el interior de la nariz y la
garganta. (pág. D46)

**muscular endurance/resistencia
muscular** Capacidad para usar los
músculos durante un tiempo
prolongado sin detenerse. (pág. C23)

muscular strength/fuerza muscular
Capacidad de los músculos para
levantar, tirar, golpear y lanzar
objetos con fuerza. (pág. C22)

natural resource/recurso natural
Material que se encuentra en la
naturaleza y que es necesario o útil
para la vida. (pág. E27)

nearsighted/miopía Afección en la que
se tiene una visión clara de objetos
cercanos y borrosa de los lejanos.
(pág. C6)

neuron/neurona Célula nerviosa.
(pág. B18)

nicotine/nicotina Droga estimulante
que se encuentra en el tabaco.
(pág. D17)

noise/ruido Sonido alto o constante.
(pág. E30)

nutrient/nutriente Sustancia en los
alimentos que usa el cuerpo para
estar saludable. (pág. B39)

**one-mile run/walk/carrera/caminata de
una milla** Prueba para medir la
resistencia cardiopulmonar. (pág. C29)

organ/órgano Parte del cuerpo constituida por diferentes clases de tejidos. (pág. B5)

outpatient/paciente externo Persona que recibe tratamiento en un hospital pero que no necesita permanecer en él. (pág. E20)

overweight/sobrepeso Peso superior al que se considera saludable. (pág. B68)

over-the-counter (OTC) drug/ medicamento de venta libre Medicamento que se puede comprar sin receta médica. (pág. D6)

pathogen/agente patógeno Germen que causa enfermedades. (pág. D39)

peer/compañero Persona de la misma edad. (pág. A71)

peer pressure/presión de los compañeros Influencia que los compañeros ejercen sobre alguno de ellos. (pág. A71)

percent body fat pinch/pellizco para saber el porcentaje de grasa corporal Prueba que mide la cantidad de grasa en el cuerpo que una persona tiene. (pág. C29)

permanent teeth/dientes permanentes Dientes que, si se cuidan, duran toda la vida. (pág. C11)

personality/personalidad Manera única de una persona de lucir, pensar, actuar y sentir que la diferencia de los demás. (pág. A11)

physical fitness/buen estado físico Estado óptimo del corazón, los pulmones, los músculos y las articulaciones de una persona. (pág. C22)

poison/veneno Sustancia que daña o mata si se traga o se pone en contacto con la piel. (pág. C50)

pollution/contaminación Presencia de sustancias nocivas en el suelo, el agua o la atmósfera que hace que no sean saludables para el ambiente ni para la gente. (pág. E27)

posture/postura Manera en que una persona se sienta, se para o se mueve. (pág. B9)

premature heart attack/ataque cardiaco prematuro Ataque cardiaco que ocurre antes de los 60 años. (pág. D64)

prescription drug/medicamento con receta Medicamento que sólo se puede comprar con una orden del médico. (pág. D5)

preservative/preservante Sustancia que se agrega a un alimento para evitar su descomposición. (pág. B51)

primary teeth/dientes primarios Primer grupo de dientes de una persona. (pág. C11)

protective factor/factor de protección Cualquier situación que aumenta la posibilidad de un resultado positivo. (pág. D31)

protein/proteína Nutriente necesario para el crecimiento y reparación de las células del cuerpo. (pág. B39)

psychiatrist/psiquiatra Médico especialista en tratar y prevenir los problemas de la salud mental y emocional de las personas. (pág. E18)

puberty/pubertad Etapa de la vida en que el cuerpo de una persona cambia y queda apto para la reproducción. (pág. B27)

pull-ups/flexiones en barra Prueba para medir la fuerza y resistencia de la parte superior del cuerpo. (pág. C28)

radon/radón Gas incoloro e inodoro que se forma en algunas rocas y el suelo arcilloso. (pág. D67)

recovery/recuperación Punto en que una persona vuelve a estar bien. (pág. C67)

recycle/reciclar Transformar productos de desecho de modo que puedan usarse otra vez. (pág. E42)

reduce/reducir Usar menos de lo que produce basura. (pág. E42)

relationship/relación Vínculo que una persona tiene con otra. (pág. A45)

resistance skills/destrezas de resistencia Maneras de decir NO a comportamientos arriesgados. (pág. A19)

respect/respetar Tratar a otros como uno quisiera ser tratado. (pág. A45)

respiration/respiración Proceso mediante el cual las células usan oxígeno para obtener energía. (pág. B17)

responsible/responsable Se dice de la persona en quien se puede confiar para un trabajo, obligación u otro asunto. (pág. A13)

responsible decision/decisión responsable Elección segura y saludable y que cumple con las normas familiares. (pág. A17)

reuse/reutilizar Usar nuevamente algo en lugar de desecharlo. (pág. E43)

ringworm/culebrilla Enfermedad de la piel causada por un hongo. (pág. C18)

risk behavior/comportamiento arriesgado Acción que puede ser perjudicial para una persona y para los demás. (pág. A6)

role model/modelo de persona Persona cuyo comportamiento imitan otras. (pág. A48)

─────────── Ⓢ ───────────

sadness/tristeza Sentimiento de pesar o infelicidad. (pág. A27)

safe touch/contacto apropiado Contacto que es correcto y respetuoso. (pág. C67)

safety equipment/equipo de seguridad Conjunto de elementos que protegen a una persona de lesiones cuando practica deportes o realiza alguna otra actividad física. (pág. C38)

sanitary landfill/vertedero sanitario Lugar donde se mantiene la basura mientras se descompone. (pág. E35)

sealant/sellante Cubierta de material similar al plástico que se aplica sobre los molares para evitar las caries. (pág. C14)

seat belt/cinturón de seguridad Correa que sujeta a una persona por el hombro y la cintura mientras viaja en un automóvil. (pág. C59)

secondhand smoke/humo de segunda mano Humo que proviene de una persona que fuma o de un cigarrillo, un cigarro o una pipa encendidos. (pág. D18)

self-concept/autoconcepto Opinión que una persona tiene de sí misma. (pág. A23)

self-control/autocontrol Capacidad que una persona tiene para no decir o no hacer algo que no debería. (pág. A51)

self-respect/autorrespeto Opinión elevada que una persona tiene de sí misma. (pág. A11)

self-statement/autoafirmación Recordatorio que una persona tiene para sí misma sobre qué debería hacer en determinadas circunstancias. (pág. A14)

separation/separación Situación en que una pareja sigue casada pero sus integrantes viven separados. (pág. A65)

short-term goal/meta a corto plazo Objetivo que se puede alcanzar en corto tiempo. (pág. A24)

shuttle run/carrera de ida y vuelta Prueba que mide la coordinación total del cuerpo. (pág. C28)

sit-ups or curl-ups/abdominales Prueba que mide la fuerza y resistencia de los músculos del abdomen. (pág. C28)

smog/esmog Neblina que se forma cuando la luz solar reacciona ante la contaminación atmosférica. (pág. E36)

smokeless tobacco/tabaco que no se fuma Producto del tabaco que puede aspirarse o masticarse colocándolo entre la mejilla y las encías. (pág. D19)

snack/refrigerio Alimento que se ingiere entre una comida y otra. (pág. B55)

sprain/esguince Lesión en el tejido que conecta los huesos a una articulación. (pág. C82)

steroid/esteroide Sustancia química que se produce naturalmente en el cuerpo o que se prescribe por razones médicas. (pág. D29)

stimulant/estimulante Droga o medicamento que acelera las funciones del cuerpo. (pág. D17)

stress/estrés Forma en que responden el cuerpo y la mente ante los cambios o exigencias de la vida. (pág. A33)

stressor/factor estresante Algo que causa estrés. (pág. A33)

symptom/síntoma Cambio en el cuerpo de una persona que es señal de una enfermedad. (pág. D51)

tar/alquitrán Sustancia viscosa que se encuentra en el humo del tabaco. (pág. D17)

thunderstorm/tormenta eléctrica Tormenta acompañada de relámpagos y truenos. (pág. C56)

tissue/tejido Grupo de células que funcionan juntas. (pág. B5)

tornado/tornado Tormenta poderosa con vientos que giran en forma de embudo. (pág. C56)

treatment/tratamiento Cuidado que se brinda a alguien que está enfermo. (pág. D52)

unconscious/inconsciente Se dice de la persona que no sabe qué sucede porque no está despierta. (pág. C76)

underweight/bajo peso Peso inferior al que se considera saludable. (pág. B68)

universal precautions/precauciones universales Pasos para evitar el contacto con fluidos corporales que podrían estar contaminados. (pág. C81)

unsafe touch/contacto inapropiado Contacto que no es correcto. (pág. C67)

V

vaccine/vacuna Sustancia que da inmunidad contra determinada enfermedad sin adquirirla. (pág. D47)

values/valores Ideas que guían el comportamiento una persona. (pág. A11)

victim/víctima Persona que ha sido lastimada con violencia. (pág. C67)

violence/violencia Daño que una persona se causa a sí misma, a los demás o a bienes. (pág. C65)

vitamin/vitamina Nutriente que ayuda al cuerpo a usar otros nutrientes, como proteínas, carbohidratos y grasas. (pág. B42)

V-sit and reach or sit and reach/sentarse y alcanzar Prueba que mide la flexibilidad de los músculos en la espalda y las piernas. (pág. C28)

W

warm-up/calentamiento Actividad física ligera que se hace por unos cinco minutos antes de los ejercicios. (pág. C38)

water pollution/contaminación del agua Presencia de sustancias nocivas en el agua que hace que no sea saludable para el ambiente ni para la gente. (pág. E29)

weapon/arma Objeto que se usa para hacer daño a alguien. (pág. C68)

wellness/bienestar Máximo nivel de salud que se puede alcanzar. (pág. A6)

white blood cell/glóbulo blanco Célula de la sangre que ataca y destruye agentes patógenos que entran al cuerpo. (pág. D47)

wrong decision/decisión errónea Decisión que es peligrosa y perjudicial. (pág. A17)

Index

Note: A page number in *italic* type means there is an illustration on that page.

9-1-1, C65, C76

extreme weather,
C56–C57, C76
heart attack, D63
hospital health care for, E20
insect bites, C85
national disaster, C77
Emergency Alert System
(EAS), C76
Emergency supply kit, C77
Emotion, A27
anger, A52
death and, B30
expressing, A28–A29, A75
personality and, A11
self-control and, A51
Emotional abuse, A76
Emphysema, D17
Empty-calorie foods, B56
Enamel, C11, *C11*
Endurance, *C22, C23*
exercises for, *C31*
lifetime sports for, C33
Energy, E44
food sources of, B40–B41
Entertainment, E12
Environment, A60, E27
affect on growth, B21
conservation of, E41–E44
diseases caused by factors
in, D57
friendly, E30
reducing pollution in,
E35–E39
types of pollution, E30
types of pollution in,
E28–E29
Epidermis, B12, *B12*
Equipment, C33. *See also*
Safety equipment
Esophagus, B15, *B15*
effects of alcohol on, D11,
D11
tobacco and, D17

Exercise. *See also* Physical
activity
coping with death and,
B31
for healthful circulatory
system, B16
for healthful respiratory
system, B17
for strong bones, B9, B11
for strong muscles, B11
Exhaust, E37
Expense, E9
Expiration date, D7
Extended family, A59
Eyes, B5, B18, *C6*, C6–C7
of adults, B28
pathogens and, D40–D41

Fairness, A13. *See also* Build
Character, fairness
Family, A59, A61
abuse and, A76–A77
adjusting to change in,
A63–A66
communication skills and,
A46–A47
conflict resolution and,
A53–A54
cooperation, A63
effect of alcohol on, D12
influence on decisions,
A18
influence on health,
A60–A61
making time for, E11
relationships within, A61
types of, A59
Family and social changes
during adolescence, B27
of adults, B28
during childhood, B24

friendly environment and,
E30
during infancy, B23
Family and social health, A5
abuse and, A76–A77
adjusting to change,
A63–A66
communication skills and,
A46–A47
conflict resolution and,
A53–A54
cooperation, A63
effects of alcohol on, D12
feeling left out, A75
friendships, A69
health advocacy, A48–A49
influences on, A60–A61
managing anger and, A52
marijuana use and, D25
peer pressure and, A71
personality and, A11
physical activity and, C21
relationships and, A45
resistance skills and, A70
self-control and, A51
types of families, A59
Family guidelines, A59
conflict resolution and, A54
decision making and, A17,
A19
drugs and, D31
true friends and, A69
Farsighted, C6, *C6*
Fast-food restaurant, B53
Fats, B41, B47
circulatory system and, B16
colon cancer and, D68
heart disease and, D63
Fats, oils and sweets, B45, *B45*
Fear, A27, A29
Femur, *B9*
Fever, D51
Fiber, B39, B47, D67, D68

Swim safety, C54
Symptom, D51

Table manners, B49
Talents, A11
Tamper-resistant seal, D7
Tar, D17
Tartar, C12
Taste, B18
Teacher, C5
Tears, D45, D46, *D46*
Technology link, C31
Teeth, C11–C15
    brushing, *C13*
    of children, B24
    development of, B22
    flossing, *C12*
    of infants, B22
    tobacco use and, D17, D20
Tetanus shot, D41
THC, D25
Thermostat, E44
Thunderstorm, C56, C76
Time management, E10–E11
Tissue, B5, *B5*
Tobacco, D17–D21
    as cause of cancer, D67,
        D68
    circulatory system and,
        B16
    heart disease and, D64
    respiratory system and,
        B17
Tongue, B18
Tornadoes, C56
Total health, A5
Touch, B18
Trachea, *B17*
Tranquilizers, D27
Trans fats, B41
Treatment, D52

Triggers, D60
Trustworthiness, A12. *See
    also* Build Character,
    trustworthiness
Turbines, E44
TV programs, E12
Type 1 diabetes, D58
Type 2 diabetes, D58

Unconscious, C76
Underweight, B68
Universal precautions, C81,
    D42
Unsafe touch, C67
Unsaturated fats, B41, B57

Vaccine, D47, D52
Values, A11, A18
Vegetable group, B45, *B45*
Veins, B16, *B16*, B17
Vertebrae, *B9*, B18
Victim, C67
Violence, C65–C67
Viruses, D39, *D39. See also*
    Germs; Pathogen
    diseases caused by, D41,
        D42
    treatment for diseases
        caused by, D52
Vision, B18, C6
Vitamins, B42, B51
Voluntary muscles, B10
V-sit and reach, C28, *C28*

Walking, C33, C53
Warm up, B11, C38
Warning labels, *D18*

Warnings, *D6*
Wastewater treatment plant,
    E38
Water
    conservation of, E41
    for digestive system, B15,
        D67, D68
    as natural resources, E27
    need for in hot weather,
        C56
    as nutrient, B42
    pollution of, E29, E38–E39
Water pollution, E29
    reduction of, E38–E39
Water treatment plant, E38
Weapon, C68
Weather emergencies, C76
Weather safety, C56–C57
Weight, C21
Wellness, A6
Wellness Scale, A6, *A6*, A9
West Nile virus, D39, D52,
    D57
What Do You Know, A3,
    A43, B3, B37, C3, C45, D3,
    D37, E3, E25
White blood cells, D47, *D47*
Wind power, E44
Wisdom teeth, C11
Write About It, A28, A64,
    A69, B24, B28, C82, D18,
    D20, D40, E18, E38
Wrong decision, A17

X-ray, C14

Credits

Cover and Title Page Photography: Dot-Box for Macmillan/McGraw-Hill

Illustration Credits: Annie Bissett: A06, B52, B58, D07, D43, D53. Tom Barrett: C24, C28, C29, C48, C55, C60, C83, C87. davejoly.com: A38, A56, B32, B60, C78, C40 D22, E14, E32. Garth Glazier with American Artists: D45. Paul Sharp and Alice Sharp: A09, A11, A15, A19, A20, A31, A37, A49, B07, B13, B19, B25, B48, B53, B65, C08, C19, C22, C33, C60, C62, D64, D67, E05, E13, E31, E39, E42, E45. Kate Sweeney: vi, B05, B06, B09, B10, B12, B15, B16, B17, B18, C06, C08, C11, D17, D63. Jim Spence/Illustrator Represented by Bookmakers: C83. Joel & Sharon Harris: B06, D11, D35.

Photography Credits: All photographs are by Macmillan/McGraw-Hill MMH except as noted.

vi: bc Richard Hutchings Photography for MMH. xii: bc Royalty-Free/CORBIS. iv: bl Chris Carroll/CORBIS. x: cl Eric Fowke/PhotoEdit. viii: cl Myrleen Ferguson Cate/PhotoEdit. vii: tr Doug Martin/Photo Researchers, Inc. xiii: tr Patti McConville/ImageState. ix: tr Photodisc Green/Getty Images. v: tr Siede Preis/Getty Images. xi: tr Spike Mafford/Getty Images. B01: bc, bl, br, tl, tr Richard Hutchings Photography for MMH. D01: bc, bl, br, tl, tr Richard Hutchings Photography for MMH. C01: bc, bl, br, tl, tr Richard Hutchings Photography for MMH. A01: bl, br, c, cr, tl, tr Richard Hutchings Photography for MMH. E01: bl, br, c, cr, tl Richard Hutchings Photography for MMH. B02: b Rusty Hill/Getty Images; cr, tl Jack Holtel Photographick Company for MMH. A02: bl, tl Jack Holtel Photographick Company for MMH; br Photodisc/Getty Images E02: bl Jack Holtel Photographick Company for MMH; br Michael Newman/PhotoEdit; tl Burke/Triolo/Robertstock. D02: tl Jack Holtel Photographick Company for MMH. C02: c Royalty-Free/CORBIS; tl Photodisc/Getty Images. D03: bl Alessandra Quaranta/Black Star Images; tl Amy Etra/PhotoEdit C03: bl, br Burke/Triolo/Robertstock; tc Photodisc Collection/Getty Images; tr Image Source/SuperStock A03: bl Ryan McVay/Getty Images; tl Navaswan/Getty Images; tr Felicia Martinez/PhotoEdit B03: c Davies + Starr/Getty Images; t Spencer Jones/Getty Images E03: c Jack Holtel Photographick Company for MMH; cl Eric Fowke/PhotoEdit; cl Stuart Hughs/Getty Images; t James Nazz/CORBIS. B04: b Jonathan A. Meyers/Photo Researchers, Inc. A04: b Mike Brinson/Getty Images. E04: b Myrleen Ferguson Cate/PhotoEdit. C04: bc Jose Luis Pelaez, Inc./CORBIS. D04: br Richard Hutchings Photography for MMH. C05: bc Photodisc Collection/Getty Images; c Royalty-Free/CORBIS; c Siede Preis/Getty Images; c Spencer Grant/PhotoEdit. D05: br Richard Hutchings Photography for MMH. A05: tr Rob Gage Photography/ImageState; tl Tom Stewart/CORBIS; tc Robert Brenner/PhotoEdit. C05: tc Ross Anania/Getty Images. E06: br Alan Landau Photography for MMH; br Macmillan/McGraw-Hill. D06: br Jack Holtel Photographick Company for MMH. C06: br Richard Hutchings Photography for MMH. B06: cl Richard Hutchings Photography for MMH. C07: bc Royalty-Free/CORBIS. A07: cr Ken Chernus/Getty Images. E07: cr Royalty-Free/Getty Images. B08: b Sonny Senser sonnyphoto.com for MMH. D08: bl Richard Hutchings Photography for MMH. C08: br Richard Hutchings Photography for MMH. A08: c David Young-Wolff/PhotoEdit. E08: c Sonny Senser sonnyphoto.com for MMH. B09: br Richard Hutchings Photography for MMH. C09: c David Young-Wolff/PhotoEdit. D09: cr Richard Hutchings Photography for MMH. E09: tr Bill Aron/PhotoEdit. D10: b Bob Torrez/Getty Images. A10: b David Young-Wolff/PhotoEdit. C10: b Robert Daly/Getty Images.

B10: bl Richard Hutchings Photography for MMH E10: br Jiang Jin/SuperStock; cl Jack Holtel Photographick Company for MMH. B11: bl Richard Hutchings Photography for MMH; cr John Greim/Stockphoto. E11: br David Joel/Getty Images. C11: br Richard Hutchings Photography for MMH. A12: bc Gabe Palmer/CORBIS. D12: bl Al-Anon Family Group Headquarters, Inc. C12: bl, br Richard Hutchings Photography for MMH. E12: cl Ryan McVay/Getty Images; tl Jeff Greenberg/PhotoEdit. A13: bc Richard Hutchings/Hutchings Photography. C13: bl, br Richard Hutchings Photography for MMH. D13: br Sonny Senser sonnyphoto.com for MMH. A14: b Richard Hutchings Photography for MMH. D14: bl Richard Hutchings Photography for MMH. C14: bl Spencer Grant/PhotoEdit. B14: br Richard Hutchings Photography for MMH. B15: br Richard Hutchings Photography for MMH. D15: cl Jon Feingersh/Masterfile. C15: cl Richard Hutchings Photography for MMH. C16: b Richard Hutchings Photography for MMH. D16: b Sonny Senser sonnyphoto.com for MMH. A16: bc Nicole Katano/ImageState. B16: bl Richard Hutchings Photography for MMH. E16: c Pat LaCroix/Getty Images. E17: br Bohemian Nomad Picturemakers/CORBIS; c Royalty-Free/CORBIS. B17 br Richard Hutchings Photography for MMH. C17: cr Richard Hutchings Photography for MMH. A18: bc Tony Freeman/PhotoEdit. C18: bl Macduff Everton/CORBIS; cl Myrleen Ferguson Cate/PhotoEdit. E18: bl Michael Newman/PhotoEdit. B18: bl Richard Hutchings Photography for MMH. E19: b Roger Ball/CORBIS. D19: br Alessandra Quaranta/Black Star Images; cr, tr Tony Freeman/PhotoEdit. A20: b Ariel Skelley/CORBIS. C20: bc Yellow Dog Productions/Getty Images. D20: bl Richard Hutchings Photography for MMH. E20: bl Sonny Senser sonnyphoto.com for MMH. B20: br Jack Hollingsworth/CORBIS. C21: bl Bob Daemmrich/Stock Boston. B21: br Richard Hutchings Photography for MMH. B22: b Scott Tysick/Masterfile; cl Chris Carroll/CORBIS. A22: bc Richard Hutchings Photography for MMH. C22: bl Rob Gage/Getty Images; c Michael Keller/CORBIS. B23: bc Royalty Free/CORBIS. C23: bl Sonny Senser sonnyphoto.com for MMH; cl Frank Siteman/Index Stock Imagery; t Richard Hutchings Photography for MMH. D24: b Gabe Palmer/CORBIS. E24: b Royalty-Free/Getty Images; cl, tr Ryan McVay/Getty Images. B24: bl Owen Franken/CORBIS. A24: br Richard Hutchings Photography for MMH. D25: tr Burke/Triolo/Robertstock. E25: br, cr Jack Holtel Photographick Company for MMH; cl Royalty-Free/Getty Images. C26: b Richard Hutchings Photography for MMH. B26: bc Richard Hutchings Photography for MMH. A26: bc Tony Garcia/SuperStock. D26: bl Richard Hutchings Photography for MMH. E26: br Bob Daemmrich/The Image Works. C27: br Jack Holtel Photographick Company for MMH. E27: br Phil Lauro/Index Stock Imagery. D27: br Roderick Chen/SuperStock; cr Eric Fowke/PhotoEdit; tr Christina Kennedy/PhotoEdit. B27: cr Joel Benjamin Photography for MMH A27: tr Richard Hutchings Photography for MMH. D28: bl Jack Holtel Photographick Company for MMH. A28: bl Joel Benjamin Photography for MMH. E28: bl Marcus Lyon/ImageState; tl Patti McConville/ImageState. B28: cl Anthony Redpath/CORBIS. B29: b Siede Preis/Getty Images; br David Young-Wolff/PhotoEdit; c Royalty Free/CORBIS; cr Royalty Free/Getty Images; tr Brian Hagiwara/Getty Images. E29: bc Spencer Grant/PhotoEdit. A29: bl David Young-Wolff/PhotoEdit. D29: c Jack Holtel Photographick Company for MMH. C30: b Richard Hutchings Photography for MMH. D30: b Sonny Senser sonnyphoto.com for MMH. E30: bl Arthur Tilley/Getty Images. A30: bl Burke/Triolo/Robertstock; cl Felicia Martinez/PhotoEdit; cl Tony Freeman/PhotoEdit. B30: bl Richard Hutchings